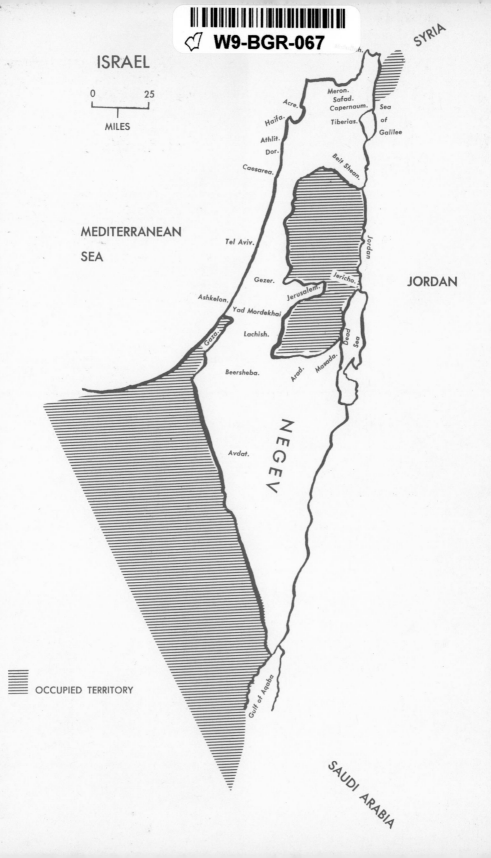

ISRAEL

SYRIA

0   25

MILES

W9-BGR-067

Meron.
Safad.
Capernaum.
Acre.

Haifa.

Tiberias.

Sea
of
Galilee

Athlit.
Dor.

Caesarea.

Beit Shean.

MEDITERRANEAN

SEA

Tel Aviv.

Jordan

Gezer.

Jericho.

JORDAN

Ashkelon.

Jerusalem.

Yad Mordekhai

Gaza.

Lachish.

Dead Sea

Beersheba.

Arad.

Masada.

N
E
G
E
V

Avdat.

OCCUPIED TERRITORY

Gulf of Aqaba

SAUDI ARABIA

The Stones of Zion

By Gerald Green:

Fiction
The Heartless Light
The Last Angry Man
The Legion of Noble Christians
The Lotus Eaters
The Sword and the Sun
To Brooklyn with Love

Nonfiction
The Artists of Terezin
The Portofino PTA
The Stones of Zion
His Majesty O'Keefe (with Lawrence Klingman)

The Stones of Zion

A Novelist's Journal in Israel

by

Gerald Green

HAWTHORN BOOKS, INC.
Publishers
New York

THE STONES OF ZION

Copyright © 1971 by Gerald Green. Copyright under International and Pan-American Copyright Conventions. All rights reserved, including the right to reproduce this book, or portions thereof, in any form, except for the inclusion of brief quotations in a review. All inquiries should be addressed to Hawthorn Books, Inc., 70 Fifth Avenue, New York, New York 10011. This book was manufactured in the United States of America and published simultaneously in Canada by Prentice-Hall of Canada, Limited, 1870 Birchmount Road, Scarborough, Ontario. Library of Congress Catalog Card Number: 72-130718.

All photographs are by Marie and Gerald Green, with the exception of two: The photographs of the summit of Avdat and of Mampsis were furnished by Robert E. Koppel, of Beersheba, Israel.

Book design by Martin J. Baumann

Acknowledgments

"The stranger did not lodge in the street; but I opened my doors to the traveller," poor old Job tells us.

One must be cautious about comparing the suffering Job with modern Israelis. Goodness knows they are threatened, tormented, and vilified daily by their neighbors; but they are not accepting these plagues with nearly the patience or resignation of the Old Testament figure. Still, they are *in precarium*, and they must have other things on their minds besides American writers, archaeology buffs, and publishing deadlines.

Nonetheless, for all their troubles, they, like Job, "open their doors to the traveller." And they do so with hospitality, generosity, the wisdom of an ancient people, and a refreshing lack of flattery. I came to the Israel Government Tourist Office in New York, almost embarrassed by my requests for assistance. A nation fighting for its life, I felt, scarcely needed me poking around Canaanite stones and Herodian walls. They thought otherwise. Their help to me was monumental. I must thank Nathan Freedman, of the New York office, and his efficient aide, Marilyn Altman, for getting me started; they could not have been kinder. In Jerusalem, Amnon Gilad and Chanan Michaeli, of the Ministry of Tourism, picked up Nate Freedman's planning and aided me in every conceivable way.

El Al, Israel's superb airline, has also earned my gratitude for many generous deeds. I am especially indebted to Peter Brunswick in El Al's New York office, and Baruch Saville, his counterpart at Lod airport. El Al, incidentally, is one of the safest, most reliable of airlines. When all the jokes about "my son the pilot" have been made, the fact remains that their crews are among the best trained in the world. The piloting of aircraft— whether 707's or Mirages—appears to be a skill at which Israelis excel.

Zev Vilnay, king of guides, teacher, scholar, soldier, patriot, deserves a special note of thanks. He and his charming wife, Esther, were gracious hosts and wise counselors.

Many of Israel's leading archaeologists were most generous in granting interviews. Among them were Dr. Nelson Glueck, Dr. Abraham Negev, Professor Yohanan Aharoni, Professor Saul Weinberg, and Mr. Meir Ben Dov.

Books on the Middle East, its history and archaeology, abound, and I shall list only those I relied on most. In the area of guidebooks, Vilnay's (Jerusalem, 1970) is obligatory for any traveler to Israel. It is accurate, profusely illustrated, and its maps and diagrams are easy to read and logically arranged. Nagel's guide (Geneva, 1969) is a good back-up to Vilnay; it is thorough on Christian places. For matters such as hotels, restaurants, and shopping, I recommend either the Bazak Guide or Fodor's (New York, 1971).

For a general orientation, several books were exceptionally helpful. An excellent one is Zev Vilnay's *New Israel Atlas: Bible to Present Day*, published by the Israel Universities Press in Jerusalem; it is a concise and graphic history-geography. *The Jews in Their Land*, edited by David Ben-Gurion and distributed in the United States by Doubleday, is a gigantic, lavish, multicolored work. Like Vilnay's *Atlas*, it is too big to take in one's luggage, but it makes for good advance reading. I leaned heavily on both of them in preparing myself for my trip.

In addition, I recommend the following, all of which I used as sources in writing *The Stones of Zion*. Like the ancient places of Israel and the rest of the Middle East, they are treasure troves, filled with unexpected gems, unsuspected gold:

Abramsky, Samuel. *Ancient Towns in Israel.* Jerusalem, 1963.

Albright, William F. *Archaeology and the Religion of Israel.* New York, 1969.

De Vaux, Roland. *Ancient Israel.* 2 vols. New York, 1965.

Freedman, D. N., and Campbell, E. F. (eds.). *The Biblical Archaeologist Reader.* Vols. 2 and 3. New York, 1964 and 1970.

Glueck, Nelson. *Deities and Dolphins.* New York, 1965.

———. *Rivers in the Desert.* New York, 1968.

Moscati, Sabatino. *The Face of the Ancient Orient.* New York, 1962.

Negev, Abraham. *Caesarea.* Tel Aviv, 1967.

———. *Cities in the Desert.* Tel Aviv, 1966.

Smith, George Adam. *The Historical Geography of the Holy Land.* London, 1966.

Talmi, Menahem. *The Dead Sea.* Tel Aviv, 1966.

———. *Lake Kinneret.* Tel Aviv, 1965.

Wright, G. E., and Freedman, D. N. (eds.). *The Biblical Archaeologist Reader.* Vol. 1. New York, 1961.

Yadin, Yigael. *Masada.* New York, 1966.

On subjects not related to archaeology or history, these works were of enormous interest and assistance to me:

Berkman, Ted. *Sabra.* New York, 1969.

Bettelheim, Bruno. *The Children of the Dream.* New York, 1969.

Larkin, Margaret. *The Six Days of Yad Mordekhai.* Tel Aviv, 1965.

Leon, Dan. *The Kibbutz: A New Way of Life.* London, 1969.

Finally, should the traveler in Israel have trouble with his camera (as I did) he should consult Gadi in the Prisma Photo Shop, Zion Square, Jerusalem. In Tel Aviv, Leon at 18 Ben Yehuda Street is recommended, and in Tiberias, Mr. Herskov in the Rassco building. Obviously I had a lot of problems with a camera, but since I am of a forgiving nature, I will not mention the New York store in which I bought it, or the name of the manufacturer.

G. G.
Stamford, Connecticut

Contents

Illustrations appear on pages 75–106 and 243–274.

ix

And Joshua wrote these words in the book of the law of God, and took a great stone, and set it up there under an oak, that was by the sanctuary of the Lord.

And Joshua said unto the people, Behold, this stone shall be a witness to us; for it hath heard all the words of the Lord, which he spake unto us; it shall be therefore a witness unto you, lest you deny your God.

—*Joshua 24:27, 28*

The Stones of Zion

CHAPTER I

The Baptists
of Beersheba

Mr. Priddy shaded his eyes. "Now when I read in the Bible that Abraham sat in the tent door in the heat of the day, I know what it means."

Mr. Priddy is one of three graduates of the New Orleans Baptist Seminary working at the excavation of Tel Beersheba. We found all of them taking a noon break from the merciless August sun—three Americans sitting silently under a khaki pup tent, sipping precious water from dusty army canteens.

"You feel you have a greater understanding of the Bible through working in Israel?" I asked them.

Mr. Priddy—he administers Baptist Sunday Schools in Moss Point, Mississippi—nods. "Oh, yes. We have seen with our own eyes, we have looked upon, and our hands have handled. We know what the Book is speaking of."

"You left out 'the land whereon thy feet have trodden,' " our

1

guide, Dani, protests. Dani is a sabra, tall, brown, hipless, wafer-waisted, broad-shouldered, with what my mother would have called a "collar-ad" face. He is an Old Testament scholar. Although his parents were born in Europe, his grandfather was the Orthodox rabbi of a synagogue on Eastern Parkway, near my old neighborhood in Brooklyn. Dani, a superb guide, who is actually an official of the Ministry of Tourism, is a compulsive arguer, especially when it comes to Scripture. Three Baptists on the slopes of Tel Beersheba are a challenge he cannot resist.

My wife and I watch, fascinated. We are about to observe one of those inevitable Israeli *mano-a-mano's*, a scholar-to-scholar duel. Never mind the enervating heat, the scorching sun, the desert dust that clogs our nostrils. There is always time for argument.

" 'Land whereon thy feet have trodden?' " Mr. Priddy repeats. "No, that is not part of it, sir. I am quoting the first chapter of the First Epistle General of St. John: 'That which was from the beginning, which we have heard, which we have seen with our eyes, which we have looked upon, and our hands have handled, of the Word of life.' "

"Ah, New Testament," Dani responds, generously trying to suppress a note of hauteur in his voice. But it creeps in; I hope our Baptists don't catch it.

The Reverend George Harrison, professor of Old Testament and Hebrew at New Orleans Baptist Seminary, enters the discussion. My wife and I are joined in connubial ignorance—she is a long-lapsed Roman Catholic, I am a befuddled rationalist, light-years removed from the Orthodox shul on Howard Avenue (Talmud Torah Tiphereth Hagro) where I was bar-mitzvahed in 1935. We listen in awe as the argument gathers force.

"I know what you had in mind, sir," Mr. Harrison says. "You are quoting Joshua fourteen nine. 'And Moses sware on that day, saying, surely the land whereon thy feet have trodden shall be thine inheritance, and thy children's forever, because thou hast wholly followed the Lord my God.' Am I correct, sir?"

Mr. Harrison is a handsome, blue-eyed man with thinning sandy hair. He has that direct, frank quality I have often encountered in southern divines. Belief is mingled with courtesy and modesty in his manner. You know at once that he is not a man to rant, or harangue, or mock. His friendliness is genuine; faith has endowed him with natural grace.

"Very good, very good," Dani says warily. "Then it goes on. . . ." And Dani speaks Hebrew.

"I'm sure that is accurate," Mr. Harrison says, "but I can only read Hebrew. I cannot respond in your language, as much as I would like to."

Dani folds his arms; score one for him. Still, I gather that he likes the Baptists of Beersheba. He appreciates their pilgrimage to his parched country. These men are a new breed of Crusaders, armed not with swords and battering rams, but with trowels, guidebooks, and open hearts.

"How did you come to be digging here?" my wife, Marie, asks. "Do you just apply somewhere, or is there an agency that gives information out?"

Our third Baptist, the Reverend Glenn Spivey, pastor of Ozion Baptist Church in Meadville, Mississippi, a fair young man built along the lines of a middle linebacker, responds. "We were originally going to dig at Mahata, but they could not get enough people, so we switched to Tel Beersheba. We are very pleased. We are getting to know the land of the Bible and the people of the Bible."

"What do you think of the people?" I blurt out. I can't help it. I shall go through life worrying how Christians—especially bedrock Christian Americans like Messrs. Priddy, Harrison, and Spivey—feel about Jews.

Mr. Harrison, senior man of the trio, answers. "We admire them," he says. "This is the nearest thing to a classless society in the world. No one shirks hard work or menial work, and no stigma attaches to it. Back in the United States, it is now almost impossible to get people to work as mailmen, an honorable and respected job. But Israelis know what it is to work, and that it is to be admired."

Is it the sun? Or is the marvelous, inspired illogic of this vignette rendering me giddy? The Protestant ethic, dead in America, is alive and flourishing in Israel, a nation of laboring Jews!

"One of the hardest jobs we have in America," Mr. Priddy says, "is convincing people that their work is of value, and that no matter how ordinary it is, it contributes to society. Not here. Here they all know that they are making a contribution."

I find I am in agreement with the Baptists, and with the Israelis. I am forever grateful that America has permitted me to be a writer, an idle, scribbling parasite—that she has "let me get away with so much," as my mentor the late Joseph Wood Krutch put it. (Krutch wrote that he could not believe that society let him earn a living writing, exactly what he wanted to do all his life, and, moreover, writing on subjects that interested *him*. Sometimes, he mused, he expected to be shaken by the scruff of the neck and admonished, "Root, hog, or die!") I am astounded by the willingness of masses of people to deliver mail, run computers, drive taxis, work as cops and firemen. I feel forever in their debt, forever grateful. I have never in my life sneered at a civil servant or a union man. I thank God for them, and I not only support my local police, but I will support any move to raise their salaries.

"We have no choice," Dani says. "We work or we perish."

Of course all arguments in Israel return to that grim point. Among themselves, the Israelis do not talk much about dying or extermination. But they remind foreigners about their precarious existence. ("There is no question of our losing a war," a guide in Arad told me. "Where do we go if we lose?")

"Yes, we can appreciate that," Mr. Harrison says. "We also approve of the priorities in your country. All necessities are provided for, but luxuries are hard to come by. And perhaps that makes for a better society."

Dani makes no response, but a faint, disbelieving smile turns the corners of his mouth. Israelis would welcome a few luxuries, anything to sweeten their lives. They live, the majority of them, at a minimal level of comfort. Of course, they have all the food they need, adequate clothing, some amenities. But there is never quite enough of the *other* things—the vacation, the extra piece of furniture, the car.

We have already visited the summit of the dig, and we have talked to Professor Yohanan Aharoni, one of Israel's most eminent archaeologists. Now, my wife asks Mr. Priddy what he thinks of the American student-diggers working on Tel Beersheba.

Mr. Priddy frowns. "Not much. They aren't much for working,

and there is too much fooling around." He does not elaborate, but we have a fair idea of what he has in mind. Americans in Israel always appear somewhat misplaced. Most of them—I say, *most*— are middle-class, comfortable, lackadaisical kids. There are almost no Israeli youngsters at archaeological sites. They are all in the army.

"The Bible is the great welding knot between East and West," Mr. Harrison says. "It is the timeless book. We have come to know it better here. Every weekend, when we have time off from the excavation, we travel. Last weekend we went to Jaffa, Ashdod, and Ashkelon. Next weekend we will tour Jerusalem, and after that we will spend two days in Tiberias."

"In my case," Mr. Priddy, Sunday School administrator in Moss Point, says, "I will earn four credits towards my M.A. for this work. I can't think of a more satisfying way to learn about the Bible."

I try to create an orderly pattern out of what I am hearing. These men are southern Baptists. They *believe*. They believe in the Word, in the Book created by those old desert wanderers, the Children of Abraham. The thought of Abraham chills me, even though we are wilting in a hundred degrees of shriveling heat. We are standing on his hill, the place where he watered his sheep.

"I truly understand now," Mr. Priddy tells Marie and myself, as Dani embarks on a biblical debate with Mr. Harrison, "why Abraham chose this spot, a natural area for his encampment. If you'll come down a way with me I'll show you the confluence of the Wadi Beer and the Wadi Hebron, the two streams. This was a prime source of water, just the place for a man with flocks."

We stare out at the bleached, burned land. How did it manage to sustain life? Indeed, how did so much vitality burst forth? All those cities built (and leveled), wars fought, dynasties founded, legends nourished, ethical and mystical systems evolved. And yet I have trouble getting through a day. The blinding heat, the sun that burns through my wilted white golfer's hat, the endless vista of scorched, pebbly, rocky land, those undulant beige-rust hills; all these conspire to render me exhausted and limp at the close of the day. I am filled with wondering admiration for those ancient desert tribes, those cranky Hebrews and Idumeans and Naba-teans who did so much with so little.

As Mr. Priddy, Marie, and I start walking back to the sheltering tent, where Dani is engaged in brisk debate over scriptural
meaning with Mr. Harrison, I begin to think about Father Abraham, on whose home grounds we are now strolling. (One tends to
stroll or amble in Israel in August. The phrase "walk humbly with
thy God" takes on special meaning here. Bold, arrogant, energetic
strides are not appropriate on these hot, pulverized hillsides.)

"As I recall, sir," I gasp, "God commanded Abraham to take his
son Isaac and go to the land of Moriah and offer him up as a
burnt offering on one of the mountains."

"That is correct. Genesis twenty-two two."

"I suppose a God-inspired man, the founder of a new religion
and a man who would make a covenant with the Lord, would
not hesitate to follow the Lord's bidding."

"So the Bible teaches us," Mr. Priddy said.

"But what astounds me," I said, "is the struggle involved
merely in getting to Mount Moriah. If it is in Jerusalem, on the
site of the Mosque of Omar, imagine the effort! Abraham was
over a hundred years old, and he had to saddle up his asses, taking two of his servants and little Isaac along, chop wood for the
sacrifice, and start the long ride to Moriah. Who knows that some
of Abimelech's Philistines might have been laying in wait for
them? So there they go—over fifty miles of rugged desert—old
Abraham, the boy, the servants, in search of the white rock of
sacrifice."

"But it's all a myth," my wife protests. "Anything can happen
in a fairy tale."

"I'm not sure it is a fairy tale," I answer. "It's got to have some
basis in tribal history. We know the old desert people practiced
human sacrifice. Scholars say the story of Abraham and Isaac has
to have some basis in human history. It's a civilizing step, a turning away from human sacrifice. What I find difficult to understand is how all these things happened in *this* place, in *this* heat,
under *this* sky. If I were Abraham, I might have told God it was
just too hot to take that donkey ride to Mount Moriah, no matter
what He had in mind. At the age of a hundred—hell, at the age of
forty-seven, I'd be content to sleep in my tent and let the world
go by."

"I'm not sure I follow you," Mr. Priddy says, as we approach his Baptist colleagues and Dani who is reeling off Hebrew in declamatory tones and swiftly translating it to English.

"Just that I wonder how they got from day to day, that's all," I mutter. "Herding, milking, pitching tents—let alone thinking about new religions and treaties with God. And after God stayed Abraham's hand at Mount Moriah, He blessed him and promised to multiply his seed—"

"Like the stars of the heaven, and as the sand which is upon the seashore," Mr. Priddy adds.

"—and then they trekked back to Beersheba and lived here for a long, long time. In this barren place. Have you seen the lands that the Bedouin cultivate just south of here?"

"We have," Mr. Priddy says.

"You wonder how they manage to feed a single sheep or goat with them, even though they have tractors and jeeps now," I go on. "I don't know that modern desert peoples produce any immortal legends or covenants with God. I think they're more like me. They get hot and thirsty and irritable and tired. But not old Abraham or the rest of them. There they are—saddling up the asses and doing God's bidding."

Of course what astonishes me even more—and this is a sensation that will intensify the longer I am in Israel—is the boundless energy and courage of the present inhabitants of the land. They grow apricots and split atoms; argue child-rearing and theology; fight an endless bloody war; stage plays and ballets; and talk, talk, talk about it all. Where does the energy come from? Someone should do a study of the growth of fatigue in modern life. Lethargy and lassitude are worldwide problems. Look at England —nobody really wants to work, the French are drunk by noon. . . .

These speculations trail off as I begin to hear a lively discussion between Dani and Mr. Harrison. Mr. Spivey, a younger man and presumably a former student of the professor of Old Testament, listens respectfully, as do Marie and I.

"No," Harrison says, "I have never felt that Saul got a fair shake from the scribes. If you read the Old Testament too quickly, you don't realize that the man had stature. He was a good military leader. He had charisma. He had to be a good leader because the Philistines were pushing in from the coast, and he had to rally the Israelites."

"Yes, I agree," Dani comments, a bit reluctantly it seems. He does not appreciate being lectured; *he* is the lecturer. "Saul blew the trumpet throughout all the land, saying let the Hebrews hear."

"They must have heard him clearly," Mr. Harrison says. "Look what he accomplished. He defeated Moab and Ammon and Edom and Zobah and the Philistines. As the Bible says, he *vexed* them."

Dani nods his head. "Yes, in Hebrew it goes like this." He utters the ancient words. He is a splendid actor—gestures and inflections match the dramatic recitation.

"I feel sorry for Saul and the way he comes across," Mr. Harrison says. "After all, he didn't ask to be made the first king. It was Samuel, acting on God's commands, who anointed him. The Book says God gave Saul another heart after that, and he was higher than any of his people from the shoulders upward. Then along comes young David—handsome, a musician, a warrior, also anointed by Samuel on the Lord's orders—and it's hard to blame Saul for acting the way he did. Then he kills Goliath, and the women start crying, 'Saul hath slain his thousands and David his tens of thousands.' You can almost sympathize with Saul wanting to get rid of that upstart, for becoming slightly paranoid."

I am drawn into the argument. Mr. Harrison, I am now certain, is a first-rate lecturer. For him, the people of the Book are alive, and vibrant, and full of salt and pungency. I add, "Isn't it a classic story of the old order being replaced by the new? I mean, even if one doesn't believe that God inspired these events, can't we understand Saul's bitterness? He was the first anointed. He unites the people. He wins the first battles. And here's this fresh kid with his harp and his slingshot, getting all the praise. Of course, Saul didn't have to go that far—to try to kill him—but he had a right to be angry. It's also one of the soundest and most dramatic of literary themes: the old leader giving way to the new. Ibsen used it in *The Master Builder*."

"That's true," Harrison agrees. "But I still feel Saul never gets the best of the account. That affair with the Witch of Endor. Nightmare Alice, I call her, when I lecture my students. Heck, we've only *her* word. It's her account of what Saul saw—Samuel summoned up from the dead, and the prediction that Saul and

Jonathan would be killed by the Philistines. Samuel didn't console Saul very much. The poor man could not have gone into battle with any confidence the next day at Mount Gilboa. Samuel'd already told Saul the Lord had left him and had given the kingdom to David. But, as I say, there was probably something funny going on there. The Witch of Endor was the only witness to this, and she probably told people about it after Saul was dead. So we have only Nightmare Alice's word, and that isn't too good."

"Are you suggesting that perhaps the Lord *hadn't* departed from Saul?" I asked.

"No, there's other evidence on that score. I'm just suggesting that Saul be regarded more charitably. To be honest, I don't think the witch ever did succeed in calling Samuel back from the dead. I don't believe her story. Which is not to say that I don't believe in the Word of God in those days. It existed then, and I believe it was given directly. But not to people like the Witch of Endor."

Dani is squinting under the glare of the noon sun. Above us, at the dig, a handful of workers labor in the five-meter-square pits. Up the side of the tel runs the cut, the test diggings made to establish different strata. I see Professor Aharoni's bright orange shirt and straw sombrero as he leads another party of visitors around the site. As I watch him I realize again that there is simply too much history to cope with in Israel. Millennia here are telescoped into hours. It takes manly concentration and a casual attitude toward eternity to walk these ancient hills. One's mind must be uncluttered, and mine is quite the opposite. But I must try to answer this.

"In those times?" I ask hoarsely. "Do you believe, Mr. Harrison, that God no longer talks to people?"

The professor of Old Testament history pauses. "Let me put it this way. I believe there are no longer any new revelations. But I believe he still speaks through *certain* people."

"In Israel?" I ask.

"The Spirit of the Lord is very much in this place. What the actual Word of God *is*, is debatable. For example, I don't believe that even Scripture is the actual Word of God. It *conveys* the Word of God, and as we read it, we must bring to it our own faith and commitment." He smiles at all of us. "You see, we are not quite as conservative and fundamentalist as others. We believe Scripture exists to be interpreted, and we are always ready to reexamine and reinterpret. That is why we are here."

"There are no more prophets and no more prophecies," Dani says flatly. "Not even here."

Mr. Harrison ponders this. His honest American Baptist face seeks a response to Dani's challenge. "I would call Herzl a prophet," he says. "Surely his prophecies have been fulfilled."

"But not a prophet in the true sense of the Bible," Dani responds. "A great political and national leader, yes. Not a prophet. I don't believe he conversed with God."

The dispute leaves me breathless. Surely Israel is the only country in the world where a Baptist clergyman from New Orleans will argue that Theodore Herzl, the father of Zionism, was a prophet—and be contradicted by the sabra grandson of an Orthodox rabbi from Brooklyn.

We bid good-bye to the three Baptists. And I feel better about the American South and the fundamentalist Protestants who rule there.

There are friendly Baptists all over Israel. Like the three diggers we found on Abraham's hill, treading the earth where walked Sarah, and Hagar, and Ishmael, and Isaac, and Abimelech, they come in search of confirmation, of substantiation, of evidence. Since even in middle age I spend about fifteen minutes a day (no more) worrying about what Christians think about Jews, these pilgrimages by quintessential Gentiles to Israel cheer me considerably.

"What," I asked my friend Zev Vilnay one day, "is the Christian attitude toward Israel, at this moment?"

Vilnay—king of guides, author, scholar, Orientalist, explorer, military strategist, and fellow Bessarabian—wrinkled his nose. "Friend Green," he boomed at me, "the attitudes vary with the faiths. The Catholics, the ones who have been in charge in Jerusalem all these years, the Franciscans and so on, are not too happy with us. Medium friendly, but not too happy. You see, according to them, Jews are supposed to suffer. We should be weeping and wailing and kvetching and pulling out our hair and getting tortured, paying for our sins, for our rejection of Christ. That's how they like us.

"But nobody weeps anymore. We are too busy. What they see here, and that includes everyone from the Pope on down, is a revival of the Jewish state, but also, a revival of Judaism as a vigorous *religion*, and this is disturbing to them. It makes them nervous. But mostly, they are upset because we aren't miserable. Let me be frank, Gerald. When the Pope came here, he smiled and he was polite, but he seemed to me to be swallowing hard. He wasn't *kvelling* to see the Star of David flying over the holy places. And now it must be even harder for them, with the Holy Sepulchre and Nazareth and Bethlehem under our administration—though these places are more accessible than ever, better maintained, easier for the whole world to see. Still, they are not happy. We aren't suffering."

"And the Protestants?"

"A better attitude," Zev Vilnay said. "The Anglicans, the Dutch, the Scandinavians, they are great believers in prophecy. Many of them, including their leading scholars, look upon Israel as the fulfillment of their own prophecies about the Bible. The Jews must return to the Holy Land before the world can be saved. So, here we are. We are returned."

I told Zev that I had read about the arrival in Israel of the Reverend Billy James Hargis of Tulsa, Oklahoma, a pillar of extreme right-wing sentiment in the United States, leader of the Christian Anti-Communist Crusade. Although I knew of no evidence indicating Mr. Hargis himself was anti-Semitic, I felt reasonably sure that certain of his backers were.

"The interview I read," I said, "quoted Mr. Hargis as praising Israel to the skies. He said he comes annually on his pilgrimage, and that he regards the Jews of Israel as the salvation of the world. That is, their return to Israel is the first part of the fulfillment of prophecy. The next part will be their conversion to Christianity, which will be followed by the conversion of everyone in the world, after which Christ will return."

"He shouldn't," Zev Vilnay said, "hold his hand on his mouth until it happens."

Israel needs all the friends she can get. And I suspect the Baptists and fundamentalist Christians, who represent a good chunk of America, may prove good allies—better surely than some of the kids who find it invigorating to consort with Al Fatah,

fellow "participatory democrats" busy "restructuring" society.
Shortly after my return to the United States, I found this item
in my airmail edition of the Jerusalem *Post*:

CONSERVATIVE PASTOR
WITH ARCHAEOLOGY BUG

"I'm a conservative. That means that I have a point of
view," says Dr. William S. McBirnie, who is heading a
group of 200 Americans, many of whom share that point
of view, on a 10-day visit to Israel.

A pastor, lecturer, news analyst with a life-long interest in archaeology, Dr. McBirnie first came here in 1950
and has been back at the head of what he describes as
"study groups" 16 times since. . . .

Dr. McBirnie has a daily radio news analysis program,
and has 150 publications to his credit in the fields of
world events and religion. "I'm a conservative political
news analyst," he emphasizes, putting himself in the
right wing of the Republican Party with Senator Barry
Goldwater and J. Strom Thurmond. He is also pastor of
the United Community Church of Glendale, California,
and a lecturer on archaeology and biblical studies at the
California School of Theology. . . .

He attributes the increased size of his present group
of tourists firstly to Israel's "monopoly" on the Holy
Land and of course the reduced cost of travel. "People
are interested to see what's happening in Israel. For the
Evangelical Christians Israel is a second home. Our
people have a life-long acquaintance with the Bible as
our religion concentrates on its study rather than ceremony."

Dr. McBirnie pauses reflectively. "It is a pity that
there is no real way for the non-Jewish tourist from the
U.S. to show friendship and solidarity with Israel. We
come and visit but we seem to be no more than visitors
who pass in the night. There does need to be some way
in which the tourist's natural affection for this land can
be given expression. You should give the people of
America—and not just Jews—a stake here."

Sometimes, when my thoughts are blackest about America, I am cheered by Dr. McBirnie's candid expression of affection for Israel. Or Billy James Hargis's kind words. Or the three Baptists on Tel Beersheba. Israel, in terms of American backing, has all the liberals she can handle. Maybe too many. Some strong voices on the right are very much in order. Welcome, *shalom*, and a hearty good *yontiff* to Messrs. Hargis and McBirnie and anyone else who regards Israel as "a second home." May they go back to Glendale and Tulsa and New Orleans and spread the word.

CHAPTER II

Stirrings

Old stones have always fascinated me. As a boy I wandered
through the magnificent Egyptian collection of the Brooklyn
Museum. My father, a Thoreau-reader in Brownsville, once found
an arrowhead in his field of corn in our backyard on Prospect
Place. I can recall the cool cindery dusk of a November day,
my father in dirty overalls and a battered homburg, raking the
dry stalks of his last crop, and coming upon the perfectly flaked
stone. Algonquin? Mohawk? We didn't know. We both handled
it with the respect due the old warriors of the eastern woodlands.

Later, because of my love for the boulders and ashlars of antiquity, I wrote a novel about Peru and immersed myself in Sacsa-
huaman and Macchu Picchu. The book suffered from too much
archaeology and not enough sex. I also wrote one about an archaeological dig in Florida; it was diffuse and overburdened with
trivia; it was a qualified success.

When I lived in Europe for four years, I found the ruins of the
classical world marvelously comforting. I knew all about the

14

bloody wars and the slaves, the treachery of Romans and the duplicity of Greeks. But I never overcame my sense of wonder and respect for old stones—the pale gold temples of Paestum, the utilitarian majesty of the Pont du Gard, the elegant theaters of Epidaurus and Syracuse and Verona, the streets of Ostia Antica and Ercolano. The relics of the dead world assured me: *It hasn't all been bad. There has been beauty, and grace, and orderliness and community.* If this be Panglossian, a Pollyanna-ish view of history, I plead guilty. As for Mr. Ardrey's killer ape, it has never seemed to me a shocking or original assertion that man is capable of monstrous crimes, that he may covet his neighbor's wife, land, food, indeed, possibly murder him and eat his brains and heart. Mr. Ardrey's hairy hominoids, stalking the African veldt, pointed bone in hand, in search of a *fleishikeh* lunch, don't surprise me at all. Even a cursory reading of history will tell us that man can be a bloody-minded fellow, that his first instinct on seeing a species not his own, or even a stranger, is often, simply, *kill it.*

But there must have been something else. Cities have been built. Families raised. Fields cultivated. Machines invented. Art and music and theater and literature have been created. Had we all been preoccupied with the compulsion to smash our neighbor's skull and sup on his liver I doubt that a single seed would have been planted, a single child suckled. There must be *other* instincts and conditions at work besides the homicidal ones. People want to get through the day, love a child, sleep in a warm place, admire a sunset or a painting, and have a little peace of mind.

Once, on a chill fall afternoon, in southern France, I saw a sign on a country road pointing to "MONUMENTS PRIMITIFS." I turned off the road to a dirt path and followed it to a barren yellow field. To one side, beneath a handful of gnarled trees, on an elevated place, I saw the old stones—a dolmen I suppose, a Stone Age altar, one horizontal boulder balanced on two vertical ones, the relic surrounded by a semicircle of curiously shaped smaller stones. The pessimist will tell me that those old Cro-Magnon hunters probably bloodied the place with human entrails, but I doffed my beret to those dawn hunters who tried to make some sense out of a bleak and harsh world.

So, some years ago, I decided to visit the stones of Zion, the major archaeological sites of Israel, my putative homeland. In the spring of 1969 it appeared that I would have a free summer—no television commitments, my novel on schedule. I promptly made contact with the Israel Government Tourist Office in New York in the person of their able public-relations chief, Nathan Freedman. I began my research, decided on a general itinerary, and wrote airmail letters to people in Israel who might be of help to an aging American-Jewish novelist with a youthful addiction to ruins.

Airborne and sleepless at three in the morning, my wife challenged: "Why you? Why should you write about Israel?"

"Because everyone does."

"You changed your name. You haven't participated in a religious service since you were bar-mitzvahed. You married a *shiksa*. You were embarrassed when they showed the vulgar wedding in *Goodbye, Columbus*. I saw you shrinking into your seat."

"Being Jewish is a state of mind," I said.

The El Al superjet cruised along gently, a giant technological miracle owned by, run by, managed by a new breed of Jews. Up front, a Jewish crew; serving us, Jewish stewardesses. Did it matter? Did I feel uplifted, amazed, inspired? I did not. Unlike Portnoy, who marveled at Jewish policemen and soldiers, I am never surprised by the mutability and variations possible in man—and even Jews. Ghana and Ethiopia and Nepal have airlines. Why not Israel? It is less surprising to me that the Israelis can run an efficient, safe, comfortable, and rather elegant airline than it would be if the men who govern Russia woke up one morning and announced that writers could write anything they pleased. Technology and industrial skills and the manipulation of things, I fear, can be mastered a lot easier than a willingness to liberate the mind and spirit can be achieved.

What makes Israel so endlessly intriguing is that her people are striving to achieve *both*—to plant their feet in the modern world of science and technology, and to nurture the ancient ethical standards, to endow them with new significance. A rather ambitious charter for a small nation; but they are a people who possess a very, very old mandate.

Lod airport: a great plain shed. I learn soon not to expect luxurious surroundings. Frankly I like simplicity. Besides, these people are at war, I have to keep reminding myself. It is not a source of distress to me that Lod is a dreary place; rather it is a source of amazement that things function as swiftly and as efficiently as they do considering Israel's terrifying priority— survival. How in heaven's name do they find enough people to handle baggage, issue tickets, drive taxicabs, direct traffic, when they are threatened daily with extermination? Shouldn't every one of them—the overweight elderly men in open shirts, the dark-eyed Oriental women at the coffee stand, the ruddy, rude cabbies—be manning guns at some border outpost? I keep think- ing about those 100,000,000 Arabs, and I grow weak in my knees.

"Mr. Gray?"

"Green."

A Sherut Shalom hostess—snub-nosed, brown-eyed, vivacious, carrying a clipboard—was addressing me.

"Oh. I am looking for Mr. Gray. An American journalist. He was supposed to be on El Al 401."

"I am an American journalist, but I am Mr. Green. It's proba- bly an error, and you want me after all."

"I don't think so. I am sure I want Mr. Gray."

As Marie and I searched for our luggage, a slender young man, tanned the color of a Gucci suitcase, presented himself. This was our first meeting with Dani, the man from the Ministry of Tour- ism. He helped us locate our bags, presented me with a sheaf of handouts, booklets, maps, and other literature from the Ministry, and advised me that there was a car waiting outside. Did I know Sam Levenson? Slightly. Noah Gordon? No. James Michener? No.

"Are you sure you aren't Mr. Gray?" the little girl asked as we made our way outside to the car. It was turning dark, that soft, melancholy Holy Land dusk, the air charged with ancient secrets.

Dani berated her in Hebrew: I was Mr. *Green.*

"You are sure you aren't Barry Gray? He was due on the same flight."

"I am not Barry Gray. See—I don't even have a tape recorder."

We walked out to the automobile, through crowds of talkative, arguing, kissing, hugging, agitated Israelis. I heard a lot of New York-accented English, almost as much French, a great deal of Hebrew, and almost no Yiddish. I had trouble orienting myself. In the dry heat, the fading light, the clotted crowds—men in sports shirts, women in printed frocks—the atmosphere was Mediterranean. We might have been in Italy, except that there were more blondes than one usually finds in an Italian crowd. I think "controlled hysteria" would be the best description of the motion, the cries, the noise. I wondered how these excitable, loquacious people would react if Arab terrorists started shelling the Lod airport. Oddly, I was confident they'd do the right thing, that they would, magically, change into disciplined fighters. In Israel paradox is paramount, and outward appearances confuse. The fat woman in the ill-fitting yellow dress, weeping and smothering a pale boy with wet kisses—I had little doubt that she would, at someone's barked order, man a machine gun.

"This is Lod," Dani said, as we drove off from the airport. "Or Lydda. As Lod it is mentioned in the Bible for the first time in Chronicles. How are you on biblical history?"

"I am a total ignoramus."

"Good."

Dani was delighted. A biblical scholar could have argued him down; in me, he had a true idiot, an American writer but a *dummkopf* when it came to Old Testament.

"Marvelous grapes just outside of Lydda," Dani said. He ordered the driver to stop at a farm stand just beyond the Crusader bridge.

We made a detour and found the farm stand, but it was closed. "Too bad," Dani said. "We have the best grapes in the world in Israel. Also the best figs and melons."

I would learn to accept this boasting, especially from guides. It is done with such innocence, with such confidence, that it is hard to take offense. And as I learned, Israeli fruit is very good indeed, perhaps not the best in the world, but a match for French and Italian fruits, which I had long considered supreme.

"This road was closed to us before the Six-Day War," Dani explained. "Now it is a much shorter ride to Jerusalem."

All along the way, I saw road-building equipment— earthmovers, graders, cranes. I doubted that the road was being improved for Hussein's benefit.

"Look," Dani said. "We left the old armored trucks where they were shot up during the War of Independence."

The reminders are everywhere in Israel. There is no shame or hesitation about preserving the artifacts of war. I counted four of these immobilized, rusting wrecks—old armored buses and trucks, destroyed by Jordanian gunners in 1947. The road had been a bloody trap for the Israelis. Now it was secure.

But for how long? Soon we were stopped at one of the road-blocks between Lod and Jerusalem. A strange contraption is utilized to block traffic: an accordion mechanism, like the barrier placed at the head of a flight of stairs to restrain babies. But instead of sitting vertically, it is placed flat and extended across the roadway. From it rise long, wicked spikes. Any vehicle attempting to barrel across the nails would suffer crippling blow-outs. Two policemen in tan uniforms were checking cars. Apparently any vehicle with Israeli plates (orange, as opposed to the Jordanian green) was moved through quickly.

"We have the best police in the world," Dani said.

Was it whistling in the dark? Do they keep assuring themselves of their excellence because they live on the edge of disaster? I hoped not. They do seem aware of their problems. Aware, but not at all frightened. They shrug; it's life; they'll manage. And this cockiness, this rugged courage, is contagious.

Abruptly, the sandy, evergreen-dotted hills around us darkened. A canopy of ultramarine blue, purpling, blackening, covered the sky. The stars gleamed for us as they had for Abraham.

"Why does the sky seem lower here?" Marie asked. "I feel as if I could touch the stars."

"Many sensitive people remark about that," Dani said. "The sky seems closer. The stars are in your hands. It is why the Bible was written here, why religion was born in these hills."

I myself wasn't quite sure whether the sky was any closer or not. Bluer, darker, brighter with stars, perhaps. But not closer. As far as I am concerned, the sky is just about where it should be, in the Judean hills or in Stamford, Connecticut. When it starts approaching us, either actually or as an optical illusion caused by atmospheric or climatic quirks, I get uneasy.

Suddenly we were in Jerusalem. The dark slopes, sprouting cypresses and pines—all, I assumed, planted and nourished by the

Israelis in recent years, for they had the look of planned groves—
gave way to paved streets and endless rows of small, cluttered
shops.

"My Jerusalem," Dani said. "My beautiful city. It is the most
beautiful city in the world."

One learns quickly not to contradict the sabra. I said nothing.
Most beautiful? I found it moderately attractive, and too
crowded. The streets swarmed with people, most of them young,
boys in shirtsleeves, miniskirted girls. I was impressed first by the
uniformity of the building stone, a pale-beige, irregularly hewn
block of great beauty. It appeared to be basic, unvarying, and
omnipresent, yet it did not become repetitious or boring. Perhaps
it retained its attractiveness because it was an intrinsically handsome stone. It was stone that required little art and manipulation;
a material of inherent beauty.

But the streets themselves—we were on the busy Jaffa Road—
seemed to me a disconcerting amalgam of Middle European and
Mediterranean. The lively, agitated crowds, the orderly mobs at
street crossings, the residual heat, the neon lights of cafés and
kiosks, suggested Palermo or Athens. But the shops—small,
jammed together, not graceful in decor or design—looked more
like Belgrade or Budapest. There was a further peculiarity that
lent the city (we were in West Jerusalem, the busy, commercial,
established Jewish section) a strange air of compartmental-
ization. All streets were separated from sidewalks by endless blue
and white barriers constructed of stout metal pipes. This was to
prevent illegal parking and jaywalking. One had to cross dutifully
at corners.

I'd heard a great deal about the individuality and eccentricity
of Israelis, that they are people who go their own way, do what
pleases them at any particular moment, circumvent laws in a
humorous, original way. I'm afraid that is myth. There are stiff
laws and regulations in Israel, and they are *obeyed*. A frontier
society this may be, but there is nothing lax, casual, or offhand
about the way its citizens regard the laws of the land. I was to see
Dani bawl the daylights out of two frightened teen-age girls after
they littered the grounds of the Ashkelon park with candy-
wrappers. It's perfectly understandable. A threatened society, a
young one, building, experimenting, aware of the rigors

demanded in order to survive, Israel has small tolerance for jay-walkers or illegal parkers or currency black marketeers. I'm sure they exist. Israel is no Nirvana. But there is damned little law-breaking, and little tolerance for it when it crops up.

We were to spend one night in Jerusalem and then embark on a week's orientation of the major archaeological sites under Dani's firm guidance. The week of hosted rubbernecking would prove exhausting—too much in too short a time—but it would have its advantages. I am a firm believer in the accuracy and acuity of first impressions. We were soon to be inundated by them, and with them would come a feel for the people and a sense of the land.

"They don't like us too well here," Dani said as we unloaded our bags under the handsome porte cochere of the American Colony Hotel. "This is East Jerusalem, formerly Jordan. They are pro-Arab. But it doesn't matter. We're in charge now."

The American Colony is superb; the kind of old-fashioned hotel which, I am afraid, is vanishing. It was once the palace of a Turkish pasha. The small lobby is bright with blue peacock tiles. There is a marvelous Oriental garden, full of flowers, cacti, and date palms. The rooms are lofty, cool, and huge, with absolutely no need for frigid artificial air. The couple who own and run it are an unusual Anglo-American family, long active in charitable work in Jordan, particularly in looking after Arab children. They were remarkably refreshing people—possessing the confident, long-legged, florid look of the eternal Britisher abroad. They are optimists, diplomats, scholars, people operating with a kind of ease and charm that comes only through a happy racial memory of the Empire. The Empire is gone, but the self-assurance and style are not. I never saw our hosts without thinking enviously of the Relief of Mafeking or Younghusband's expedition to Lhasa. No wonder Dani was a bit stiff as he spoke, in flawless Arabic, to the night clerk.

"So. We will call for you at nine in the morning," Dani said. "Sleep well, and *shalom*."

He smiled at the Arab desk clerk. But I sensed an evident unease, a maladroit quality that Dani never exhibited when with Jews or Christians. I was to observe this often in the occupied areas. Territorially, Jerusalem may be nonnegotiable, as the Israe-

lis contend, but there is a good deal of negotiating to be done in
people-to-people relationships. Not that the Arabs of East Jerusalem, notably the hotel employees, are not models of polite-
ness and charm. Moreover, as my host advised me, most of
the West Bank Arabs, not just East Jerusalemites, have no use for
King Hussein, and while they are not necessarily delighted with
the Star of David, they have no regrets about being free of the
Hashemite's Bedouin rule.

Our week of orientation began the next day. At once the light
staggered me. It burns. It blinds. Never in my life have I seen
sunlight so bright, so invasive, so total. Normally I am impervious
to dry desert heat. I have worked long hours in 110 degrees in
Baja California and in the Sonoran desert of Arizona, and I have
had more energy than I thought possible under such conditions.
But the heat of Israel is different. I suspect it has to do with the
intense overwhelming light. For one thing, it affects the visual
sense. Burning out colors and shadings, it endows shapes with a
hard new outline. The effect on the eyes is that of a faintly tinted,
sharply defined drawing. I have stared at the Damascus Gate,
that pale handsome creation of the much-maligned Turks, at
noon, and been convinced that some artist has used a brush and
black paint to outline the battlements and walls.

Mostly it is the power of this supernal light to diffuse a golden
cloud over the visible world. It is not easy to accept. One longs
after a while for dusk and shadows and a slow, subtle darkening
of the eternal golden walls and tan stones and honey streets. The
colors of the day, the golds and yellows and beiges, become
oppressive after a time; grayness and shadows are desired.

Since I am a great believer in absorbing the essential truths of
any country I visit (in France I will not eat sliced bread, in
Greece I wear rope-soled shoes) I resented the icy air conditioning of the Ministry's snappy new Dodge. I wanted to subject
myself to the hot gusts, the desert furnace. Part of traveling is a
reasonable amount of suffering: it endows the traveler with a virtuous martyred coating.

"Look at the right-hand side of the road," Dani said in his usual
peremptory way. "Look!"

"Big stones. Overgrown with weeds."

"*Herodian* stones. Superb, superb. Ah, what a country. Yes, Herodian stones. They call that section Khal-Unia. What does that suggest?"

"I don't know."

Dani snorted. He would do a lot of snorting and frowning during our week together. I took offense at first; later I realized that this is routine sabra impatience. "Khal-Unia. Colonia. Colony. It was a Roman colony of some kind. Those are the foundations of Herodian buildings. You can't mistake those huge boulders. Herod knew how to build."

This was my first encounter with the love-hate relationship Israelis have with Herod. They concede grudgingly that he could build, he could get things done, he could handle his Roman masters, he could manipulate his cantankerous Jewish factions. But they aren't quite sure they like him. In this they are conditioned by the traditional view of Herod as archfiend, killer, monster. Still, I get the feeling that some Israelis would like to come right out with it and declare him, bloody as he was, a national hero.

"This place, Colonia," Dani said, "was related to the Castellum Romanum, on the other side of the road, just ahead. The Colonia refers to a party of Roman army veterans who were settled here, under the protection of the Castellum. You see those remains of Herodian stones? There used to be many more. They were taken to build Arab houses over the years, and all that's left are those foundations."

Dani had the driver stop at a fruit stand—we never seemed to pass one by—within view of the great white, bleached, grass-covered ruins of Khal-Unia. We bought small sweet pears, delicate apples, juice-heavy peaches. As I chewed on a perfumed chartreuse pear I contemplated the remains of Herod's building—temple, domicile, whatever. There they were: old stones—old mysteries, old civilizations. People couldn't have been murdering each other all the time, even though a reading of Josephus seems to give that impression. There had been time to hew and transport and set in place those massive white blocks, each one neatly flanged at the edge—a sure indication of Herodian work—and build their places at the side of the road.

We moved on. "On your left," Dani said, "the Castellum Romanum, or the Castel. Old Crusader fort. It was a big victory for us in 1947. But a lot of Jewish soldiers died fighting for it. We didn't have a damned thing to fight with, and the Arab Legion was inside with heavy guns."

Farther on, we left the road and parked at Aqua Bella. "You should see this," Dani said. "A Crusader monastery, twelfth century."

Surrounding the honey-brown remains of the monastery was an extensive park, coursed by a swift-flowing stream, small waterfalls, and cultivated meadows, covered with benches and picnic tables. It was Saturday, the Israelis' day off, and even at nine thirty in the morning the park was jam-packed with people in casual clothing—shorts, swimsuits, loose dresses. Here a volleyball game was in progress, there some men pitched horseshoes. There was a good deal of card-playing. Transistor radios sustained a musical hum. Yet there was a subdued and modulated quality about these Jews. Apart from the emotional scenes I saw at the airport, I rarely witnessed exuberance, excessive loquacity. I suspect most of the people are profoundly, almost mystically, satisfied merely with being in the land. They are rarely in need of wild outbursts. Their pinochle and soccer games have a restrained quality. Or perhaps they are thriftily saving their energies for more arduous tests than the turn of a card or booting a ball?

The ruins of Aqua Bella rested amid pomegranate groves nourished by the clear stream in which Israeli kids in blue shorts and kibbutz hats played. There were Gothic-style arcades and a few sculptures on ruined columns, lions, falcons, crosses, reminders of those brutish, bloody soldiers of the cross. All of the area's ruins—the Castellum, Colonia, Aqua Bella—must have been part of the same complex of buildings in Crusader times.

In the Aqua Bella parking lot a very young couple were carefully draping a plastic covering over their tiny Fiat to protect it from the scorching sun, the abrasive dust. Where once savage Templars and hairy Knights of St. John tethered their armored mounts . . .

Farther along the road north we came to Abu Ghosh, the site of a magnificent Crusader church. Dani explained that Abu Ghosh was a village of friendly Arabs.

"And it is the place where David danced," he added.

"Danced?"

I crisped under one of his most disdainful glances. "Yes. When the Ark was returned. Read First Samuel, four, five, and six. For goodness' sake! The Philistines got the Ark at Aphek, after killing thirty thousand Israelites including Hofne and Pinhas. The Philistines took the Ark to Ashdod and put it in front of Dagon, their god. The next morning Dagon was flat on his face. They stood him up, but the next day his head was chopped off, and the palms of his hands. A lot of the Philistines in Ashdod died, so they decided they didn't want the Ark that badly. They took it to Gath, and the Lord struck them down there also, with hemorrhoids."

"Hem——?"

"Yes! The word in the Bible is *emerods*. 'Hemorrhoids.' God struck the Philistines of Ashdod and Gath and Ekron with emerods. It says so. 'They had emerods in their secret parts.' "

"No wonder they were in a hurry to get rid of it."

"Gath passed the Ark on to Ekron, and Ekron to Beth Shemesh. The people put golden emerods on the Ark, and golden mice, as an offering. But the Lord smote fifty thousand of them, because they looked into the Ark. By now, the Philistines got the idea. The Ark wasn't for them. So it was returned, according to First Samuel, to this place, Kiryat Yearim, or Abu Ghosh, to the house of a man named Abinadab, which is supposed to be right in this area."

"But what about David dancing?"

"That came later. David brought thirty thousand men here, and they took the Ark from Abinadab's house, put it on a cart, and brought it to Jerusalem. When they brought it out, David played on instruments—harps, psalteries, cornets, cymbals—to celebrate. Later, when the Ark entered Jerusalem, the Bible tells us that David danced with all his might before the Lord. One of his wives, Michal, Saul's daughter, saw him dancing and despised him and denounced him for jumping around half naked in front of God. David didn't like her tongue, and neither did the Lord. She was stricken barren. But the procession started here."

"What does it mean?" I asked. "What do the sages say about it?

I can understand the dancing. A logical reaction. But why did Michal deny him his fun? And why was she punished so harshly?"

Dani shrugged. "David was a king. He could do what he pleased. He even told Michal he'd act worse as soon as he got a chance—with the maidservants in front of whom he had undressed himself."

We walked through the garden of the Crusader church, examining old tombs, one oddly shaped like a toadstool, another decorated with a cross. It was a peaceful, cool oasis, a quiet end to the bloody, red-faced brawling of the Crusades. Linear history was choking me; I wanted it spatial, spread out, like a Breughelian landscape. From David's dance of joy, I was now marching with Godfrey de Bouillon and Baldwin the Leper.

The only other tourists in the garden of the Abu Ghosh church were two American women: a young nun of startling beauty and grace and an older blond woman who seemed to be a surly duenna. Dani spotted the nun at once, and his face lit up. "My goodness, look at her. No wonder she had to have a friend travel with her."

The sister was indeed attractive, a tall slender woman in her thirties with a clean, angled face on the style of Katharine Hepburn's. She had a shy sweetness about her. If she taught school, she was surely the most popular teacher on the staff. Dani winked at me. "Watch me talk to her," he said roguishly. "They love to talk to Israeli men. Wait . . ."

Alas, he deceived himself. As soon as he moved his lithe figure toward them, they abruptly turned away and walked toward the parking lot. Evidently the need of Roman Catholic sisters to converse with sabras was not as overwhelming as Dani had imagined.

"I wonder what kind of dances David did?" Marie asked when Dani returned.

"I don't know," I said, half seriously. "I sort of see him in a kind of wild *kazotzki* or taking those leaps like the Red Army dancers. A lot of heel-clicking and finger-snapping. He was God-inspired. He must have soared." The notion excited me. "And if he were anything like Michelangelo's David, or even Verrocchio's, what a sight he must have been, his chest uncovered, those muscled limbs gleaming in the sunlight!"

History was still refusing to behave for me in progressive, extended fashion. Dani had told me about David. But I kept seeing David in Italianate Renaissance form, Michelangelo's corded athlete, Verrocchio's slender ephebe. Then, for some ghastly irrelevant reason, I even—forgive me—saw him dancing the way Groucho Marx does, with those fancy kicks and unexpected thrusts of arms and hands. But how *does* a man dance in front of the Ark of the Covenant?

"Why should Michal have been so bitter about David dancing?" I asked again.

Dani scowled. "She was Saul's daughter. Isn't that reason enough?"

"Like father, like daughter. They didn't care for David. But you couldn't say the same for Jonathan, even though he was Saul's boy. He loved David like his own soul."

We stopped to buy postcards from an elderly French monk in the vestibule of the Crusader church. I thought about the Ark of the Covenant resting in this village, and King David escorting it back to Jerusalem as he played the pipes and cavorted about the cart, clicking heels and performing entrechats. Dimly I recalled something I had read in Dr. Homer W. Smith's iconoclastic *Man and His Gods*, speculation as to what the Ark contained. Stones, Smith had argued; probably phallic stones.

Our next stop, as the sun rose and flooded the world with hot light, was at Tel Gezer. From the road we could see a fragile-looking tower on the crown of the gently rounded hill. Dani explained that it was the archaeologist's photographic tower. There was a dig in progress on Tel Gezer. Work had begun in 1964 and was to conclude in 1971.

We parked and I saw my first Bedouins—three black-clad, mysterious women, a few children, some scrawny sheep. They drifted by, gliding with the aloof, silent indifference of the nomad. I always have the feeling that they view everyone else with condescension and hauteur.

Tel Gezer was a big operation. There were several large army-style barrack buildings and opposite them an open-air mess hall in which one of the shifts of diggers was having an early lunch. In the main shed, amid sorting tables, filing cabinets, desks, we found Miss Carol Bohn, a pretty brunette in her twenties, one of the supervisors.

"I'm a student at Harvard Divinity School," she told us. "I'm working on my Ph.D. in Old Testament. I got my M.A. there in New Testament. I first came to the Holy Land after I graduated from college. I worked at an Arab school in Jerusalem run by the Quakers."

We strolled along the dusty path—pale gray dust, the millennial powder of history—and I asked her, "Are you a Quaker?"

"No. I'm a Roman Catholic."

"And who is in charge of the dig?"

"The Hebrew Union College of Cincinnati. The boss is Bill Dever. He's resident director, but he's in Jerusalem with Dr. Glueck today."

This was the legendary Dr. Nelson Glueck, college president, rabbi, archaeologist, philosopher, former O.S.S. operative in Transjordan.

"This is ecumenism of a high order," I said. "All faiths unite at the digs. Doesn't dogma ever get in the way of the digging?"

"No," she said. "We're concerned only with the evidence. How others interpret what we find is something else."

A series of trenches five meters square dug to varying depths, the average about five or six feet deep, marked the site of the excavations on the summit of Tel Gezer.

"We call this the High Place," Carol explained. "It was first excavated by MacAlister in 1902. He spent seven years working here. His most important finds were the *masseboth*, the sacred pillars. You'll see them on the other side of the hill. Unfortunately he ruined the stratification by dumping the fill from one trench into another and muddling the layers hopelessly. This makes the work here difficult."

We paused at one of the stone-lined pits. A bearded young man was making notes on a clipboard, jotting down measurements read to him by an extremely pretty blonde girl. She was measuring sections of the interior walls of the trench with a small plumb line and a ruler. He was John Warrell, a teacher at Hartford Theological Seminary, a graduate of Phillips University in

Enid, Oklahoma. The girl was Linda Ammons, a student at Phillips.

"Find anything interesting?" I asked.

"A beautiful oil press," Mr. Warrell answered.

It *was* beautiful, an old stone of honorable lineage. I took some photographs, and envied Warrell and Miss Ammons their luminous summer working in the ancient confines of Tel Gezer.

"In First Kings," Carol said, as we strolled around the trenches, "we are told that Pharaoh conquered Gezer, burned it, killed the Canaanites who lived here, and then gave it to his daughter, who was Solomon's wife."

"That's the first hopeful thing I've heard about Israeli-Egyptian relations since I've been here," I said. "Wouldn't it be nice if Nasser had a daughter, married her to Moshe Dayan's son, and then gave them the Sinai peninsula as dowry?"

Dani didn't think my theorizing was funny. He'd already told me he resented the jokes inspired by the Six-Day War. The poster of the Hasidic student changing into a Superman suit had enraged him.

"Unnecessary," he said. "We already have the Sinai. Nobody has to give it to us."

"Solomon rebuilt Gezer and made it a major fort," Carol said. "Along with Hazor and Megiddo. I have to get back to the dark room. You'll find the *masseboth* over there, also the Solomonic gate."

She left us amid the ruins. Dani explained to me the strategic importance of Gezer. Its summit towered above the surrounding plains. From it, a clear view of the valley of Ayalon and the plains toward Lydda are visible. Not far from Gezer passed the Via Maris, the "Way of the Sea," the main road that led from Egypt to Mesopotamia. Gezer functioned as a frontier town between the hills to the east and north, and the littoral. For the lowland residents, whether Canaanite or Philistine or Hebrew, the hill of Gezer, with its natural fortified position, was a stepping-stone toward the Judean hills. For those who held Jerusalem, it was a forward defense station.

The gray-white stones of the Solomonic gate—Dani called it a "chariot gate," built for the entrance and departure of war wagons—seemed surprisingly small. Indeed, I had the feeling that everything was on a smaller scale in biblical times. Beds, rooms, homes, artifacts, all testified to a race of little people.

"How old is this site?" I asked.

"There have been traces of late Chalcolithic," Dani said. "That would be about 3300 B.C. I think the main evidence from the *masseboth* was Early Bronze, about 3200 to 2600 B.C. That's the period right after the Chalcolithic. Think of the Bronze Age as the Canaanite period, about 3200 to 1200 B.C. Then, although it is a simplification, you can think of the Iron Age as the Israelite period, about 1200 to 587 B.C."

"But . . . if the Bronze Age is Canaanite and runs up to 1200 B.C., what about Abraham?" I asked.

"He's about 1900 to 1750 B.C.," said Dani. "But he was no Canaanite. He came up from Ur. The Bible is precise. He came into Canaanite territory. You remember Abimelech and Phichel. The more we learn from archaeology, the more we see how exact the Bible is."

I'm not so sure. All those fundamentalist Christians, not to mention the Israelis themselves, running around the diggings disturb me. Is it possible they sometimes find what they *want* to find? Or interpret what they find in such a way as to make Scripture stand up?

"And there are the *masseboth*. Steles. Those pillars." Beyond the trenches they stood, ten rough-hewn phallic stones, pale gray in color, the tallest of them over nine feet, mute monuments to some god unknown. They stood in grand isolation on Gezer's famed High Place, and although far more is known about them today than in MacAlister's time, they still remain cloaked in a good deal of pleasurable mystery.

MacAlister (I read later in an article by Dr. Dever) considered the *masseboth* the most important single find in seven years of labor at Tel Gezer. Nearby he also found eight infant burial jars. These, together with two caves discovered below the steles, convinced him he had found the main cultic area of ancient Gezer.

MacAlister dated the *masseboth* 1800–1400 B.C., placing them in the Canaanite Middle and Late Bronze periods, beginning in the Age of the Patriarchs, through the Hyksos invasion and the Egyptian periods in the Holy Land. He then reburied the area, covering the steles so that they would remain secret until such time, as he put it, that "a national pride in monuments of antiquity such as this shall have been developed locally." Sixty years later, excavations sponsored by the Hebrew Union College rediscovered the *masseboth*. As for "a national pride" in such monuments, I doubt that the old Scot could have foreseen the national obsession that archaeology would become in modern Israel.

In the summer of 1966, operating only with MacAlister's sketchy information, the Hebrew Union diggers located the first stele beneath several feet of MacAlister's fill. Two years later, under the direction of Professor Anita Furshpan of the University of Connecticut, excavation of the High Place was completed. The key to much of the work was an effort to isolate what Professor Dever calls "elusive bits of undisturbed debris"—that is, material not subjected to MacAlister's stew of strata and stones. Luckily some original plaster surface around the pillars and a stone socket had not been disturbed. Material sealed under this surface was found to date from the Late Middle Bronze period, 1650–1550 B.C., thus the steles belonged to a period of great cultural expansion at Gezer. There was a reuse of the cultic area in Late Bronze, but by the time Solomon took over Gezer and rebuilt it, the old Canaanite shrines were no longer of importance to the hill fortress. Monotheistic Solomon and his proud Hebrews had their Ark; they had no use for pagan pillars, whatever they represented. But were they left standing as reminders of a more primitive age? Buried? Or perhaps they were tolerated, in the manner in which Catholic missionaries often permit pagan structures and primitive customs to survive so long as they can be decently incorporated into Christianity.

"We've left those crazy *masseboth* standing, Your Majesty," I can hear the Gezer Captain of Chariots telling Solomon as he comes around on his monthly inspection. "Nobody is sure what they are, but we think they serve as a warning, in case anybody gets any funny ideas. Who in his right mind would want to pray in front of one of those stupid things?"

An infant burial jar found beneath one of the steles, Professor Dever writes, was interpreted as a burial jar of a much earlier period, and not a human sacrifice. Beneath the founding level of the *masseboth*, the Hebrew Union diggers found materials dating to Early Bronze, and beneath that an even older layer with traces of Chalcolithic. This led to speculation that the High Place may have had a long tradition as a sacred area, possibly predating the Canaanite period.

Professor Dever concludes: "One may walk among the towering *masseboth*, pausing to examine the basin or the socket and musing about what moved men in the long-distant past to erect such monuments. Unfortunately, the archaeologist is better equipped to answer 'What,' 'When,' or even 'How' than he is that perpetual 'Why.' "

I doubt that I'd use the word "unfortunately." Perhaps the past has the right to keep some secrets from the probing spade and the curious trowel.

Gezer speaks to us of battles and bloodshed: She was conquered by the Pharaoh Shishonk in 926 B.C., later by Assyrians, Persians, Seleucid Greeks, in A.D. 143 by Simon Maccabee, who built a house there, and in 1948 by the Israelis. But perhaps its most charming legacy is the Gezer calendar.

This small flat stone, eleven centimeters long, is preserved in the Museum of Antiquities in Istanbul, Turkey. In ancient biblical script dating from about 950 B.C., in the time of Solomon, it defines, with eminent good sense, the seasons in terms of agricultural labors:

> These two months are [olive] harvest.
> These two months are planting [grain].
> These two months are late planting.
> This month is hoeing up of flax.
> This month is harvest of barley.
> This month is harvest.
> These two months are vine-tending.
> This month is summer fruit.

As often happens when I wander around the ruins of old cities, I begin to wonder: Where were the ordinary people, and how did they get their work done? So many stones of antiquity tell us of battles, death, military works, kings and priests and generals. Without the grains and the olive oil and the flax, the bloody battles wouldn't have been worth a damn. Is it possible that nine-tenths of the people, perhaps ninety-nine per cent of the time, were engaged in simple pastoral jobs? Perhaps the ruins of forts, chariot gates, and walls—not to mention the written and oral traditions of warfare—tend to distort our recollections of the past. I suppose it can't be helped. There are few monuments to agronomists and cattle breeders, even in modern times.

Our next stop was Megiddo, in the Jezreel Valley. We were on our way to Upper Galilee to spend the night at a kibbutz in the Huleh Valley. Greedy as ever for more ruins, I asked Dani if we could make two stops on the way up, at Megiddo and Beit Shean. He agreed reluctantly. What he really wanted was to stop at a dude ranch run by an Israeli from Chicago.

"They serve the best coffee, real American coffee, in Israel," he said, "and we can go horseback riding."

I told him I hadn't come to Israel to drink American coffee and ride horses. We agreed we would try to do some of both: brief stops at Megiddo and Beit Shean, followed by a stop for coffee at the dude ranch. The notion of a dude ranch in Israel bothered me. There are, I think, limits to acculturation. At a certain point such intrusions muddy the waters of national character, of the appearance and flavor and texture of a land. While I am not against progress, I am still offended when I think of the splendid Etruscan tomb in the courtyard of the Museum of the Palazzo Vitelleschi in Tarquinia. The stone noble on the sarcophagus gazes out across the street to a café where he can read, eternally, the advice: "BEVETE COCA-COLA."

The remains of Megiddo had a polished, finished look. The Department of Antiquities had done its work well. There was a small reception house with souvenirs and refreshments, and the site itself had the manicured, well-kept look of an old ruin, long excavated, charted, and labeled.

"You know, of course, that Megiddo is Armageddon," Dani said as we began to stroll about the hard-packed paths.

"Yes. The last battle of the world is supposed to take place here."

"That is all you know?"

"Well . . . Theodore Roosevelt, when he split from the Republican Party in 1912 to form the Bull Moose Party, told his convention delegates, 'We stand at Armageddon and battle for the Lord.'"

Dani did not want to hear about Theodore Roosevelt. He plucked a long, dark-brown pod from a tree and showed it to me. "You know what this is?"

"Carob. The Spaniards call it *algarroba*. They used to sell it on the Prospect Place market when I was a kid—the appetizing store always had a few of them in a glass jar. But I don't remember what they called it."

Dani's eyes narrowed. His brows had arched. Nodding at Marie, he said: "He knows a great deal about trees."

"I don't know a damn thing about botany, but I know a carob when I see one. I think the seeds are a laxative."

He waved the mahogany-colored pod under my nose. "This is *Johannesbrot* in German. St. John's bread. In Hebrew, *buksa*."

"That's the word. That's what they called it in the Prospect Place markets."

On a dirty street in Brooklyn, thirty-five years ago, I had sucked at a broken pod of *buksa*, the cathartic fruit of the carob tree, and now I saw it again on the mound of Megiddo.

"Megiddo was one of Solomon's chariot cities, like Gezer," Dani said as we approached the huge stone silo, reputed to have been built by King Jeroboam. "Long before that, it was a Chalcolithic site, dating back to 4000 B.C. It was mentioned in Egyptian writings, because King Thutmose of Egypt made war against it in 1478 B.C. Like many cities around here, it was in danger all the time because it was on the Via Maris, the 'Way of the Sea,' in Hebrew the Derekh Hayam, the highway between Egypt and Assyria."

I would hear this often in Israel, references to the land as a crossroads, a buffer, a wedge, an arena placed sorrowfully between the two great powers of the ancient world. Embattled, ravaged, leveled, it had still maintained its own character, developed its own religion, created its own stubborn identity. Ancient Egypt and ancient Assyria, these survive only as eroded stones, chipped monuments. But the Hebrews, those cantankerous, stiff-necked, disputatious Children of Abraham, those wandering ass-nomads, as one archaeologist describes them (as distinct from camel-nomads) survive. Why? They had the *Book*. I admit this freely, even though I am a rationalist. It is comforting to a writer to feel that survival is connected to a written tradition, words and sentences and concepts *written down*. I am not so certain that endless rolls of caramel-colored videotape will ensure the survival of modern man, simply because these fruits of technology, of the "global village," are generally devoid of any moral force. They are mere mirrors (often distorted ones) of a limited and fragmented reality. For all the blood and death and hate in the Old Testament, it is its ethical force, its concern with standards of human behavior, that ensured its survival.

"Solomon fortified this place. The Bible says he had a thousand and four hundred chariots in his cities and twelve thousand horsemen. After his time, many battles were fought here. Shishak of Egypt destroyed it when it was ruled by Jeroboam. Jeroboam the Second restored it. In 732 B.C. the Assyrians conquered it. The last big fight here was between the Egyptians and King Josiah. The Egyptians were on their way up to fight the Babylonians as usual, and Josiah tried to stop them. Josiah was killed. It's in Second Kings: 'His servants carried him in a chariot dead from Megiddo and brought him to Jerusalem.' That was the end of Megiddo. By 400 B.C.—deserted."

It was late afternoon. We wandered listlessly amid the stones, which some say were Solomon's stables (though Professor Yadin thinks they were built after Solomon), through the scant remains of the old Canaanite temple, the massive circular walls, the palace, and most impressive of all, the deep, cool water-tunnel, 180 feet below the ground, 360 feet long, redolent of centuries, industry, and a clean, cold mountain-spring.

Megiddo has been attractively restored, not quite as flamboyantly as Knossos on Crete, which hints at the rather florid imagination of Sir Arthur Evans, but in a subdued and understated way. It is a good place to wander about in the late afternoon of an August day, amid carobs and cypresses.

Our first day—too crammed, too detailed, delicious but slightly indigestible, like fruitcake—was drawing to a close. Dani wanted his American cup of coffee and wanted to show me the dude ranch. I wanted to gawk at more stones. He agreed to a brief stop at Beit Shean, the main city of the fertile Beit Shean Valley, where there was a well-preserved Roman amphitheater.

Beit Shean is one of the most continuously occupied cities in Israel. Excavations of its tel have revealed no less than eighteen different strata of civilization, from prehistoric times to the Arab conquest of the eighth century A.D. Under the Arab occupation, it eventually became a swampland, and agriculture died out in the previously productive valley. With Turkish rule, the barren lands reverted to the government, then became crown lands under the British mandate. The British awarded the land to Bedouin farmers, who used it for sheep pasturage, and it remained uncultivated. A familiar pattern followed. Wealthy city Arabs with no interest in farming acquired the land from the Bedouins, and in turn sold large tracts to the Jewish National Fund. Today the area flourishes as an agricultural center.

"You remember when Saul was killed by the Philistines after Mount Gilboa," Dani said as we drove down the modern main street of Beit Shean. We could have been in a new suburban section of Milan or Rome as we passed modern bus stops, pale gray modular apartment houses, shoddy, stark, but enlivened by vivacious, dark people, and lots of noisy kids running about the streets. "The Philistines found Saul and his sons dead on Mount Gilboa. So they stripped his armor and cut off his head. They put the armor in the house of Astaroth and fastened his body to the wall of Beit Shean. Right in this city, probably somewhere near the tel. You'll see it when we get to the amphitheater. At night, the Bible tells us, 'all the valiant men arose and took the body of Saul and the bodies of his sons from the wall of Beit Shean and came to Jabesh and burnt them there.' The main street in this city is Shaul Street, in honor of our king."

Our King. He said it as if Saul had reigned a few years ago. One encounters this frequently in Israel. David is just a few decades dead, and Moses (always Moshe Rabbainu, Moses our teacher) is fondly remembered. These people are masters at skipping centuries, millennia. Somehow it is all eminently sensible and logical. The smudged, black-eyed children I saw running around the streets of Beit Shean—mostly Orientals, Dani advised me—could give lessons in hereditary one-upmanship to the snootiest of Philadelphia Main-Liners or the loftiest Bostonian.

(Whenever I heard Dani or some other sabra discuss biblical heroes as if they were recent relatives, familiar *meshpucheh*, I had a memory of my boyhood at a camp in the Adirondacks. A frail, doddering nonagenarian, one Jack Bennett, was the local carpenter, who occasionally performed odd jobs around the camp. Bennett was a trembly ninety-two or ninety-three. He would often relate, nails secure in his lips as he repaired the siding of the dining hall, how his "granddaddy saw an Injun t'other day, a dang Mohawk, come all the way up from Saratogy." We would roar at this. But then we would understand that it was quite possible that Bennett's grandfather had indeed seen an Indian, if not the other day, then surely in his distant boyhood. We imagined Bennett's grandfather in a tricorn, knee britches, hunting shirt, shouldering a muzzle-loading blunderbuss. What stunned us was the immediacy of the event in old Bennett's mind. His "t'other day" was like Dani's "our king.")

"Springs, water all around here," Dani said, as we drove away from the residential quarter, with its brown-skinned children and gaudy Oriental women, toward the amphitheater. "They can grow anything. The biblical scholars used to say that if the Garden of Eden, Gan Eden, is in Israel, then the gateway is at Beit Shean."

I said nothing. The modern city was, as I have mentioned, stark and hard-outlined. It had the standard look of all new urban sites in the Mediterranean—light stones, hard concrete sidewalks, a sense of efficiency and simplicity imposed by practical bureaucrats on the hothouse disorderliness of the lower classes. No doubt it makes for living conditions cleaner and more comfortable than these people have previously enjoyed. And they seem perfectly adapted to it. The waiting lists for new high-rise apartments are shamefully long in Israel. Esthetically, though, something is lost.

"Beautiful girls, beautiful," Dani said. "Algerians, Moroccans, look at them. The Moroccans are flirts. They do things with their eyes."

"No wonder you like to go out on tours," my wife said.

"I only look. It's free. Israeli girls are the most beautiful in the world."

I did not argue. They were certainly attractive, these Orien-

tals of Beit Shean, and like the girls of Hungary and Czechoslova-
kia they seemed to accomplish marvels with minimal money and
with enormous demands made on their time and their energies.
But the most beautiful in the world?

The amphitheater was magnificent. The soft yellow light of late
afternoon turned the old stones an orange-gold. We walked
through a verdant park, where Dani revealed a new skill: he was
a bird-watcher. "Look, look," he cried. "A bulbul, a Persian night-
ingale! Beautiful, but a pest. It eats too much fruit. The farmers
hate them."

A black and red bird darted in and out of a pomegranate tree.
In the short walk across the little park to the Roman theater Dani
also identified a lark and a goldfinch. A protean fellow, he, like
so many Israelis, had an active, energetic, sometimes exhausting
mind. Ornithology, archaeology, linguistics, history, politics—all
these were stored in his alert brain and imparted freely to any listener.

We rested on the comfortable stone seats of the Beit Shean
theater. It is quite handsome, built in the traditional semicircle,
gently inclined, certainly no Colosseum but a match for the
impressive Verona theater or the Teatro Marcello in Rome. I
gazed out to the distant tel of Beit Shean, shadowy and mysterious. It is a perfect small plateau, a flat, massive mound. Again, I
felt the compression of time. The Holy Land has this disturbing
tendency. Centuries are shrugged off. Civilizations are reduced to
a line or two on an archaeological chart, a few inches of red or
black detritus.

"This theater was only recently excavated," Dani said as we
rested our aching bones. It seemed an eternity since we had
climbed Tel Gezer that morning and looked at the mysterious *masseboth*. "In 1962, by a man named Applebaum. He decided it
dated from the third century of the Roman period, and that it
could seat five thousand. The Arabs in the Middle Ages used it as
a multiple dwelling. We preserved it, and built new apartments
on the other side of town."

"Can we climb the tel?" I asked. Sheer bravado on my part.
Light, heat, dust, rocky ascents, and sandy descents had worn me
down. A joyful weariness devoured me.

"We can, but there is not much to see, and we have to press on.

I don't want to get to Kfar Blum too late. They are fussy in kibbutz kitchens, and I don't blame them."

We proceeded northward on the road that parallels the Jordan Valley. The tawny brown hills to our right were Jordan—enemy territory. Dani warned us, almost gleefully, that we might hear a shell go off, as if to gauge our reactions. Did he expect a wince, a shiver? Far from being a hero, I am a sneaky avoider of danger. A boyhood in Brownsville taught me not to seek confrontations when they could be avoided. But I felt absolutely no fear. The Israelis' calm, offhand, and unblinking attitude about the terrors that surround them is contagious.

The names of villages and kibbutzim sped by us: Gesher, Degania, Kinneret. Later, I would read about mortars and explosives falling on them daily, almost routinely. Riding by them, in an air-conditioned Dodge, listening to Dani's scholarly accounts of the biblical history of the valley, I found it impossible to accept the likelihood of danger.

Marie had become friendly with our driver, Avram. He was an Iraqi Jew, come to Israel by way of Turkey, and he spoke but a few words of English. Hebrew was his mother tongue, and he could get by in Arabic and Turkish. Dark, bald, mustachioed, short, muscular, he had a frank, innocent countenance. Avram was married, had five kids, and had served his hitch in the Israeli army as a tank driver. But communication with him was well-nigh impossible. He had studied English in night school, but his limits were the names of a few objects—"tebbel," "cherr," "menn," "voomin"—and the ability to read phonetically a few words. Marie, an inveterate conversation-maker, valiantly engaged him in chatter as he drove, but then she surrendered when Avram kept mentioning something that sounded, as nearly as she could figure out, suspiciously like "Chiang Kai-shek" and pointing to his head.

"What's he saying about Chiang Kai-shek?" she asked Dani.

"That was his nickname in the army. Because they decided he looked Chinese."

I could not tell whether Avram resented the name or was proud of it. He spoke about himself, his family, his life, with such open, candid good nature, a kind of happy acceptance of his world, with such an evident joy in being a citizen of Israel, per-

mitted to practice his religion and raise his kids as free Jews, that
there seemed to be no peaks and valleys in his emotional makeup.
Perhaps I underestimate him: but to me, at least, he possessed
an admirable equanimity of character, a resolute happiness with
his lot, all the more worthy of esteem because it was rooted in
faith and a sense of honor and service and community. I was told
later that this kind of hard pure loyalty is characteristic of many
Oriental Jews, the Yemenis, the Iraqis, and others. (It is essential
to distinguish these peoples from the Moroccan Jews, who, for
the most part, are *French*, more French than the French, less
Jewish than the average Israeli. This is a rank value judgment,
but it deserves respect. Having lived among the French, I think I
know their attitudes and manners, and Moroccan Jews are, *au
fond*, French.)

On our right was the cool blue of the Sea of Galilee, the Kinneret, the Lake of Tiberias. It was dusk, with slate-gray shadows
descending like a translucent curtain over the rust-brown hills
and green fields. Christ's sea appeared to change from ultramarine to gunmetal blue even as we sped by. It was all much too old,
too ageless, for comfort. Along the shoreline were signs of settlements, or a stretch of sandy beach amid the thick grass. I noticed
at least three signs in firm Hebrew and English forbidding swimming.

"All this beautiful shoreline," I asked Dani, "and swimming is
forbidden along so much of it?"

"One is permitted to swim in the lake only when a lifeguard is
present."

"It's a shame. You'd never get Americans to abide by those
rules with all those beaches, all that open water."

"We are a small nation. Every life counts."

I soon understood him. I soon understood the strict rules
against swimming unguarded. They all lived with memories of
the six million. Sabras did not like to talk about it, but the holocaust colored their lives every waking moment. Life having once
been held cheap by their enemies, they were in no mood to
squander it now.

"You think we are too careful?" Dani asked. "We value every
life. They are all precious. At eleven every night the radio broad-
casts the names and home addresses of the boys killed on the bor-

ders—by shelling from Egypt, mortars from Lebanon, machine-gun fire from Jordan—and the entire country listens, and the entire country weeps. When Shmuel Katz of Tiberias is killed in the Sinai, people in Jerusalem and Eilat also cry for him. We are one family. We are all related."

Weeks later I understood. I rode one day in a *sherut*, the seven-passenger taxicab, and we listened as the radio broadcast the name of a soldier killed in a bombardment on the Suez Canal. An attractive girl seated next to me began to sob.

"Did you know him?" I asked.

"I don't have to," she said. "He is one of us."

CHAPTER III

From Blum
to Bebele

It was dark when we reached Kfar Blum, a prosperous kibbutz six miles south of Metullah, the northernmost town in Israel. We were in the Huleh Valley, an area of fertile land enriched by the draining and rerouting of the waters of Lake Huleh. As a result of this processing of the land, one must often ride over dikes and along embankments separating squared-off ponds in which carp and bream are bred.

"Kfar Blum, I take it, is named for Léon Blum," I said.

Dani simply nodded. He was tired also. A long day of successfully topping me and of pounding biblical lore into my thick, cluttered head had worn him out. I thought of Ionesco's play *The Lesson*, in which a female pupil's intransigent stupidity drives the teacher mad; he ends up murdering her.

"Léon Blum," I mused. "Socialist Premier of France. Jew, victim of the right wing, prisoner of the Nazis. He died after the war. He's one of the dim faces out of those scary newsreels of the thirties. All the helpless European politicians who couldn't do a thing about Hitler, or weren't allowed to by home-grown Nazis and Fascists."

Blum. A tall man with a sorrowful face, a droopy moustache, sensitive eyes mangled by eyeglasses, and a floppy artist's hat. He had always seemed to me an inevitable victim, a man who, for all his humanity and decency and intelligence, was fated to be defeated—by the anti-Dreyfusards he had battled as a youth, by the French industrialists who refused to arm the country against Hitler, by the Lavals and the Pétains who overcame him, by the Nazis who jailed him. I was the last man on earth not to give Léon Blum his due, and I certainly did not begrudge him his memorial in this wealthy kibbutz; but he did not seem to me of the heroic mold. A too soft and too reasonable man, intellectual, pacifist, a man wrong for his time. . . .

(Ridden with guilt, I ran to the *Britannica* when I got home and discovered that Blum was not quite the bookish mollycoddle I had imagined him to be. When the Vichy regime tried him for treason, his testimony was of such a forceful and discomfiting nature to the right-wing collaborators that the trial was suspended, and Blum was quietly spirited off to a concentration camp where he could no longer embarrass Laval and Pétain with the clear voice of truth. A good man.)

I had read that many kibbutzim did a lively business running guesthouses and resorts. Still, I was rather unprepared for the pleasant, homey, Catskills atmosphere at Kfar Blum. When one says "kibbutz," an image of sun-seared, thick-thighed pioneers, hauling stones and driving oxen, comes to mind. It was puzzling to find myself in a modern motel room that suggested a night's lodging outside of Schenectady, New York. The dining room was crowded—mostly with American teen-agers—and Marie and I sat on canvas chairs on the lawn, listening to the nocturnal hum of strange insects. Distantly, muted American rock music was issuing from a record player. On the slopes to the east of Kfar Blum, a thousand jewels winked and gleamed on dark blue velour. This was the new village of Kiryat Shemona—the "Town of the Eight"—named for heroes killed during the War of Independence.

Dani, showered, shaved, in a clean shirt, appeared with Avram. He studied my face in the moonlight. "You didn't shave?" he asked, annoyed.

"I'm sorry. I prefer to shave in the morning."

"It would be better if you shaved at night."

A troupe of American youngsters—gangly, long-haired, loud— came out of the dining hall. I could see Dani stiffen slightly. A mocking smile curled his mouth. "*Americanski*," he said softly, with no attempt to hide his disapproval.

Dinner was simple, ample, and excellent. We were waited on by two people, a young, dark, pretty sabra and a middle-aged American woman. The sabra went about her business briskly and silently, frowning faintly, a girl impervious to flirtation or stares. She had flowering hips and thighs, and she wore minuscule blue shorts. As she bustled about, barely looking at us, and avoiding Dani's mild flirting, several of the American youths held a prayer service in a corner of the dining room. Here was the essential, contradictory, Israel: the beautiful Amazon, round of flank and firm of flesh, irritably parading her unreachable beauty—while young Americans *dovinned*. I pondered this. Would it have been appropriate if they had read from the Song of Solomon? "*I am the rose of Sharon and the lily of the valleys. . . .*"

The other waitress was a dark attractive woman from Chicago named Esther. *Haimish* was the word for her. She had read my books. She liked to talk, and she talked with wit and vivacity and great warmth. In fact, she talked to us so much that the sabra, the voluptuous frowner (why did the shorts have to be *that* short?), bawled her out for not serving the meat course.

"Lots of Americans at Kfar Blum," Esther told us, "and English. My husband and I have been here since 1949. We love it. My son is down in the Sinai."

"In the army?"

"No. He's starting a new kibbutz. It runs in the family. My little Danneleh."

She said this not with the standard Jewish mother's lip-smacking but in a self-kidding way. Still, her concern was evident. Dani began to sing: "*Danneleh, Danneleh, nehm a banan-eleh. . . .*"

"I wish he were here so I could give him a *bananeleh*," Esther said. The girl in the tight shorts summoned her to clean tables. Esther excused herself and invited us to her home that evening to meet some kibbutz leaders.

Two couples were present: Esther and her husband, Harry, and a man named Akivah Skidell, principal of the Kfar Blum secondary school, which served several kibbutzim in the Huleh Valley, and his wife. Skidell was a New Yorker who had spent a great part of his life in Canada, working for the Jewish Agency.

"We came here twenty-three years ago," Skidell said, "and we have no regrets."

Skidell said this casually, as if it were hardly necessary for him to put this feeling into words. In contrast to the intensity of the sabras, their professions of patriotism, their almost hyperthyroid love of country and compulsion to praise it, many American (and English) Jews who have become Israelis tend to treat the experience with a jocular offhandedness. Skidell had this engaging quality. He was a tall, well-built man, with gray hair and light-gray eyes and a serene, tolerant, faintly amused look on his face. He reminded me of a good-natured summer-camp director.

"There are about seven thousand American Jews coming to Israel to stay every year," he said as the ladies served us apple cake and tea. "I am told that there are seven hundred Jewish schoolteachers from New York City alone coming over this year because they can't take the school situation there. They'll be a problem until they learn Hebrew. A few may know a little, but it's different when you have to speak it every day."

Inevitably this led to a discussion about the Negro-Jewish problem in New York City.

"What is all this about backlash?" Esther asked.

"And what about those Black Panthers—are they really anti-Semites?" her husband, Harry, asked. Harry, a slender, bespectacled man, was the kibbutz accountant.

Marie and I attempted a brief summary of the racial scene in New York: the polarization of ethnic groups, the resentment at Mayor Lindsay's alleged favoring of blacks, the "Jewish revolt" against traditional liberal positions because of the tensions resulting from the school strike, the fury of victimized taxicab drivers, and so on.

I could see that the nuances of urban life in America were lost
on them. They listened politely, asked questions, but they were
light-years removed from Ocean Hill–Brownsville and the South
Side of Chicago. They could not get exercised over backlash candidates and the New Left; their life was here, on the Lebanese
border.

"I can see how things have changed in America," Akivah Skidell said tolerantly. "I taught school there years ago. Mathematics. Well, we get lots of Americans kids here for the summer, and
they aren't like the kids I knew. We've got a bunch from Los
Angeles now. The stuff they bring over! Guitars. Record players.
Amplifiers. Tape recorders. They blew every fuse in the kibbutz
the first night they turned those things on."

"And pills," said Mrs. Skidell.

"Pills?" I asked.

"Pills," she said. "Those American kids—these are tenth-
graders, mind you, fifteen-year-olds—they come with dozens of
bottles of pills, all colors, pills for everything."

"Not just pills," Esther said. "Let's face it, drugs also."

These people were a pioneer society still—innocent, pure,
uncontaminated.

"And how do your children feel about these Americans with
their amplifiers and pills and tape recorders?" I asked.

Akivah Skidell put a sage's hand to his forehead and closed his
eyes. "They love them," he said wearily.

"Love them?"

"They're crazy about them. They envy all that electrical stuff.
They want to learn all about the pills . . . and the drugs. You see
what we have to contend with?"

This conversation about affluent Americans led me to reflect on
the lack of luxury, of ostentation, of excess, in Israeli lives. Skidell
was a school principal. Harry was an accountant. In the United
States, they would be comfortable middle-class people, living in
good-sized houses or apartments. Here, on Kfar Blum, their
apartments each consisted of three tiny rooms in a simple one-
story concrete building. They were spotless, airy, light, but
smaller than the tiniest apartment in any low-cost housing project
in Harlem. Everything was diminutive—the plain furniture, the
lamps, the paintings on the wall. I noticed, however, as I did in

many Israeli homes, no matter how simple, a well-stocked book-shelf and a rack of records. This was not a country of wall-to-wall carpeting, of Tiffany lamps, of brocade bedspreads and interior decorators who frightened housewives into flocked wallpaper and carved breakfronts.

And yet I was certain that the two American couples—and other kibbutzniks I met later—were reasonably satisfied with the marginal fulfillment of their material needs. They surely had worries and problems and deep concerns (not the least of which was mere survival). But the color or thickness of carpeting, the veneer of a mahogany dining table, were not among them. Here there is an exhilarating sense of release, of surcease from pointless obsessions, and one realizes that Thoreau's admonition to "simplify, simplify" is sound. This is not to say that most Israelis, particularly the younger women, do not often yearn for some heady luxury, some adornment to house or person which their Spartan way of life prohibits. More of these accessories to living will come to them in time. But I am concerned. If they become too much like us—creatures of the Sunday *Times* advertisements —I will begin to fear for their survival.

The conversation got around to Bruno Bettelheim's new book about kibbutz children, *The Children of the Dream*. No one (including myself) had read it, but everyone (except myself) had strong ideas about it. One encounters, and is swept up in, a great deal of furious debating in Israel, especially among the older generation.

"He is too simplistic," Akivah Skidell said. "I understand that he claims that our kibbutz kids don't have any imagination, that they function well in direct situations but that they are not interested in subtleties, in complexities, in situations that require analysis and individual initiative."

"And that isn't true," his wife added. "Look at all the jet pilots and high-ranking army officers who were raised on kibbutzim."

"I don't think it's a very scientific work," Harry said. "Interesting to an outsider, but not scientific."

"How do you mean?" I asked.

"From the reviews I've read, he only spent seven weeks at the so-called Atid kibbutz, and that isn't enough. Besides, he didn't use a control group, the way a sociologist should."

"He also says," Skidell said, "and I read this in the same review, that kibbutz education has a leveling effect, that it favors the middle achiever, and in so doing it succeeds in elevating the dull kid, but it has the effect of bringing down the possibilities of the talented child. I don't agree with that."

"And some of the things I read!" Esther added. "Kibbutz children are inarticulate; they suspect big ideas; they aren't ardent Zionists! Also, that they're rude, offhand, and their personal relationships are shallow."

"Well," I ventured, "as another nonreader of *The Children of the Dream*, which qualifies me as another expert, I got the idea that Bettelheim is extremely laudatory about the kibbutz concept of child-rearing. He is full of praise about the way these children adjust to life, unlike kids raised in American institutions. Also, he apparently felt that kibbutz children were less neurotic, because rather than a pair of intense parents on whom the child can operate with a child's selfishness, there's also the housemother——"

"The *metapelet*," Esther said.

"——and the other children in the peer group. In short, all the *mishigas* that comes from familial strangulation is diluted and spread thinly. Hence, better-adjusted kids."

"Generally true," Skidell said—a bit reluctantly.

"And," I went on, "I gathered that Bettelheim was so impressed with the kibbutz system of child-rearing and education that he saw the possibility of extending it to certain urban communities in America. In fact, the purpose of the book was to challenge American middle-class child-rearing patterns and present what he felt was an alternative."

Dani, who had been silent throughout this argument, shook his head slowly. "No. No. He didn't spend enough time. Of course, I haven't read the book either."

"All I can say," I said, "is that Dr. Bettelheim isn't getting a fair shake. He writes a book to show all the great things the kibbutz does for kids, and you Israelis knock him for saying maybe the kids don't grow up sufficiently imaginative or artistic."

"You're learning about Israelis," Esther said. "You have to be all for us, one hundred per cent."

"I'd hate to have to answer Bettelheim's mail," I said. "All those angry jet pilots raised on kibbutzim, those articulate deputies in the Knesset, denying they lack imagination or are incapable of handling subtle matters."

Late as it was, they walked us back to the guest house. The love of the land is always with these people: Nothing pleases them more than a stroll about the kibbutz lands, a pause at a river bank, a visit to an orchard. It is, of course, a mystical ritual, but it is done with a simplicity that makes the rootless American a bit envious.

The sky was blue-black. Lights winked in jeweled ridges on the slopes of Kiryat Shemona. Abruptly we heard two loud, reverberating blasts. The detonations had a thick, dull quality; they were mindless stupid intrusions.

"Oh," Esther said—and I still do not know whether she was joking or attempting to mislead me—"they must be working in the quarry again."

I grabbed Marie's hand. We exchanged astounded stares.

"Nothing, nothing," Harry said. "Somebody was careless."

At the guest house, we said our goodnights. Dani looked at me archly. "That came from over there." He pointed northward toward the Lebanese border. "Al Fatah. Every night they drop a few in. Probably on Kiryat Shemona."

In the morning, the radio newscast in English confirmed his suspicions. Two mortar shells had been dropped on Kiryat Shemona by infiltrators. No real harm had been done; a storage building had been slightly damaged. But a few weeks later, two people in Kiryat Shemona would be killed in the same kind of nocturnal attack. Six months later, it was a frequent target.

At breakfast there was no discussion of the incident. It had happened; it had been expected; it would happen again. These border farms had lived under attack and the threat of attack almost since their founding. They do not enjoy their vulnerability. They suffer with each death. But they are determined they will live with it, master it, resolve it—and survive. There is simply no other view to take. As I was told many times, Israel's actual borders, for all the guerrilla bombing and infiltrating, have never been more secure, more defensible, more geographically sound. They will accept the daily bloodletting, the tension, the need to remain armed, alert, economically lean, for they have no alternative, absolutely none. If it takes a hundred years of this kind of existence, they are prepared. You cannot (and I wonder that the Arabs, the Russians, and our State Department are so obtuse as to not comprehend this bedrock truth), cannot frighten or bully a people who have been tempered in Auschwitz.

As we lined up at the breakfast buffet table, there was not a word spoken about the shelling. Even the voluble American teen-agers from Los Angeles were not interested in the fact that the village across the road had been bombed. It was considered as unworthy of discussion as a minor jeep accident in the next town.

Set out on a long table were platters of mild cheeses, varieties of smoked sardines and herring, raw sliced peppers, carrots, and cucumbers and the more familiar fruit, juices, cereals, bread, rolls, and butter. The first few days Marie and I found ourselves loading up with everything in sight. I ate my way through bland yellow cheese, creamy white pot cheese, smoky brown sardines, and several varieties of bread. Soon the novelty wore off. The meal began to seem excessive. And for all the hiking and climbing we were doing, we simply did not expend the energy necessary to burn up all that nourishment. It occurred to me that these enormous breakfasts were intended originally for farm workers, for men and women going out at dawn to harvest melons and milk cows and clean chicken coops. Failing to absorb the rich meal in honest toil, one suffered a cementlike congestion of the diaphragm, cheeses and fish congealing in the abdomen and rendering speech, locomotion, and thought difficult. We soon were on a regimen of juice, oatmeal, and coffee.

Mr. Skidell was waiting to take us on a tour of the kibbutz. He was wearing a white open-collared shirt—the nearest thing to a uniform that the old-timers affect—gray shorts, short black socks, and black oxfords.

"The problem of many kibbutzim today is diversification," he told us. "Some of us have been too successful from an agricultural standpoint. We overfeed the country. Eggs, chickens, milk, fruit—more than the population can absorb without running the danger of high cholesterol."

"What's the answer?" I asked.

"Light industry. We have started a factory, electric control boards. This way we absorb our labor, and we offer attractions for the younger people who might want to leave. With mechanization, new fertilizers, new farming methods, a lot of kibbutzim found themselves with labor surpluses. Almost every kibbutz now has some kind of industrial operation."

"And I take it," I said, "that salaries, that earnings in this industrial work are equivalent to farm pay?"

Akivah looked at me with his amused, gently cynical eyes. "Salary? *Pay?*"

We had stopped at the vast Olympic swimming pool. It dazzled us with its blue-green purity, glinting in the morning sun. The temperature must have been close to a hundred degrees Fahrenheit. Dani shaded his eyes. If Akivah's were amused, his were not. "Pay? Salaries?" our guide asked incredulously. "What are you talking about? Nobody gets paid on a kibbutz."

"I—ah—nobody?" I asked.

"Of course not!" Dani shouted. "That's what is different about it!"

As soon as he told me this, I realized I had known it for many years. And I understood my inability to accept this central fact about the communal farms. At heart, we Americans are Protestant-ethic, free-enterprise, money-making people. There is nothing more incomprehensible to us than the notion of working without monetary reward, whether it be good pay or high profits. We are a nation motivated, for better or worse, by the old *Saturday Evening Post* slogan, "Boys, turn your spare time into cash." The concept of the kibbutz demands a turnaround in our thinking, a rejection of all we have ever learned. The Yiddish expression *parnosseh*—earning a living—is, incidentally, as alien to the kibbutz as our Yankee notions of cash on the barrelhead. Frankly, I was ashamed of my conditioning. I realized that the notion of people working for no salary, no cash payment, is as repugnant, as alien to us, as incest. We reject it. We are frightened by it. Our minds refuse to entertain it. I suspect it is one reason why the kibbutz concept, as noble, as intriguing, as successful as it has been in

Israel, has no application on a worldwide basis. It presupposes a highly motivated, highly sophisticated people, determined to function as a community.

We strolled down another tree-shaded street. The small gray houses with their tiny lawns and gardens gave me the impression of an Adirondack or Catskill adult camp. I knew about the struggles of the early kibbutzim, the endless labors, agonies, frustrations—not to mention the present bombings, threats, terror—and I marveled at the air of pastoral peace. The kibbutzniks seem to be saying, *Do your worst. We will beat you; we will survive.*

"The prohibition against earning money," Akivah said, "applies even to money from sources outside the kibbutz. For example, I am paid by the state, since I'm principal of a school that serves this area. I turn my salary over to the kibbutz. Many of our people work outside the farm. They, too, turn their pay over. So do many members of the Knesset—our Deputy Prime Minister, Yigal Allon, for example, is a member of the kibbutz at Nof Ginnosar. He gives his salary to the kibbutz."

"And how much does he earn?" I asked.

Skidell thought for a moment. "Oh, about five thousand dollars a year."

"How much does Mrs. Meir earn?" Marie asked.

"Six thousand dollars," Akivah answered. "But understand they are not interested in money. They are interested in power, in nationhood, in an idea."

We passed two tennis courts, a basketball court, a soccer field. "What happened to your soccer team?" Dani asked. "You used to be one of the best kibbutz teams in Israel."

Skidell shrugged. "It got to be a burden. It got out of hand. All this recruiting of players, deals, underhand stuff to sign up athletes. I got sick of it. We deemphasized soccer. We still play, of course, but not to go out and win every game, no matter what."

It was like the Ivy League. Having done some random football recruiting for Columbia, my alma mater, I could appreciate Skidell's disgust. He sounded like a Columbia alumnus discussing Dartmouth's and Yale's greedy harvesting of high-school stars.

Our tour of the kibbutz took us to the irrigation canal at the easternmost border of the village, a dark-green, stagnant-appearing stream. Two sun-browned members of the kibbutz, in faded blue shorts and pointed kibbutz hats, were laying sections of terra-cotta pipe.

"We are lucky here, and prosperous," Skidell said. "Lots of water, good fresh water. And beyond, we have the Golan Heights now. We can never be hurt again. You know, when Israeli farmers from this valley go to visit the Golani, they wonder how they survived all those years when the Syrians were up there. Now, life is much easier."

No sooner had he said that than he led us into a concrete bomb shelter. Paradox never ceases in Israel. They were more secure than ever (a comparative security, to be sure), but mortar shells had fallen on Kiryat Shemona last night, and every kibbutz had its underground shelters.

"Canvas cots," Skidell said, showing me a room filled with triple-tiered bunks. "For the children and their *metapelet*. Also, food supplies in that locked cabinet, radio communications, medical supplies, blankets."

"Have you had to use them recently?"

"No. We are fortunate."

I thought about the man's casual confidence. But what else was he to do? Tear his hair and wring his hands and weep? As I was to learn, apart from a sprinkling of older people still suffering from ghetto conditioning, there is very little indulgence in self-pity, in breast-beating. Long before the present crisis, the kibbutz pioneers had buried the old European fears, the old patterns of submission. There is too much to be done, there is too much recent history, too many iron lessons of the past, to permit wailing, hair-pulling, the show of fear. Sackcloth and ashes have long been out of fashion.

"Let's look at our 'unimaginative' children," Akivah said.

The first house into which we walked was a typical communal dwelling, where the youngsters ate, slept, played, and attended nursery school. These were three-year-olds. The young girls in charge, the *metapelets*, paid no attention to us: no greeting, no interest. They were all business.

A curly-headed blond girl, no more than three, small even for a three-year-old, was standing on tiptoe, attempting to clean a table top with a moist rag. I did not believe I have ever seen so small and so young a child so earnestly engaged in a task. Her tiny arms could barely reach the plastic surface. She frowned, strained, her immense brown eyes (a common combination in Israel, these dark brown eyes, butter-yellow hair) a study in concentration.

"They all have jobs to do," Akivah said. "As soon as they can get around they know they have responsibilities."

Another mini-kibbutznik, a black-haired girl, was attempting to sweep the floor, successfully rearranging a layer of fine sand. When I read Dr. Bettelheim's book some months later I discovered that the work ethic stays with these children right on to adulthood—though not all of them appreciate the hard life.

My wife is a card-carrying Latin sentimentalist, when it comes to children. She began to cry. Not noisily, but sneakily. Tears rimmed her eyes. "I can't stand it," Marie muttered. "They're so tiny. And beautiful."

We walked toward another children's house, a home for the four-year-olds. It seemed to me that beautiful was not quite the correct word. Goodness knows they were handsome enough kids, smooth-skinned, sturdy, bright-eyed. But what impressed me, and it was evident even in a group of a half-dozen four-year-olds, was an unmistakable air of confidence, of certainty, in the children. Perhaps I was merely transferring to them my own swift impressions of the stability, directness, and orderliness of kibbutz life. Or maybe it was the immutable groupings of six and the ever-present *metapelet*—combined nurse, teacher, housemother—which suggested a variety of social rightness. Whatever the reason, these kibbutz children appeared to me a singularly perky, sassy, unworried gang.

"My grandson is in this house," Akivah said.

A sturdy, dark-haired boy toddled over to the multicolored barrier that closed off the play area in front of the dwelling, and began to chatter to Akivah. As soon as this was noticed by the other infants, a second boy, a tough-looking towhead, waddled up to the fence and shouted something in Hebrew. Both Dani and Akivah began to laugh.

"What did he say?" Marie asked.

"He told the nurse not to let me in," Akivah said. "He knows I'm the grandpa of one of them, and he doesn't want me around."

Mr. Skidell obeyed the tot's order. We strolled away. Marie asked if the child's reaction were a reflection of a need for more parental love. "He didn't want you there," she theorized, "because your grandson would have an edge, a little more attention."

"I don't think so," Skidell said. "It was a normal competitive reaction. They spend afternoons with their parents. It seems to give them all the affection they require. If a child needs special attention, the mothers are allowed to sleep in the children's dormitory with them. And any parent is absolutely free to come and go as he pleases to the children's houses, and in fact bring other kids to visit. It's a lot more informal than it appears.

"In fact, there is a great deal more flexibility to child-rearing on a kibbutz than Dr. Bettelheim realized, since we regard the kibbutz as a dynamic form of social engineering. If we can't change and experiment, we are failing. The mother stays with the child for the first six weeks of the baby's life. After this, she goes back to her job, usually beginning with four hours a day and gradually working up to a full day's work, to coincide with weaning."

"She has the child for only six weeks?" my wife asked. "Only *six weeks?*"

"Mrs. Green, she has the child forever, but under what we consider healthier conditions, for children, parents, and——"

"And for Israel," Dani said quickly.

He had put his finger on it. For all the values of a kibbutz system of child-rearing, for all the advantages of a voluntary collective existence, there loomed, in back of all the trial-and-error systematizing, a certain mystique. And the mystique was spiritual intoxication with the concept of Jewish statehood, of Jewish survival, of the perfection and elevation of whatever Judaism meant—culture, religion, ethical system—to these determined Zionists. Which was not to say that the missionary zeal, the inspired idealism, the absolute belief in the concept of Israel, were harmful to the children. Given the history of the movement, the ordeals, the obstacles, the conspiracies and horrors with which they have had to contend, the kibbutz system, as a useful social structure, as an agency for creating a cadre of devoted, selfless citizens, has been an astounding success.

"We do have trouble getting enough trained *metapelets,*"

Akivah said. "We do not settle merely for people who like children. They must be professionals and have the right temperament for the work."

"But it's economically sound," I said. "I mean—releasing all the mothers to work."

"Not true. It is expensive. It has all been costed out, and it is more expensive to organize this sort of communal child-rearing and education than if we used the traditional family system. Still, it is worth it.

"After six weeks, the child progresses through a series of different homes. First there is the infant's house—birth to a year and a half. Then, the toddler's house, up to four years—that's where we saw the little girls cleaning up. Then, kindergarten and transition, four to seven—my grandson and his jealous friend. Ages seven to twelve are the children's community. Twelve to eighteen are the high-school group.

"Some kibbutzim are varying the technique. At a few places the children are in communal living only until four in the afternoon, and then go home, and spend the night with their parents. At others, the evening meal is not eaten communally, but with the parents, in the home."

"I thought the community dining hall was a hard and fast rule of kibbutz life," I said.

"No longer. You can get your food from the kitchen, anything you want, and take it home for your evening meal. And the children can join you. You see, privacy, or the lack of it, is one of the big problems on a kibbutz. Many people can't take the constant close association with others over the long haul. So we try to make it easier for them."

We walked through more tree-shaded clusters of one-story bungalows, all of the same rather drab gray concrete, brightened with flowers, painted window boxes, individual touches. At one point, Akivah, passing his own apartment, noticed that the sprinkler on his small lawn had been turned off. It appeared to be the only aspect of our morning tour that disturbed him; for the first time I saw him look annoyed. He fiddled with a subterranean control. Soon the sprinkler was scattering water on the grass and beds.

"Flowers are an obsession with us," he said. "In fact, many kib-

butzim are now producing them on a commercial basis. Flowers
for the market. It's a good business. In this region, we also do a
lot of carp-breeding. You'll see the fish weirs when you ride out.
The standard crops have been almost too successful, so we diver-
sify."

I noticed a flourishing cactus garden and recognized some spec-
imens from the Sonoran desert of Arizona, where I had directed
nature films with Joseph Wood Krutch. "That's a pincushion
cactus," I said, "and a Teddy-bear cholla."

"Don't ask me," Akivah said. "One of our members is an
Englishman, and he's crazy for cactus. This is his own landscap-
ing project."

"It's excellent. As good as the cactus gardens at the desert
museum in Tucson."

"I'll tell him. He'll be delighted. You see, he even made a moat,
a water channel between the small section up there and the rest
of the garden. We all say he did that because he's an Englishman—he had to have his private island. Privacy again, you see."

The collectivity of kibbutz life struck us full force in the dining
hall of Kfar Blum. It was high-ceilinged—spotless, modern,
efficient, the ideal communal dining hall. Again I thought of
Copake and Grossinger's and a thousand Jewish summer camps in
upstate New York. And I wondered, could it be that the summer
camps of American Jews, for all their determined fun-seeking,
round-the-clock cha-cha-cha bands, coronary-inducing cuisine,
garish ostentation, are in some weird manner searching for a lost
innocence, simplified communal life, that has eluded guests and
hosts?

Bruno Bettelheim points out that the community dining hall
was central to kibbutz philosophy in the early days. A deliberate
attempt was made (and it succeeded) to break the tyranny of the
mother-dominated ceremonies of eating. It was decided that the
old ghetto patterns of family closeness, the regulated, ritual meals
in the kitchen or dining room, were destructive and debilitating.
In the early days, and perhaps even now, husbands and wives
were advised not to sit together in the mess hall. Food was
simple, almost crude, and was taken quickly, eaten quickly, and
never discussed. Once and for all, it appears, the kibbutz pioneers
were determined to smash the image of the food-oriented, orally

satisfied Jew. "Eat, eat" was apparently the first Jewish cliché
that the kibbutzniks destroyed. Man did not live by bread alone,
these pioneers understood. In time the kibbutz dining hall—
symbolically—became much more than a mere eating room: It
became a community center for important meetings, entertain-
ment, and so on.

It was close to noon, and the short walk around the kibbutz
grounds had parched our throats. Akivah greeted the girls preparing the huge tables for lunch. He led us to a spotless aluminum
cooling apparatus, at which were three black elongated spigots
shaped like Indian clubs—the old-fashioned candy store soda
dispensers.

Akivah placed his hand on one of the spigots. "Water or
seltzer?" he asked.

All the bad jokes tumbled through my mind. Jewish explorer
dying of thirst, dragging himself through Sahara, muttering,
"Seltzer, seltzer . . ." And Marie, brought up in the Italian-Jewish
littoral of the East Bronx, became hysterical.

"It's a small enough vice," Akivah said. "There's always seltzer
on tap."

Nectar, celestial liquor. Seltzer was to us what ice-cold martinis
are to a Madison Avenue luncher. A small enough vice. We re-
freshed our throats with glass after glass of bubbly icy seltzer,
fresh from the storage tanks, the aluminum coolers of Kfar Blum.
Old Hemingway, according to the young writer who followed him
around in his declining years, keeps telling us about the "crackling
cold" white wines they drank on picnics. Faulkner and his bour-
bon bottle. Fitzgerald and Zelda, boozing it up in Paris. What
they didn't know. There we stood soothing our shriveled gullets
from Kfar Blum's bottomless well of cold seltzer!

I thought of Hemingway, old soldier, old brawler, afraid of
nothing, as I quaffed my seltzer. He never liked Jews. Jews could
not fight. Effete, sniveling, climbing intellectuals. (On learning
A. E. Hotchner's name, he remarked, "That's a suspicious name";
but the biographer curiously makes no comment, either unwilling
to admit to his hero's anti-Semitism or unaware of the import of
the great man's sneer.) On the hills beyond, Arab guerrillas were
dreaming of murdering the children of the kibbutz. But they
would never succeed. A race of seltzer-drinking, chicken-raising

farmers was showing them what courage meant, how wars are fought. And as Hemingway mocked his detractors, how do you like it now, gentlemen? All the Scotch in the world, all the hard booze and heroics of literary killers, suddenly seemed to me the most meretricious of poses, trashy and pathetic in its insistence on its courage and ferocity. Steinbeck went around bragging to sycophants that he once "killed a man with my own hands." Read Mailer for advertisements in a similar ballsy vein. But a man can drink carbonated water and fight like hell.

At breakfast that morning, someone mentioned that a certain Professor Weinstein was digging at a tel near Shamir.

"Shamir?" Dani asked. "Shamir? Ah, we must see Shamir. But I don't know of any digs up here."

Part of the fun for me on these archaeological hunts is searching for the obscure site, the place the guidebooks know nothing about, the hidden treasures which require map-reading, interrogation, jouncing rides over dirt roads. All proved necessary to locate the elusive, mysterious Professor Weinstein.

Shamir could not have been more than a mile from Kfar Blum, a border kibbutz in the northern Israeli "finger" once dangerously close to Syrian guns but now relatively secure by virtue of the occupation of the Golan Heights. (Shamir, like all these northern settlements, is in double jeopardy, on Lebanon's doorstep and threatened by Syria.)

Despite the closeness of Shamir to Kfar Blum, it took us a good deal of turning and backtracking to locate it, even though the roads are good, and well marked. We stopped once and spoke to a young kibbutznik driving a tractor. He had legs like stone pillars, a chest of oak, and the laconic manner of the farmboy. Yes, he was from Shamir, but he had no idea who Professor "Veinshtein" was; he had never heard of him.

At Shamir—another prettily landscaped, bungalow-and-lawn kibbutz—we stopped again to ask instructions. A thin, long-haired youth in tight blue jeans came out of the kibbutz office. "An American," Dani sniffed. "I can spot them a mile away."

He also knew about Professor "Veinshtein," but he had no idea where he was digging; he thought he lived in a bungalow at the other end of the kibbutz. Since I tend to wax compulsive when I

am on the track of a witness, an interviewee, a new site, we were
soon grabbing children off the street and demanding where they
had hidden the mythic Veinshtein. We halted a bearded young
man on a bicycle (I believe I accused him of *being* Professor
Veinshtein); stopped housemothers herding the inevitable six
chicks; halted two fat teen-agers carrying egg crates from a ram-
shackle hatchery. No luck. Finally, a woman from the kibbutz
office gave Dani detailed instructions in Hebrew.

Avram wheeled the Dodge around, and we bounced out of
Shamir. Dani scowled. "I've never heard of this place where he's
digging. But she said there was an American archaeologist living
at Shamir. It doesn't mean anything. There are American
archaeologists everywhere. She said his helpers are staying somewhere else, and besides, she thinks they aren't working at the
place anymore."

"A shame," I said. "I feel as though I've known Professor Veinshtein for years."

We were back on the blacktop roads. Beyond us rose the
ridged, sun-brightened hills of the Golan, rust-brown, tawny,
beige. The luxurious green fields of the Huleh Valley below were
of such dramatic contrast, so obviously a different terrain, that it
was as if a topographical map had come to life. Indeed, when I
consulted the Ministry of Tourism's detailed map (provided to
me in New York by the efficient Nate Freedman), I realized
that this was one of the few places in the world, thanks to the
smallness of distances, the dazzling clarity of the air, and the
abrupt changes in coloration and conformation, that a topographical map could be checked and matched with the actual countryside.

"*Shamir* means adamant," Dani said. Avram made a sharp turn
off the main road. We drove along one of the raised earthen dikes
I had seen, a narrow ridge of hard-packed dirt bordered with
papyrus, partitioning the fish-breeding ponds. "Adamant, you
know what it means?"

"Immovable. Something that can't be broken."

"Right. *Shamir*—adamant. The stone that can't be moved. Not
by the Lebanese or the Syrians or the Fedayeen or the Al Fatah
or the United Nations or the Russians. It's in Ezekiel."

"All that? All that about the U.N. and the Russians?"

"No, no. Adamant. 'Behold, I have made thy face hard against their faces. . . . As an adamant'—in Hebrew, *shamir*—'harder than flint have I made thy forehead: fear them not, neither be dismayed at their looks.' "

We kept traveling, at about five miles an hour, over an extremely narrow dike. Where was Veinshtein? We had seen no signs, no evidence of a dig. On either side of us the swamp vegetation grew high and thick, blocking our vision. Normally Dani was able to spot a tel from a distance. At length the road ended in a cleared area. A rusting engineless bus leaned against a hillside. Next to it was a flimsy shack of corrugated tin. Both were evidently used either as offices or for storage.

"Ah," our guide said, "we are *on* the tel. There it is above us."

The ground rose from the clearing, that familiar mound, sloping upward, dotted with scrub and stunted trees. "I see no Veinshtein," I said. "I see no diggers. No students in shorts."

"Ahead, ahead," Dani said. "There they are."

But there was no "they." Only a solitary person, one man alone, seated beneath a tremendous old tree, gently and lovingly sorting hundreds of potsherds spread across a plank table and placing them in brown paper bags.

"Dr. Vein—Dr. Weinstein?" I asked.

"Weinberg."

"They told us your name was Weinstein. That was at Kfar Blum."

"Weinberg. I'm Professor Saul Weinberg, of the University of Missouri."

We introduced ourselves. He invited us to stay for a while and chat. He had dismissed everyone for the day. It was Sunday, and while Saturday is the normal Israeli day off, he had decided to give his helpers a day in town. Most of them had gone to Haifa.

"I even gave Mrs. Weinberg the day off," he said. "So I am all alone here with my potsherds. It is rather pleasant here. This tree, incidentally, is a great help. It's a Palestinian pistachio, the nuts of which are inedible, but it more than makes up for its lack of nourishment in the splendid shade it provides."

No Great Neck living room, no king's chamber, could match Saul Weinberg's plot of earth beneath the leafy branches of his Palestinian pistachio. Alone, on his folding camp chair, mulling over sherds and assorted artifacts, he was a man in harmony with his environment and the distant past. I asked him to tell us something about the dig.

"This is a rather modest affair," Professor Weinberg said. "You see, I am a classics specialist, a Greek man. Most everyone in Israel is digging the Bible. My interest is in the Greeks. The problem in the Holy Land is that wherever there was a Greek culture, the Romans followed in short order and destroyed it. What I find intriguing about this place is how extremely Greek it is. Nothing here would be out of place in Greece."

He identified some pottery fragments for us—typical Greek designs and styles from the third to the second centuries B.C. "Very Greek, very Greek indeed," he said happily.

"What is the name of this tel?" Dani asked.

"It has two names. The Arabs used to call it Tel Alakhda, the 'Green Tel.' But more recently it has been known as Tel Anafa, the 'Tel of the Heron.' The first knowledge of it turned up during the 1956 Suez affair. The army dug trenches here, and in the course of the digging some interesting stucco decorations, overlaid with gold, were found. The geometric designs were clearly Greek, third century B.C. I heard of the discovery and it intrigued me. This would be quite far inland for a Greek settlement. It was possible, however, that it was a military outpost, and that the Ptolemies had sent soldiers and their families to settle here."

"Like a Nahal settlement," Dani said. "A paramilitary border kibbutz."

"Yes, similar to that. Now it was also possible that these farmer-soldier settlements expanded inland, and that local people acquired the material Greek culture. I tried to dig here in 1963, but this part of the country was much too hot, too close to Syria and the Golan Heights. Of course, after 1967, all that changed. I had been digging in Israel since 1964, mainly near Haifa, where I found a great deal of Greek glass. In 1968, I began this dig. We are, as I said, a modest operation, only thirty-five volunteers and a staff of ten, five of whom I brought from Missouri with me."

"Do you have any Israeli diggers?" I asked.

"No. It's very hard to get them to dig anything but the Bible. Besides, their young people are all in service. In a way, I'm lucky being a Greek specialist. I have places like Tel Anafa to myself."

Professor Weinberg was a man to envy and admire. Around us, in the reeds, in the scrub, in the lofty reaches of the pistachio tree, insects buzzed a cheerful threnody. It was hellishly hot. But beneath the sheltering branches, the air was dry and cool.

"I enjoy being by myself now and then," he said. "It concentrates my mind. I shall be very busy this fall. I'm taking over as director of antiquities at the Israel Museum in Jerusalem."

We were all impressed, especially Dani. He raised his eyebrows and darted a knowing glance at me, as if to say, *Here is a man, a first-class man.*

"Come along, I'll show you around," Professor Weinberg said.

I asked if he would rather forgo the tour, if we were intruding on his splendid solitude. "Not at all. It's a pleasure to find someone interested in Greek antiquities."

We climbed the grassy slopes of the tel. Dr. Weinberg walked with the help of a cane, and he shaded his head with a huge straw sombrero. A thoroughly civilized man, I realized. A gray-haired man, he had a warm, wise face, bespectacled, with generous features. Somehow he put me in mind of the great physicist I. I. Rabi—or the actor Sam Jaffe—or, perhaps, Sam Jaffe *playing* Rabi, in a movie whose title I have forgotten.

At the summit, we walked along the edges of the five-meter-square pits. Around us we could see a bright vista of dikes, reeds, carp ponds, and canals shimmering in the morning sunlight.

"Thus far," Professor Weinberg said, "we've gotten down to the Persian period, 586 B.C., and the Hellenistic, roughly 330 to 75 B.C. The Seleucid Greeks of Syria, you must remember, went right down to the first century B.C., to the Maccabee period. We surmise that the Maccabees, specifically Alexander Janneaus, conquered this area, but he did not destroy the settlement. Rather, he just let it go out of existence. So that after the Hellenistic period, the tel ceased to be inhabited. At least we have found nothing beyond that time."

I asked what was the earliest sign of habitation.

"We have excavated down to the Persian period, but we have

found some Early Bronze pottery, which would indicate occupation in the third and second millennia B.C."

We strolled around the unearthed boulders, the dark pits with their signs of kitchen middens, the blackened remains of hearths, the demarcations of walls and doorways. "We plan to keep digging here until 1972. I am interested in cultural relations and trade contacts between Greece and Palestine. You see, when the Greeks came in they Hellenized this part of Palestine in a short period. They imposed a new, vigorous culture. They brought in enough people and established communities like this to set up a simulacrum of Alexandrine life. But of course there's a paradox there, too." A smile lit the archaeologist's face. "You see, Alexander's campaigns were to a great extent anti-Hellenistic. It was a means of getting rid of Greek religion on the borders of Israel. He was much involved with the Eastern religions—Egyptian, Persian —and he tried to create an amalgam, a combination of Hellenistic and Eastern civilization. To be pure Hellenist, that was anti-Hellenistic."

We walked slowly across the rocky roof of the tel back toward the Palestinian pistachio. "There's a splendid granary," Professor Weinberg said, pointing to a circular group of stones at the bottom of a trench. "And a fine oven. We've also found enormous quantities of Greek glass here. It's possible there was a glass factory on the site. And all of it very, very Greek."

Dani asked him, with a good deal less of the challenging tone he had adopted with the Baptists of Beersheba: "You mean there was no occupation of this area by the Jews after it was conquered by Alexander Jannaeus?"

"Oh, yes. We are pretty certain that habitation, except for the usual sporadic Bedouin habitation, ended when the Greek settlement vanished."

"But you are not completely certain?"

"No." His eyes crinkled. "But that's the nice thing about archaeology. Nobody ever died for it—or of it. If we aren't absolutely accurate, so what?"

Now, archaeologists can be towers of dogma, positivists, champions of their own special area. But not Saul Weinberg. He was a model of tolerance and good humor, a man free of certainties and pet theories. The earth of Israel to him was no mere tool to buttress New or Old Testament assertions, or a place in which "to dig the Bible," but a wondrous, rich source from which to embellish and expand our knowledge of the ancient world. We left him joyfully sorting his Greek glass and pottery atop the Tel of the Heron.

Hazor was our next stop as we drove south through the Galilean hills. I had been told this was the biblical site that James Michener studied as the basis for his novel *The Source*.

"Hazor is mentioned in the Book of Joshua," Dani said. "Jabin united the Canaanites against Joshua. The kings of Canaan gathered their army near Meron, and Joshua made a surprise attack and defeated them. Then he took Hazor without a fight and burned it, because its king had been the head of the Canaanite alliance. Much later, Hazor became one of Solomon's chariot cities. You remember?"

"Yes. Like Gezer. And Megiddo."

"You are learning. Hazor was always an important city. It stood at the gateway to eastern Galilee. It was on the main route between Egypt and Assyria. Yadin did the main excavations here in 1955 to 1958. Some of his people are back here now, digging out the underground water systems, although he's back in the United States."

We drove up to the gate. A chain barred our entrance. An attendant came out of the sentry shed and spoke to Dani, who showed him his identification card from the Ministry of Tourism.

"He says it is closed to the public. They had a bad accident here the other day. Landslide. Five of the workmen were injured and two are still in the hospital. No archaeologists here, just the laborers. He says we can go in, but we're on our own, and we shouldn't get near the edge of the water tunnel."

Walking up the site, we realized how elevated it was, how it dominated the surrounding area, like Gezer and Megiddo. We looked at the ruins of the fortress, the tower, the thick, forbidding city walls.

"It is barren," Dani said. "But in Jerusalem, go to the Israel Museum, and you will see the beautiful things they found here—the Solomonic gate, the Canaanite lion, the Canaanite steles."

After touring the gray-white walls, we walked toward the site of the excavation. Several huge earth-moving vehicles were at the edge of the pit: a giant grader, a pay-loader, a crane. A half-dozen workmen in sweat-stained, dust-coated blue were removing loads of earth from a dark, yawning cavity in the tel. At one side could be discerned a flight of steps winding toward the bottom.

I could understand how the accident had occurred. The sides of the great pit were slippery. The sandy soil, divested of its scrubby vegetation, made for difficult footing. Even my Abercrombie and Fitch hiking shoes failed to give me a purchase. The heavy motorized equipment, I noticed, stayed a respectable distance from the edge of the pit.

By taking the elevated position on a mound of excavated soil—it was bleached earth, dead gray, and it made it difficult for me to conceive of this same dirt producing fruit and wheat and vegetables in abundance—I was able to see the start of the underground channel.

"It is similar to Megiddo," Dani said. I saw him only dimly, his lean figure distorted by heat waves. "You see the steps?"

I did. "What period?"

"This tunnel, I don't know. But there are tunnels here that go back to Middle Bronze——"

"Canaanite."

"Ah, an expert. Yes, this was a great Canaanite city six hundred years before Joshua."

"I'm beginning to feel sorry for the Canaanites. They built a considerable civilization, but where are they?"

"Where are any of them? Amorites, Edomites, Kenites, Rechabites. They did not have a book."

Dani shied a flat stone into Yigael Yadin's bottomless cistern and tunnel. "Let's go to lunch."

Later, worrying about my Canaanites—they seem to have been shortchanged by history—I turned to George Adam Smith's classic *The Historical Geography of the Holy Land:*

> Israel was everywhere a mixed race, but while in Samaria and Galilee the foreign constituents were mostly Canaanite, in Judaea they were mostly Arabian . . .

when history first lights up within Palestine what we see
is a confused medley of clans—that crowd of Canaanites,
Amorites, Perizzites, Kenizzites, Hivites, Girgashites,
Hittites, sons of Anak and Zamzummim—which per-
plexes the student but is yet in such harmony with the
natural conditions of the country and with the rest of
history. Again, if we remember the fitful nature of Semitic warfare—the rush and if this be not successful, the
resting content with what has been gained—we can
appreciate why, in so broken a land, the invasion of the
Hebrew nomads was partial, and left, even in parts it
covered, many Canaanite enclaves.

George E. Mendenhall, in an article entitled "The Hebrew Conquest of Palestine" (*The Biblical Archaeologist Reader*, Vol. 3,
New York, 1970), further discounts the notion of total military
conquest. Mendenhall reasons that the word *Apiru* (*Hab/piru*),
the presumed root of *Hebrew*, means, in effect, "I hate my king
and my city," and that those inhabitants of the ancient world
so called were rebels against the kingly authority and cities of
Canaan. These people, argues Mendenhall, were not distinct
racially or culturally, and no one was born a "Hebrew." Rather,
one *became* one, by withdrawing from or rebelling against the
existing social order, in this case, local monarchies and urban units.
As for the conquest of Canaan by the Hebrews, he writes:

> There was no statistically important invasion of
> Palestine at the beginning of the twelve-tribe system of
> Israel. There was no radical displacement of population,
> there was no genocide, there was no large scale driving
> out of population, only of royal administrators. . . .
> In summary, there was no real conquest of Palestine
> in the sense that has usually been understood; what
> happened instead may be termed, from the point of
> view of the secular historian interested only in socio-
> political processes, a peasant's revolt against the net-
> work of interlocking Canaanite city-states.

And, Mendenhall goes on, the moving force in this revolt

against Canaanite kings was the Hebrew concept of God. The old power of the kings, the rebels maintained, was "an illicit assumption of the prerogatives of God alone." The peasants got their land, their animals, their birthrights not from some ruler but from Yahweh, as part of the covenant. The notion evidently appealed to many Canaanites (and, I assume, other dwellers in the land); anyone who made covenant with Yahweh now had title to his own land. God's communities tilled their soil under divine protection. Church took over from the state, and the kings of Canaan fell. Thus, as I interpret Mendenhall, a religious movement—which had its origins in the escape from Egypt—created a new political and social order, and indeed, a new ethnic identity: Hebrews, or Israelites. But the people who converted to the new God and turned against the monarchs were the same people who had always tilled the soil of Palestine. Mendenhall writes: "There could hardly have been any considerable contrast linguistically or ethnically between the Israelite tribes and the population of the Canaanite cities."

In short, Israel was a religious movement, a popular uprising, an indigenous force that rose in Canaan. As for the notion that the twelve tribes were descendants of a single ancestor, Mendenhall states this was *ex post facto* genealogy—an attempt to create a historic unity to enhance a religion.

So maybe we Jews are part, or all, Canaanite. Those Bronze Age pioneers live yet in our blood. As we dined in the elegant restaurant of Ayelet Hashahar, on spicy gefilte fish and aromatic blintzes, I was glad that the Canaanites had not been obliterated but had apparently survived in the blood of modern Jews (at least according to Mendenhall).

Ayelet Hashahar—"The Morning Star"—has earned its high marks. Its guest house was where James Michener stayed for several months while working on *The Source*. As one enters the grounds of the kibbutz on the usual tree-shaded road, one passes a small museum containing some of the finds from Hazor. It is one of the best small museums I have ever seen and certainly worth a visit before enjoying the charming dining facilities of the kibbutz.

"They call this place the Grossinger's of Israel," Dani said. I had forgotten his Brooklyn grandfather. As a boy he had spent a year or so in New York.

"Yes, everything but cha-cha-cha lessons and weekends for singles," I said.

Marie kicked me.

"Oh, I know what he means," Dani said. His dark eyes took in the crowded dining room. It was filled with Americans, noisy, joyful, loudly appreciative of the cuisine.

"Look at those waitresses," Dani said. "Aren't they beautiful? Bebele gets the best-looking girls to work here. They're all Orientals. Here, I'll ask this one."

A teen-age girl with skin the color of iced coffee and eyes like two Krasne's jumbo-size black olives answered him with a warm smile and a gentle voice.

"An Indian," he said. "From Bombay. Beautiful, beautiful." He pointed to another dusky girl, this one wearing her hair in long ebony braids. "She's a Persian, and that one, an Iraqi. Oh, what marvelous girls."

"You love your people," Marie said.

"Yes, yes! They are all so different, so unusual."

He was right. The colorful diversity intrigued him. As it did us in a few days. But it went beyond that. Dani was manifesting an essential trait of the Israeli citizen, the one thing above all that makes him sui generis: a finely developed sense of community. In the truest, deepest sense Israelis are united; they feel responsible for one another's welfare; they are endlessly interested in one another. They gossip about each other, brag, praise, exaggerate, color the truth slightly, weep when a soldier dies, applaud when a scientist triumphs. This is not to say they do not have their rivalries and their antagonisms. Cultural and ethnic differences abound, as well as the traditional prickliness and single-mindedness of the Jewish intellectual (or shopkeeper, for that matter). But these are piddling, insignificant matters even though writers still are tempted to magnify them until one gets the impression that Israelis spend their time squabbling and snarling, a disunited, irritable breed of people, determined to prove John Dryden's estimate of Jews as "a headstrong, moody, murm'ring race."

For example: Some months after my return from Israel, after I had been telling anyone who would listen how impressed I had been with this palpable, pulsating air of community, this remark-

able solidarity, I read an excellent popular history of Jerusalem by
a young American-Jewish writer and found these words:

> Most of the Jews in the city look down on their fellows.
> . . . Among the old settlers, the Sephardic or Spanish
> Jews, as the senior group, tend to patronize the Ashkena-
> zim. The Ashkenazim on their part also look down on the
> Sephardim, since in Israel, Ashkenazim control the coun-
> try's political and intellectual life. The European Jews
> look down on Jews from Arab lands, and the Jews from
> Arab lands resent the European Jews. The German Jews
> despise all the other Jews, considering them crude, and
> all the other Jews detest the German Jews for their Teu-
> tonic arrogance.

As I read this, I blinked in disbelief. I am quite sure that these
jealousies and snobberies exist. Moreover, the writer was discussing the situation only in Jerusalem. But the verbs: *detest?*
despise? patronize? I had the feeling that the author and I had
visited two different countries. Many people had told me about
the problems of assimilating Orientals, but not a single Israeli
ever spoke to me in disparaging or bitter tones about the Yemen-
ites and the Iraqis. Indeed, I was often told, "They make great
soldiers" or "They practice a true Hebrew religion." As for the
rivalries between German Jews and others, Dani sometimes used
the derogatory term *yecke* to refer to them, but he did so in an
offhand manner, with no real conviction. But after reading this
account of the hatred nutured by Jerusalem Jews, I began to
wonder how in God's name they had won the Six-Day War or
built a single apartment or plowed a hectare of land.

I worry a great deal about my opinions. And so I was pleased
to find confirmation—in almost the exact words I had been
using—in the pages of *Commentary*. Robert Alter, in the February, 1970, issue, in an article entitled "Zionism for the 70's," wrote:

> Perhaps the most important contextual change [since
> 1967] is a new sense of confidence in the viability of
> Israel's national consciousness, in Israel's inner coher-

ence as a society. Especially coming from America,
where we seem to live more and more in a state of
mutual suspicion, estrangement, perhaps even dread of
one another, one is struck by the solidarity—and I mean
solidarity, not nationalistic fervor—that makes itself felt
now in Israeli society. Israelis have long been known for
the abrasive, abusive, intrusive ways in which they tend
to relate to each other . . . but one is more frequently
aware nowadays of the obverse side of this abrasive-
ness—a familial assumption of familiarity, an involve-
ment in one another's fate not just as fellow citizens but
quite simply as fellow men.

As I read these words, months after my tour of Israel, I thought
of Dani in the dining room of Ayelet Hashahar, intrigued and
delighted with the Indian and Iraqi waitresses. And I decided
that the writer who had perceived so much hatred, so many
ethnic jealousies in his Jerusalem Jews, might do well to go back
and take a second look. There is, I suspect, a vast difference
between an offhand insult (my own childhood was filled with
rude remarks about Galitizianers and Litvaks) and *hate*.

"Every kibbutz tries to imitate Ayelet Hashahar, to run as good
a kitchen, as good a rest house. It's the standard. Wasn't the
lunch terrific?"

We agreed that it was. There had been all sorts of gourmet
touches: relishes, side dishes, a freshness to the bread, the subtle
white soft cheese, the vegetables. And the perky Oriental waitresses in their yellow dresses were a distinct asset.

"And here's the man responsible," Dani said as we got up to
leave.

A slender doll-like man in his sixties wearing a white shirt and
dark trousers came over to greet us.

"Mr. and Mrs. Green, this is my friend Bebele Eshkol, who
runs Ayelet Hashahar."

Bebele asked us if we had enjoyed our lunch and invited us to
take a swim in the kibbutz pool before resuming our sight-seeing.
Normally I am immune to the bonhomie of innkeepers and res-

taurant owners. Headwaiters put me on guard. I never trust their good nature. Their merriment, like that of parsons (*vide* Samuel Johnson) is "an offensive thing." But Bebele Eshkol was not merely a greeter. He had dignity; he had command presence; he had *style*.

Later, as we swam in the kibbutz pool—I seem to recall it was close by a redolent chicken hatchery, an odd kibbutzian arrangement—I asked Dani about his friend Bebele.

"Yes, he is quite a man. He built this place's reputation by himself. You say 'Ayelet,' people think of Bebele."

"What did he do before?"

"I'm not sure. But during the War of Independence he was one of our top officers. I should have called him by his title. He was *Colonel* Eshkol."

After a while one stops being surprised. I will say this for Colonel Bebele Eshkol: No military man in the world serves up a tastier gefilte fish.

CHAPTER IV

Where Jesus Preached

"The name Capernaum," Dani said, after he had shown his Ministry of Tourism pass to a bearded Franciscan at the gate, "is from the Hebrew Kfar Nahum, which means the village of Nahum. Who Nahum was, no one is certain. It's not mentioned in the Bible. In the New Testament, Capernaum is famous for the synagogue where Christ preached."

"How are you on the New Testament?" I asked.

"Not interested."

We walked slowly around the reconstructed ruins of Capernaum on the northwest shores of the Sea of Galilee. The place is quite lovely, haunted, full of mystery: it is the site where Christ walked on the water. I looked out at the darkening blue surface of the Galilee and tried to formulate some rational explanation for the miracle, something to do with atmospherics, topography, the lay of the land. "And it was now dark and Jesus was not come

73

to them. And the sea rose by reason of a great wind that blew. So
when they had rowed about five and twenty or thirty furlongs,
they saw Jesus walking on the sea and drawing nigh unto the
ship, and they were afraid. . . ."

Of course, it had been at night, and the lake was stormy. Visibility was poor. Andrew, Simon, James, and John were distraught.
In their state, it was quite possible they *saw* him walk.

We walked through the grove of eucalyptus trees—imported
from Australia to combat erosion and, from all indications, a great
success—past the Franciscan monastery, toward the restored synagogue.

It is an imposing structure, monumental, gracefully proportioned. It consists of a main prayer hall with three double doors
and a one-story annex, the house of study, or *beit midrash.*

"A rich synagogue, a rich congregation," Dani said. "Like
Scarsdale. The stones are white limestone, beautiful stones,
almost like marble. But it isn't local stone. They had to bring it
from four miles away, from the Vale of Arbel."

"What about the black stones in the base?"

"Basalt. That is the local rock, softer, blacker. But the Jews of
Kfar Nahum were too high-class for black basalt. So they used it
only in the foundation, and they *shlepped* fancy limestone all the
way here. That was a lot of work for a small Jewish community in
the third century."

"Third? I thought Christ preached here."

"He did, he did, but much earlier. What you are looking at is
not the original synagogue. That one, the one where Christ spoke,
where the miracles were performed, was destroyed by the
Romans either in the Jewish War, 73 c.e., or the Bar Kochba
War. This one you are looking at was probably built around 200
c.e."

"c.e.?"

"Christian Era. We don't use a.d."

"Ah. Of course. *Anno Domini.* Not your—our—*Domini.* Theirs."

"It was leveled by order of Septimius Severus or Severus Alexander. The third century was a good time for Jews in Galilee.
There are more than thirty major synagogues from that period
around here—Meron, Bar'am, Chorazim, Beit Shearim. This is the
most luxurious."

Crusader tombstone shaped like a toadstool; Crusader church of Abu Ghosh.

Tel Gezer: the trenches.

Tel Gezer: two volunteer diggers, Christian seminarians from Oklahoma. The young lady is measuring the depth of strata.

"We stand at Armageddon and battle for the Lord." Marie resting against the walls of Megiddo.

The great tel of Beit Shean, overlooking the remains of the city's Roman amphitheater.

A group of young kibbutzniks at Kfar Blum. Already (or was it our imagination?) they had that calm, confident look about them.

Professor Saul Weinberg, of the University of Missouri, shows us around his dig at Tel Anafa, near Shamir. "A very Greek place."

A man at peace with the world and the centuries: Professor Weinberg sorting his find in the shade of a Palestinian pistachio tree.

A major excavation: digging deep for the ancient cistern of Hazor.

The unmistakable black basalt ruins of Chorazim, unique in Israel.

The head of Medusa from one of the stones of Chorazim.

Beautifully carved and preserved tomb door from the vaults of Beit Shearim.

A standard of all Israeli travel literature—the Roman aqueduct of Caesarea.

Like huge coast artillery, ancient Roman columns have been used to buttress the sea wall of Ashkelon.

The memorial at Yad Mordekhai. In the distance one-dimensional plywood Egyptians charge across the kibbutz fields. On the hill in the foreground stand the handful of rifles and machine guns that repelled the invaders.

The summit of Avdat. Almost all the visible ruins are Byzantine.

One of the ancient cisterns of Avdat, probably Byzantine work on top of Nabatean engineering.

A view from Avdat. The dark cultivated patch in the distance is Professor Evenari's famed experimental acreage in the Negev.

Ruins of a Byzantine church, Avdat.

Masada in profile. The different levels are Herod's three hanging palaces.

The palaces viewed from above: the circular wall of one of Herod's pleasure domes.

After Herod, the zealots. Another view from the heights clearly shows the Roman camp and the siege wall.

A tour group on the summit of Masada gives an idea of the huge area.

Resting amid the remains of the synagogue on Masada.

The descent. Contrary to tourist mythology, it is not a very arduous hike.
Elderly ladies and children manage it daily.

The bare bones of an old, old civilization: Tel Arad.

Guide studying Arad's drainage system.

The dig at Tel Beersheba. The cut in the slope of the tel reveals history;
centuries speak through exposed stones.

In the trenches of Tel Beersheba: a bikini where Abraham once sat in his tent in the heat of the day.

The mosque in Hebron. The purported tomb of Abraham, it is sacred to Jews and Moslems. The lowest stones in the interior wall are Herodian.

A view of Jerusalem from the Hotel Intercontinental. The great globe is the Dome of the Rock. The area around it gives some idea of the spacious, tree-lined Noble Sanctuary.

TV aerials adorn a handsome stretch of Turkish wall around the Old City.

Some say this is the well where David first saw Bathsheba. No one really believes it, but it adds a touch of romance to the grim Turkish citadel.

The procession along the Via Dolorosa commences with a prayer by the Franciscans at the first station, where Christ was condemned by Pilate. It is now the courtyard of an Arab school.

We wandered among the huge stones and columns standing around the open porch and steps. Many of these have unusual carvings, well preserved in the hard, gold-tinted limestone. On the keystone of an arched lintel we saw a graceful scallop shell, enclosed in a wreath of acanthus leaves. A fallen Corinthian capital displayed the ornaments of temple ritual: a ram's horn, a seven-branched candelabrum, an incense shovel. Other ruins were decorated with palm trees, pomegranate flowers, the Star of David, eagles, and Capricorn, the mythical sea-goat.

"All have significance," Dani said. "The palm tree symbolizes Judean Jewry. The wreath is a victory symbol. This is the most interesting of all. What does it look like?"

We stared at the carving on the yellow-gray stone. "It looks like a temple, or a house on wheels."

"It's a *carrucca*," Dani said. "Probably Roman. It was a wheeled carriage, a sort of synagogue on wheels. There are several theories about it. One is that it was used to move big shots around. The other is that it was a portable shrine for the scrolls of the Torah. Maybe it's what they thought the Ark looked like. In the old days, you remember, it was brought from place to place, into battle, and so on. Professor Sukenik thinks maybe it is a symbol of the mystic chariot that is mentioned in Ezekiel. In any case, that is our *carrucca*."

As we stood on the stone porch of the Capernaum synagogue, he explained that the upper story of the main building was the women's section. ("Just like at my grandfather's shul on Eastern Parkway.")

A long row of well-preserved benches he identified as the honored seats of the elders. "Ah, the east wall," I said.

Dani glared at me. "No! In Europe, in America, it would be the east wall. Why?"

"Facing Jerusalem," I stammered.

"Right. But from here, which way is Jerusalem?"

"South."

"Now you are showing some intelligence. Naturally. So these benches face *south*. In synagogues in Galilee, the seats of the elders always face south."

Dani pointed out an ancient Greek inscription on one of the columns. A certain Herod (not the famous one) and his son

Justos had paid for the erection of that particular column and were memorialized on it. An Aramaic inscription had to do with one Halphayi, who contributed the column on which his name appeared.

"So it's an old custom," I said. "Names of the donors."

"And here is an inscription we could do without."

It was in Latin, and it looked new, sharply incised into the stone. "What do you have against it?"

"It's out of place. It's a memorial to Orfali, the Franciscan monk who did the restoration."

"He deserves something for all that work."

"I know, I know. But it's out of place. It's too modern."

Dr. Gaudence Orfali had died on April 20, 1926, two days after completing the work of restoration. He was a Galilean-born Christian Arab of Syrian origin, whose family probably was from the Turkish-Syrian border city of Urfa, hence the name. There had been digs at the site of Kfar Nahum before, including several run by the indefatigable Englishmen Robinson and Wilson. Under a young English lieutenant named Kitchener, later to gain fame at Khartoum and in World War I, the Palestine Exploration Fund did further work at Capernaum. This, according to Baruch Sapir and Dov Neeman in a superb guide to Capernaum, "aroused general interest, mainly in Christian circles, who saw . . . an unprecedented opportunity to unearth the center of Christ's ministry in Galilee."

The Franciscans purchased the site in 1894 and promptly buried the exposed ruins to prevent further thefts of the stones by Arabs, who had by now carried away anything that was portable. (I am reminded of Damon Runyon's description of Sam the Gonoph, who was so honest he would not steal anything, provided it had an armed guard around it and was nailed down.)

Enter the euphonic Orfali. In 1905 the Franciscan Arab began his systematic excavation, apparently a monumental job. Orfali unearthed the main building with its three doors, the walls that were still *in situ*, and the *beit midrash*. Many of the key limestone blocks had found their way to Arab buildings in neighboring villages; the tireless Orfali bought them back. He was less successful looking for a basilica that, according to early Christian tradition, had been built on the site of St. Peter's house. No such basilica was found, but he did unearth the remains of a curious octagonal structure paved with mosaic. Orfali decided it was a baptistery. Contemporary scholars are not certain.

We paused at the octagonal ruin, which had been partially restored. Dani said it was probably Byzantine. "When Pope Paul visited here," he said, "one of the monks decided to dress this up, to give the idea that this really was St. Peter's basilica. A terrible thing to do. The Department of Antiquities put a fast end to that, though generally they don't like to intervene with the Franciscans."

As we left Capernaum, I asked Dani about the proliferation of images on the buildings of Capernaum, all of them part of the third-century synagogue. Wasn't this against Jewish law and tradition?

"They took over notions from pagan temples," he said. "Mostly the animals, the birds. You'll notice a lot of these have been rubbed off. Later, the Jews decided these carvings were an abomination."

In Sapir and Neeman's work, I came across this bit of information:

> The external appearance of some synagogues was so similar to that of pagan temples that even pious Jews, when strangers in some unfamiliar place, bowed to a pagan temple, mistaking it for a synagogue. That such mistakes have quite often been recorded is proved by the thrice-repeated Talmud statement: "If he saw [an idolatrous shrine] and mistook it for a synagogue and bowed down to it, surely his heart was to heaven"— meaning that if he did so bona fide, he should not therefore be prosecuted for idolatry.

As we drove from Capernaum to the site of another third-century synagogue, Dani began to speculate on the prevalence of miracles in Capernaum.

"Jesus walked on the water here," he said. "He also cured the man with the withered hand. And raised Yair's daughter from the dead. He calmed the sea. He also arranged for Peter to find a shekel in a fish's mouth, to pay the tax collector."

"How do scholars explain so many miracles in one place?"

"Who knows? They're still full of miracles here."

"Such as?"

"The Franciscans insist that the synagogue you just saw is the one where Jesus preached. Nobody else believes that. Everyone else agrees it's from the third century. But listen, why should I begrudge them a miracle? If they want to believe it's the same synagogue, let them. *Seit gesundt.*"

There are archaeological sites that through a harmony of geography, color, and their ruinous state produce a sense of delectable mystery, of ineffable beauty. The Greek temples at Paestum, below Salerno, are in this sublime category. So is the Pont du Gard in the south of France. In Israel, the first site I observed that affected me so deeply was Chorazim, variously spelled Korazim, Chorazin, Korozain.

"There isn't much left there," Dani said as Avram drove the Dodge up a dirt road on a hillside. We were a mile or so north of Capernaum. "As a matter of fact, hardly anyone ever visits it."

At once my blood pumped a bit faster. Old sites that are unvisited are often the most rewarding. Isolation, unrestored ruination, inaccessibility, all these can make for a place to inspirit the heart and challenge the mind. Chorazim proved to be a classic site, one of the most memorable in the Holy Land.

"Jesus preached here also," Dani said as we walked up a narrow path. Varieties of bramble, wild grass, some malformed old trees bordered the walk. There was no entrance booth, no signs, no refreshment stand—rare and private. A ponderous dolmen, built of the brooding black native stone, stood to one side. A typical large flat boulder balanced precariously on the base stones. Obviously this Stone Age structure was not part of the third-century synagogue. I looked at Dani in puzzlement.

"Who knows?" he said. "Maybe some kids put it up."

Higher on the height we saw the tumbled black pillars and foundation stones of the old house of worship.

"Another place Jesus didn't like," Dani said. "One of the cities he bawled out. 'Woe unto thee, Chorazim!' Christ said. It's in Matthew."

Woe unto thee, Chorazim. I suppose it would have been appropriate to feel morose over the way Christ's malediction had come true. Chorazim was indeed a wreck, a dead and desolate place. Yet I did not have the slightest sensation of sorrow. Chorazim, a clutter of fallen stones and dark memories, is actually joyful! It is harmonious, colorful, at peace with the land.

To begin with—the colors. No French Impressionist could combine hues in a more daring, dazzling, eye-stunning manner. The fallen columns, the huge doorways, the lintels, the base stones, the mighty ashlars, are of that weathered black-gray that only the native basalt can produce. Where the stones have been pitted and scarred by time and wind they possess an ash-gray softness; otherwise they are a stark and dignified black. Around the clearly defined outlines of the temple, columns and decorated boulders lie in helter-skelter array. But not totally helter-skelter. For some reason, the arrangement is totally satisfying, everything resting in millennial dirt, all in pleasing proportion. Indeed, the haphazard artistry of Chorazim is more agreeable than the sedulously restored facade of Capernaum.

The blackness of the stones is accented by the brilliant yellow-brown grass that surrounds the area. I thought of Van Gogh's burning yellow meadows as I looked at the scene; I regretted that his wild brush had never come to Chorazim. And above, a diamond-blue sky. Beyond, calm, cool, lay a wedge of the Sea of Galilee, a turquoise triangle, shimmering, elusive. Black, yellow-gold, pale blue, turquoise. These were colors of such intensity, such perfection, such dazzling balance, as to stun the onlooker with the sheer potency of matched hues.

While Dani took Marie on a tour of the site, pointing out the curious carvings—Medusa, a garland enclosing the zodiac, a lion—I scampered like a madman about the blunted irregular black walls, taking photographs. My hands shook. I was intoxicated with the colors, the conformation of stones and terrain, the terrible mystery of the place.

I was able to learn very little about Chorazim. The origin of its name is obscure, according to Zev Vilnay. It survived into the early Arab period as Kereza and achieved lasting fame when Jesus denounced it. In the third century, the black basalt syna-

gogue arose, a modest affair compared with the magnificence of
Capernaum. And then came the long sleep on the tawny slopes
overlooking the Kinneret.

Woe unto thee, Chorazim! Christ's denunciation was fulfilled.
Chorazim was destroyed. But not for me. Nature and artifice
have combined to make her immortal—old stones and the intense
colors of earth, sky, and water united in one of the most breathtaking vistas in the Holy Land.

"Chorazim has made me insatiable," I said. "What else can we
see?"

"You don't know your Old Testament, but you don't get tired,"
Dani said, with grudging admiration.

We visited the Church of the Multiplication at Tabgha, the
place of the miracle of the loaves and the fishes. The mosaic floor,
with its gay wading birds—leggy herons, smug ducks, sassy cor-
morants—is a pure delight. Unfortunately it was late afternoon,
and the lighting left much to be desired. The work is fifth-cen-
tury Byzantine and has a flowing, natural style, suggesting a
tapestry.

Time was pressing. It was getting chilly and we were losing the
sun. Dani hurried us along. "Too short a visit," I protested. "I
had time for only half a loaf and one fish."

Outside the church we ran into the beautiful nun we had met
outside the hotel two days ago. She smiled wistfully at us, but
ignored Dani's attempts at conversation. A step behind walked
the portly duenna. Sister? Friend? Was she assigned to keep an
eye on the attractive sister? The two were traveling in a private
car with a private guide, a taciturn redhead who knew Dani. The
two of them exchanged some banter in Hebrew. I gathered they
were discussing the sister.

"What was that all about?" I asked as we drove off.

"Just talk," Dani said. "Such a waste. He says the blonde keeps
an eye on her. She's afraid to talk to a man. Well, that all has to
change."

On the road back to Tiberias my new thirty-five-millimeter
reflex camera broke. It was an expensive camera, widely advertised. It is an excellent camera, with many admirable features.

But the rewind mechanism is faulty. It is too delicate. It snaps under the slightest pressure. The small orphaned knob rested in my blunt fingers, the open rear of the chassis exposing and annulling an entire roll. Where in Israel would I get it fixed?

"We'll try in Tiberias," Dani said. "Our people are superb mechanics."

In the center of Tiberias we found the Rassco building, a large modern structure built around the plaza. In a café seven or eight brightly dressed young girls twittered and chattered. There was much rolling of dark eyes, a word of French here and there, extravagant gestures.

The camera shop was run by a certain M. Herskov, a minuscule man in a yarmulke. He was arranging to take portraits of a Yemeni woman and her two children, black-eyed tots. But sensing my disaster—I spoke to him in halting Yiddo-German, Dani having run off to chat with the girls—he told her to wait. Upstairs in a steamy darkroom he dismantled the camera, set the rewind knob, tested it, loaded it with new film, and wished me well. I offered to pay him. He refused. We compromised by my buying several rolls of film.

I crossed the plaza, my mind untroubled. It was dusk. In the shops, the cafés, under the arcades, circulated Druse women in gray robes, trim Israeli policemen, Orientals, bearded old Orthodox types. There was a rightness and a decency about the place. Tiny M. Herskov, a Hungarian, a nimble-fingered skilled fellow, content beneath his embroidered yarmulke, was part of it. Displaying talent, hard work, ambition, faith, kindness, he seemed to me to be a man who offered the world a great deal.

"We should be getting on to Lavi," Dani said, "but I realize what kind of a tourist you are."

"What am I?" We were threading our way through early evening traffic in Tiberias, military cars, taxis, carts, burros.

"A sponge. You want to soak up everything. So, we'll get to Lavi a little late. There's something outside of Tiberias I want you to see."

Dani's unscheduled treat was the ruins of the ancient synagogue of Hamath Tiberias, just south of the city, near the redolent sulfur baths. The light was fading. It was still quite warm. As we parked alongside the Sea of Galilee, now turning a blue-gray,

I caught the aroma of sulfurous gases, those allegedly salubrious vapors, and I felt for a moment I was in Italy on the Via Tiburtina, near the Bagni di Tivoli.

We walked through a landscaped park to the main attraction of the Hamath Tiberias excavation, an extensive mosaic floor of a third- or fourth-century synagogue. Three huge panels in the nave of the building reveal a series of well-preserved mosaic designs. The southern panel depicts the Holy Ark, a bulky two-story structure with a triangular roof and two pillars on either side. Flanking it are the familiar symbols found everywhere as synagogue decorations: the seven-branched candelabra, the shofar, the palm branches, the incense shovels. A central panel—all of them are large, perhaps fifteen by twenty feet—shows a colorful zodiac. At each corner of the wheel are women representing the seasons, and in the center of the zodiac the sun-god Helios, rays emanating from his early Byzantine face, rides his chariot through the heavens. Pagan that he is, there is a shifty quality in his dark eyes—as if he is aware that he has sneaked into the holy precincts of Yahweh only by sufferance, or perhaps error, or perhaps an attempt to propitiate the local Roman or Byzantine overlords.

A northern panel consists of Greek inscriptions flanked by two sturdy red and gold lions. These are the names of the founders of the synagogue. In the fading light the mosaic floor assumed a soft melting appearance. The tans, browns, golds, and reds appeared to run together, like the colors in a well-laundered madras shirt. Although rather crude and heavy-handed in execution—one could never compare them to the delicate artistry of the Ravenna mosaics—they had a robust, thick-legged, grain-fed honesty. They suggested rugged farmers and fat millers and red-nosed vintners, rural Jews working the fertile slopes of the Kinneret. There was nothing effete or decadent about these rustic Hebrews of the late Roman period.

In keeping with the character of the mosaics was the unique manner of protecting them from eager tourists who might be tempted to climb the balustrade for a closer look. As we walked along the wall and Dani explained the symbols to us, we heard a guttural growl, then a fusillade of angry barking. A black, mean-eyed German shepherd dog lurched toward us, and we recoiled.

"Nice doggy, nice doggy," I said shakily. But he was leashed, having the run of about half the perimeter of the mosaic enclosure, enough slack to permit him to keep the curious from crossing into the priceless floor. It saved money on guards, I suppose, but his bumptious barking was hardly conducive to meditative calm in the presence of ancient wisdom. Apparently Hamath Tiberias had been a center of learning, housing a renowned *beit midrash* in addition to the complex of synagogues. Assuredly no noisy watch dogs were tolerated by those venerable scholars.

Our room at the Lavi kibbutz looked out on the Horns of Hittim, or Hattin, the location of the momentous battle between the Crusaders under Guy of Lusignan and the victorious forces of Saladin.

It was almost dark now, but the "horns" were clearly visible. They are two curiously curved peaks with a level area between them. Actually, they appear less like mammalian horns than the twin projections on the head of a manta ray, forming that same wide, deep curve. They made an eerie, brooding silhouette in the moonlight. This was a bloody old place, the slopes where the doomed Crusader army encamped to await its destruction. It happened on July 4, 1187. Saladin had already laid siege to Tiberias and captured most of it. The Frankish army marched from their safe encampment at Sephoria, where they had ample water, to recapture Tiberias. Saladin, wily Kurd that he was, exclaimed, "That is just what we want!" The cunning avenger of Islam had besieged Tiberias in order to draw the Franks out and into battle in the midsummer heat in an area short of water. The place was Hittim.

Encamped for the night on the slopes beneath the Horns, the Crusaders realized Saladin had lured them into a trap. They were without access to water. The heat was unbearable. With the wind blowing toward the Crusaders, Saladin ordered his troops to set fire to the dry, crackling grass of the plain—the same yellow stalks I had admired at Chorazim that day. Choking on smoke, parched, roasting in their metal breastplates and chain mail, half the Crusader infantry surrendered in the first few hours, and the rest followed. A heroic cavalry charge by the Christians almost turned the tide, but it was a last gasp. Guy of Lusignan and the other leaders of the Frankish force surrendered. One group of noble lords, Raymond of Tripoli, Reynald of Sidon, and others, battled their way toward Sephoria and escaped. Christian historians judged them heroes; Arab writers called them cowards.

The Horns of Hittim, on that sweltering July day, became a great charnel house, a sacrificial altar. Thousands of corpses—human and equine—littered the earth. Christian blood drenched the ground. In addition to suffering a horrendous loss of soldiery, the Crusaders suffered the ultimate humiliation: The Moslem horde captured the True Cross. As Zoé Oldenbourg puts it in *The Crusades:* "On that one day, the power of the Franks in Syria was shattered once and for all, and the Kingdom of Jerusalem to all intents ceased to exist."

As I sat in the cheerful dining room of Kibbutz Lavi, weary, newly showered, clean-shirted, restoring myself with vegetable soup and brown bread, I ruminated on the brutal, mindless battle of the Horns of Hittim. Rarely had the monstrosities perpetrated in the name of religion been more evident to me. Oh, I have been aware of them most of my life. Whenever I find myself thinking generously of the organized faiths, moved by warm memories of Pope John or the Niebuhrs and Martin Luther Kings of our time, I shall think of Hittim and all those corpses and the whole sanguinary mess of the Crusades. After the battle of the Horns Saladin personally executed one of the most savage of the Crusaders, Reynald de Chatillon. The noble Saracen hacked off Reynald's right arm, then turned him over to his lieutenants for the mortal blows. It was a clear case of the biter bit—Reynald was an atrocious sadist and killer. Guy of Lusignan, king of Jerusalem, shivered in terror as he watched Reynald being sliced into a julienne. But Saladin spared Guy and consoled him: "One king does not kill another."

I was wondering, as I ate my pot roast, whether these violent deeds might have taken place on the spot where now I sat, waited on by chirpy kibbutz girls, listening to the hum of New York tourist voices. Then a huge bearded presence rolled up to our table.

"Wahlcome to Lavi," he said in the unmistakable brogue of Ireland.

"Ah, C.B.! C.B., old *chaver!*" Dani was on his feet, embracing

the Irishman. He was introduced to us as C. B. Kaye, former
Dubliner, manager of the Lavi guesthouse. Barrel-chested, bushy-
bearded, blue-eyed, a purple embroidered yarmulke on his
balding head, clad in khaki shorts and sandals, the man was a
compendium of contradictions.

"Of course I knew Brendan Behan," he said, "a great man, but
done in by the gargle. What an intalligent fallow he was."

I began to scrawl notes on a napkin.

"Yes, I am a Dubliner," C. B. Kaye told us. "I worked as a jeweler in the dear city and decided it wasn't for me. I came to
Israel fahrteen years ago. I was raised in an Orthodox house, and
I chose Lavi because it is an Orthodox kibbutz. My wife is an
Indian, or more properly an Iraqi. She was with the migration
from Baghdad to Bombay after the Second World War. We make
a grand couple, me from Dublin, and she from Bombay, and both
of us Orthodox."

I asked Kaye whether he found his Irish background an asset
as resort manager.

"Oh, yes. Irish-Americans are flabbergasted when they listen to
me speak, but American Jews are even more so. Taddy Kennedy
hugged me and said, 'C.B., yer a better Irishman than I am.' The
Cardinal from Dublin visited here, and when I responded to his
question, puttin' on a bit extra brogue to impress His Aminence,
he turned pale. Yes, I said, I am a Dubliner, just like you. I have a
grand time with our Gentile guests, such as the Chief Justice of
Ireland, or a party of Seventh-Day Adventists who came here.

"The Irish, you know, are varry interested in and sympathetic
to Israel. It goes back to the fight against the British. They'll cheer
for anyone who fights the British. They claimed that the Irgun
and the others learned their methods from the I.R.A. During the
Six-Day War a lot of Irishmen volunteered to fight for Israel, but
they didn't get a chance to come over here. You know, Ireland
doesn't recognize Israel, but it's not because the people wouldn't
approve. It's because the Vatican doesn't recognize us, more's the
pity. Ah well, the dear Pope has his problems also."

It was music, poetry—Joyce, Synge, and Yeats, reborn in the
Kibbutz Lavi, under the Horns of Hittim.

"This is a young place," Kaye said. "Begun in 1949. Johnny
Oberman will tell you about it later at the lecture. The govern-

ment financed a lot of us then, border settlements to discourage
the Arabs. You'll see the shelters tomorrow."

Was there any expectation of paying off the government loans?

"Oh, no. Hundred of years from now, maybe. We'll be in debt
forever and ever. But the Americans who come here tell me that's
the only successful way to run a business. By that standard, we
are a great success." And with that C. B. Kaye excused himself to
chat with the American tourists dining nearby.

The Johnny Oberman to whom C. B. Kaye had referred was the
kibbutz school principal. His lecture that evening proved enlight-
ening and more than ever convinced me of the gossamer mystique of the kibbutz. About thirty of us sat in a corner of the
dining room, tired, overfed, drowsy. But none of us slept.

"We came here in 1949," Oberman said, "and began by spending one year clearing off the top of the mountain. Nothing but
hauling rocks away so we would have land to cultivate. All we
did was move rocks and pray three times a day. We are Orthodox. Prayer is part of our lives. We kept buying land, clearing it
as fast as we could—by hand, with tractors, with horses and
mules. Although I am now the head of the school, I worked as a
farmer for many years, and I came to love the land. There is less
mystery to this than you might think. After a day spent in intellectual studies, in mental work, it is restful to go into the fields in
the fresh air and use your muscles moving rocks."

I tried to pinpoint Oberman's accent. He was a spare man in a
white open-collared shirt, khaki shorts, sandals. Like Kaye, he
wore a yarmulke and sported a flowing black beard that gave
him the look of a young Herzl.

"I am from Melbourne, Australia," Oberman went on. "I was a
mathematics teacher. I came here in 1949 with the first group,
and as I have said, all we did was move rocks. Today we cultivate
over three thousand acres. We grow wheat, melons, other fruits,
produce milk and eggs. I liked it in Australia, and I did not feel
unwanted there. I could have stayed. But I wanted something
else out of life, and I believe that my wife and myself and our
four children have found it here at Lavi. The kibbutz life is
appealing to many of us, and I count myself lucky to be among
them. You must bear in mind that only a fraction of Israelis live

on kibbutzim, no more than three per cent of the population, and about ten per cent of the farm population. But we farm about thirty-five per cent of the arable land, and the kibbutz farms are extremely productive. Orthodox kibbutzim are the exception, not the rule. The early ones were atheistic and socialist."

After he spoke about the absence of salaries, of rewards, of the abolition of private property, someone asked, "But do you control your own destinies?"

"Of course we do. But collectively. We make decisions on a group basis. We have committees for everything, maybe too many. No one can act completely independently. But it works out. One has to start with a sense of giving, of cooperating, otherwise the kibbutz idea cannot succeed."

It seemed to me that Oberman had put his finger on what is right about the kibbutz in terms of Israel's needs and what is wrong about it in terms of applying the formula to other societies.

"Isn't that the secret of the kibbutz?" I asked. "That the members enter it with this attitude, with this awareness of community cooperation, and, if necessary, sacrifice? Don't most kibbutz members *begin* with this view and so it doesn't have to be *instilled* in them? That is, you don't have to do any strenuous missionizing among your people. They know that for the plan to work they must live communally."

"True."

"Then isn't it true that as a model for other societies, especially for emerging countries with rural problems, the kibbutz has no application anywhere else in the world?"

"Probably so," Oberman said.

"Do you know of any other country that has developed a kibbutz system successfully?"

"I have heard that the Japanese are attempting it in some farm areas. But I confess I know very little about it. They were here some years ago observing our kibbutzim."

What I was reluctantly realizing was that the kibbutz is a highly specialized form. It presupposes a sophisticated, motivated, intelligent, tightly bound, group-oriented people. And only among some modern Zionists would one find these characteristics, I am forced to conclude. I have read speculations on the possibility of introducing the kibbutz to African, Asian, or Latin American farm communities, but having spent some time in these regions, I am convinced that such an undertaking in village India or rural Kenya or the Guatemalan highlands would be doomed. It takes a great deal of planning, of drive, of desire, of calculated intelligence, to make something as audaciously revolutionary as a kibbutz work. The secret of its success is that it is *voluntary*. The failure of the collective and state farms in communist states—and it has been a crashing failure—is that these are *enforced* associations. In Poland, Russia, the other communist states, these efforts at a collective society have turned into dull, inefficient, slovenly groupings of sullen people. About all that has saved agriculture in Eastern Europe has been the reversion to "household plots"—private tracts farmed independently in defiance of Marx.

"We have our problems," Oberman went on. "Many people complain of the lack of privacy. They get tired of being cheek-by-jowl with the same people all the time. We try to overcome this. The evening meal need no longer be eaten in the dining hall. I never eat there. I go to the kitchen, get anything I want, and my wife cooks dinner at our house and we eat with the children. Thus we try to create a bit more privacy. Our school is run somewhat differently also. The children don't spend the entire day at the school or sleep there. They come home at four thirty in the afternoon and sleep with the family. It's considered a radical departure by the traditionalists among kibbutz educators."

"Can anyone be kicked out of a kibbutz?" someone asked.

"Yes, but it's very rare. The only absolute reason for ousting a member at Lavi is for striking another person. That means automatic expulsion. Of course, we are selective here. And when you apply for membership you are on probation for one year. Then you are voted on and almost all candidates are accepted."

A woman had heard that many kibbutzim are suffering because young people want to leave for the cities.

"It is a problem. We are coping with it. We try to send all our youngsters who are qualified to the university. Let us say a boy is brilliant in physics. Is it fair to ask him to come back to the kibbutz to pick pears? To be honest, we want him back here. In some capacity. We are working on the problem. We regard the kibbutz as a dynamic form of organization, one that can change with the times. As you have no doubt heard, almost all kibbutzim are diversifying in industry. We have a factory where synagogue furniture is crafted, and it's more of a success than we ever dreamed it could be."

"That still doesn't take care of that brilliant nuclear physicist," the woman persisted.

"We realize that. Maybe we'll lose him, and maybe he has a right to go on to government work. But we want to keep as many of the children as possible, especially the skilled and educated ones."

I had the feeling he was being overoptimistic about keeping the brilliant youngsters, or even the merely restless ones. For all the attractions of kibbutz life—the pastoral atmosphere, the sense of achievement, the proximity of the reassuring earth, the communal mystique—the gaudy world outside beckons.

The next morning, after the traditional trip to the buffet breakfast table—yellow cheeses and silver sardines stick in my mind—we met up with C. B. Kaye again. We walked through the nursery and schools. The children, like those at Kfar Blum, had that cocky, confident appearance. It must have been my imagination, but even the infants two or three months old, snoozing in cribs, their bare behinds exposed (to prevent diaper rash), had that sassy look.

"Their day starts at six thirty A.M.," C.B. said. "But a lot of their parents are at work from three thirty in the morning, at least in the summertime. It gets too hot later in the day to work in the fields."

I mulled over the possibility of some twenty-year-old kibbutznik, a genius at molecular biology, coming back to Lavi to pick melons at three thirty in the morning. There seemed to be good arguments for his objecting to such a life. Oberman had said the kibbutz was "dynamic," that it was changing and would change more to accommodate the gifted, questing young. But how?

C.B. led us to the Lavi synagogue. "It's very simple, very modern," he said. "But notice the way it's modeled on the syna-

gogues of Chorazim and Capernaum, the same plan. We wanted
it to look like the old Galilean synagogues around here."

I asked about an elevated square of mosaics just outside the
synagogue. "Why the four holes?"

"I thought you'd guess. It's an outdoor *chupa*. We placed the
sockets in it so the canopy could be installed easily. All our wed-
dings take place under it."

"Who builds these—the people on the kibbutz?" I asked.

"No, that would take us away from farming. We get outside
contractors to do it. Of course the benches and the woodwork
come from our own furniture factory. It's Scandinavian beech,
finished in Israel. A great success, that business—can't keep up
with orders. Every shul in America wants Israeli-made furniture
from an Orthodox kibbutz."

We walked the shaded paths of Lavi and were shown, as at
Kfar Blum, the ugly gray cement intrusions: bomb shelters. "We
have been lucky so far," Kaye said. "No troubles up here."

In daylight it was apparent that the kibbutz had, as Oberman
had told us, been built smack on top of a mountain. The rocky
crest had been sliced off and flattened to make room for homes,
paths, communal buildings. Although the kibbutz was twenty
years old, it still had the look of an overnight creation, like the
nocturnal clusters of tents and stockades described by Arthur
Koestler in *Thieves in the Night*. I kept thinking of Omar
Khayyám's description of "the strip of herbage grown, that just
divides the desert from the sown."

At the edge of the summit, for example, there stood the simple
one-story homes with red tiled roofs, postage-stamp lawns, shade
trees, paths, a child's bicycle, a clothesline, a bed of wilted
flowers. And a few yards beyond, where the mountain declines,
the pebbly yellow hostile soil took over—as parched as it had
been 780 years ago when Saladin trapped the Crusaders on the
Horns of Hittim.

We walked to our car, and as we passed the synagogue once
more, C. B. Kaye asked us to admire the handsome mosaic depicting the tablets. "You know why there are two of them?" he asked.

Dani nodded. He knew the story. Marie and I did not.

"Waaal, you see, God offered the Commandments first to the

Arabs. What's in it? the Arabs asked. Thou shalt not steal, God said. Not interested. Then he offered them to the Franch. What's in it? they asked. Thou shalt not commit adultery. Sorry, not interested. So he offered the Commandments to the Germans. What's in it? they asked. Thou shalt not kill. Impossible, said the Germans, we don't want 'em. So he came to the Jews. And the Jews asked God, what do they cost? Nothin', said God. Fine, they said, we'll take two of them. That is why there are two tablets."

"Can there be any good thing come out of Nazareth?" Nathanael asked Philip (John 1:46). My friend Zev Vilnay infers from this that Nazareth had a bad reputation in biblical times. It is a bleached, colorless city, nestling on the high hills of Galilee, peopled with soft-voiced, gentle-eyed Christian Arabs who seemed to me strangely secretive. A guide will pester and importune you; a boy selling postcards will tug at you and ignore your protestations; a café-owner will serve you excellent coffee with a sad smile—and yet they all seem to be keeping everything to themselves, revealing little.

We spent most of the witheringly hot morning in the cool confines of the vast Church of the Annunciation, which, disappointingly, is an appalling mishmash of styles, materials, and concepts. It was finished in 1966, and to judge from the scaffolding and unfinished chapels and niches the work is still going on and will be for many years. The exterior is bulky, massive without being graceful. The huge square shape appears totally incongruous with the truncated bell tower. They simply don't work; the proportions are not right.

Inside, on the main level, various countries, among them Japan, Belgium, and France, have contributed mosaic and stonework wall decorations, to symbolize the universality of the church. Most of the mosaic work is of an unsubtle, garish order. Picture-postcard Christianity, peppermint piety. Moreover, there is a jumbled, mindless quality about many of the panels. An exception is a handsome black, red, and white mosaic from Africa. We chatted with two young French Canadians who were installing a wall section with terra cotta bricks in floral designs that promised to look quite attractive when finished. But overall, the nave, and its attendant mural decorations, had all the charm of Loew's Pitkin.

Below, one may look upon the grotto where according to tradition the angel Gabriel appeared before Mary to announce the birth of Jesus. A column marks the spot where Gabriel is thought to have stood. Another column marks the place where Mary sat as she heard the news. I seem to recall some eerie blue stage lighting. My feeling was that to appreciate the beauty and mystery of the miracle one would do better to study Piero della Francesca's version, or da Vinci's or Raphael's.

Perhaps it is the newness of the Church of the Annunciation as much as its ungainliness and size that bothered me. The new, the uncracked and unchipped, the hard clean lines of machine-milled mosaics and synthetically fabricated colors, are out of place in the Holy Land. Things should be rubbed down, worn, off-center; time and weather and combat should leave their mark. The Nazareth church, in its mighty Wurlitzer style, its Roxy garishness, and its execrable "dramatic" lighting, is unhappily not of a piece with the rest of the land. St. Francis himself would probably be uncomfortable in it, not to mention that modest Jewish family who are the objects of all that veneration.

The refreshment stand at the catacombs of Beit Shearim, fifteen miles east of Nazareth, is run by an elderly Litvak who looks like an old-fashioned New York stage Irishman or the comic innkeeper of an Elizabethan play. But unlike our friend C. B. Kaye, he speaks no English. Only Hebrew and an elegant Litvak-accented Yiddish. He was an old friend of Dani's. They exchanged a few jokes, some reminiscences, and the Litvak and 'his wife served us espresso and sweet rolls.

"A wonderful old man," Dani said. "Loves it here next to the tombs. He is a worthy successor to the Sanhedrin who used to meet here in Beit Shearim."

We rested from the murderous heat in the shaded patio in front of the Falstaffian Litvak's stand. Across from us, a family of six, young parents, four kids ranging from an infant to a teen-age boy, sipped soda and talked in a melange of Hebrew and Brooklynese.

"Not tourists," Dani said. "I'll bet you. Immigrants from America."

Marie walked over to them. "I thought I heard a New York accent," she said.

"Williamsburg," the mother said.

"How long have you been here?" Marie asked.

"Six months. And we love it. The best thing we ever did."

"Why did you come here?"

The father shrugged, not as if there were any doubts on his part, but because he could not conceive of anyone not understanding. He had curly *payes* and a small beard and soft, harassed eyes. Two of the boys also sported scraggly *payes*. All of the males wore *tsitsis*. They were a singularly docile group. I worried about them.

"Why?" the father asked. "We belong here. Not in Brooklyn."

I could understand. I thought of Williamsburg, a neighborhood much like my old haunt, Brownsville. Decaying tenements, angry blacks, filthy schools. Muggings, foul language, burning garbage on the dirty snow, hydrants spewing water in the summer, eternal stench and noise. Here, in Israel, they might have to worry about the Al Fatah and a rocket dropped on their home. But it seemed on balance a lot safer, more rewarding existence.

As we toured the catacombs I said to Dani, "Those were the first Americans you seemed pleased with. Present company, I hope, excepted."

"They're not Americans. They are Israelis."

No doubt they were. The children now talked Brooklyn English, but I wondered how long they would retain it. Williamsburg with its bad odors and violence and racial strife had driven them out.

"Beit Shearim means the 'House of Gates.'" Dani said. "It's fairly late, second century Christian Era. The big shots, the *k'nockers*, had their bodies sent here for burial."

We paused in front of the restored facade of one of the catacombs. It consisted of three high classical arches, the entrance through a door on the left. Inside, in the dark caves, there was a labyrinthine complex of tunnels, passageways, cul-de-sacs, containing about two hundred sarcophagi. The incalculable treasures in these graves of ancient Jewish nobles were almost all missing, stolen by grave-robbers, when the necropolis was excavated in 1936 by the distinguished archaeologist Benjamin Mazar, the man

supervising the dig at the Western Wall in Jerusalem. Beit
Shearim had enjoyed a long but not undisturbed sleep from the
time of its destruction in the fourth century until Professor Mazar
brought it to light again.

"This business of getting buried properly was a problem in
those days," Dani said as we stopped to admire a tomb door displayed in a glass case. It was handsomely carved in simple panels.

"Why do you say that?"

"During the Roman era Jews wanted to be buried on the
Mount of Olives, from where the dead are supposed to rise. But it
was forbidden to them since Hadrian's time. So they asked that
their bones be sent here, a center of learning and piety. If they
couldn't get it done right away, their descendants would wait a
while, pack up their bones in those carved urns—ossuaries—and
send them here. You'll see beautiful ossuaria in the Israel Museum
in Jerusalem."

"Isn't there a Jewish cemetery on the Mount of Olives now?"

"Yes. Hussein's *momserim* tore it up and used the stones as
building foundations. No complaint from the U.N."

In the afternoon we went swimming in Caesarea, at the public
beach off the Roman aqueduct, that honey-colored succession of
low arches which are a standard item in Israeli travel posters and
advertisements.

In between dousings in the blue-green surf, Dani gave me the
basic data on Caesarea. "Originally this was called Strato's Tower
during the Hellenistic period. The town goes back to maybe the
fourth century B.C. In 22 B.C., Herod came along and found the
place in decay, a wreck. Twelve years later, Herod completed the
job of rebuilding it, and they had a big celebration. It's all in Josephus, how Herod put up palaces, a harbor, one of the biggest on
the coast, a theater, which you'll see later, a hippodrome. Herod
went first-class when he went."

"You are an admirer of his?"

"Herod got things done. Why should he have such a rotten
reputation with everyone? Listen, he had a tough job."

I was to encounter this apologetic admiration for Herod several
times. Master builder, politician, tyrant, diplomat, he is more
admired than condemned by modern Israeli scholars. It is easy

to understand why. He built. He restored. All right; he murdered a few people. Who didn't in those days? There is almost a little shamefaced pride in Herod's strength, his enterprise, his cunning. He has, of course, no prophetic or biblical or moral stature. Born of an Edomite father and an Arab mother, he was not even a real Jew, but a convert. But he offers something to the Israeli psyche: He was a sort of admirable tyrant, a practical ruler, who for all his faults built cities and palaces and kept the Romans and others off balance through shrewd manipulation. Strange as it sounds, Israelis speak of him with the same grudging approval which many Italians to this day give to Mussolini. Oh, he was a mean, tough bastard, but he made the trains run on time. Thus Herod. Yes, he killed just about everyone who got in his way—but he built cities and temples and roads. I suppose in the case of modern Israelis, two thousand years' distance and the bloody mores of the Roman era give them a bit more justification for thinking generously of wicked Herod.

The harbor and the ruins of the Byzantine Crusader city of Caesarea are spread over a wide, flat area, and are not overly impressive. The old stones are pleasantly jumbled. There are a massive Crusader wall with high, arched gates, the crumbled arches of a Roman temple to Augustus, the foundations of Byzantine homes, and near the water's edge a small neat mosque founded in the nineteenth century by a community of Bosnian Moslem immigrants under Turkish mandate. There is even the inevitable fruit stand, nestling against the golden Crusader walls, where we purchased luscious peaches and perfumed pears.

We did not spend nearly enough time at Caesarea. I consoled myself that these shortened visits were in the nature of *vorspeisen*, rich samplings. Some day, we would return to wander leisurely through the ruins. One cannot absorb all the sensations, all the knowledge, all the mystery, in a short visit to a place as complex, as multilayered as Caesarea.

By this time I was discovering that the heat, the dryness, and American custom were preventing me from sharing in Dani's and Avram's insistence on an Israeli midday meal. No matter how hot it was, no matter where we were, they had to have their full five- or six-course lunch: appetizer or soup, meat with potatoes, and a vegetable, fruit, bread. By the third or fourth day Marie and I were reduced to a bottle of cold grapefruit juice and a plate of cold *homos*, the tasty cold chick-pea paste.

"In a little while you'll be a *homos* expert," Dani observed. "A *maven*."

I was always brought up short when he used a Yiddish word. Then I would recall the years on Eastern Parkway.

"You mean there's *homos* and there's *homos*?"

"Of course." He sampled mine. He and Avram were having fried steaks, fried potatoes, salad. "Not bad. But not enough *tehina*. Sesame paste. You see, the real *homos maven* can tell you whether it has enough *tehina*, oil, pepper, garlic, or lemon, and he has his own preferences. It's more than a plain plate of mashed chick-peas, it's an artistic production."

In the afternoon we walked around the restored Roman amphitheater of Caesarea. The restoration is almost total: there is a magnificent raised stage below, and the new tiers of seats are smooth and unmarred. The work is so thorough, so efficient, that the ancient flavor has been lost. I longed for some irregularity, some cracks and chips in the pristine limestone. Regrettably, we were not able to see a performance that evening, for I was told that the acoustics are superb and the nocturnal setting, with the moon-brightened Mediterranean as backdrop, is unforgettable.

The amphitheater on which the restoration was performed is not Herod's but one dating from the second century. It was unearthed by an Italian team whose goal was to discover Herod's theater, an account of which appeared in Josephus. Their first attempts disclosed only the large theater that is the one used today. Finally, in 1962, the Italians' patience was rewarded. Beneath the "modern" theater floor they found a Herodian floor. Curiously, it was not made of marble or stone slabs, as was customary in large public buildings, but of thin white mortar ornamented with painted geometric designs.

According to Dr. Abraham Negev, what happened was this: Herod had run short of funds. So overextended was he in his building projects that he could no longer pay for unlimited quantities of marble from Italy or the Aegean. Hence, the use of a cheap mortar floor, ornamented with colored designs to give an illusion—a very poor one—of marble. These tawdry imitations of the real thing can be seen in some of the rooms at Masada—more of Herod's ersatz construction material. (As the Italians dug down, they found no less than twelve mortar strata. Evidently, as soon as one became worn or the color erased, another was smeared on top of it.)

Further digging confirmed that the mortar levels were from the Herodian era. On the stage Herod's architects had used whatever marble was available to them. Scraps and fragments remaining showed carved details: flowers, leaves, vines, grapes, wreaths, and the traditional egg-and-dart motif. Unfortunately, few pieces of ornamented marble from the front of the stage remained. During the early Arab period almost all of the marble pillars and foundation stones were burned to make lime.

That evening we sat around the pool of the Dagon Hotel in Ashkelon sipping red wine and chatting with its Viennese owner, Franz Dorot. We might have been in Miami Beach. I found it hard to imagine that just a few miles south was Gaza, that suppurating sore, that stew of terrorism, intrigue, and mindless violence. Dani advised us against going down there. "We'll go as far as Yad Mordekhai," he said, "but Gaza we can afford to miss. It's horrible. I try not to go there myself unless I have to."

But didn't the tourist companies run buses into the Gaza strip?

"Oh, sure. The tours go everywhere—Sinai, Golan, Gaza, the West Bank. It's different on a tour bus. Nobody makes trouble with them. But some Arab might try to throw a grenade at a private car traveling alone."

At the time I learned of the blithe confidence with which the Israelis sent busloads of tourists into the occupied areas, there had not been a single attack on a tour group. Sadly, some months later the first fatality occurred. Arab guerrillas opened up with machine-gun fire on a bus returning from Hebron, and an American tourist from Brooklyn was killed. But it was regarded as a freakish accident. The tours still roll into Hebron, and Gaza, and the Golan, and the Sinai. And, I am told by official sources, there have never been more tourists, more traffic on El Al, more hotel reservations.

Even before the tragic death of the Brooklyn man, I felt a little

uneasy about these fat, defenseless, belching buses, run by Egged
or United, groaning their way up the Judean hills or into the
parched Sinai, laden with unarmed American (or French) Jews,
busy snapping photos and oblivious to the presumed threat of the
Al Fatah. There seems to be a stubborn lunacy about turning a
bloody guerrilla war into a packaged tour, but apart from one or
two incidents there is sufficient security in the Egged buses to
keep them fully booked.

I'm not sure I know the explanation. The Arabs are not noted
for selectivity or sensitivity in shooting at people. They have not
hesitated to shoot rockets at school buses. Yet the tourist buses
are usually ignored. And the Israelis, in what I am convinced is a
case of psychological torment, of flaunting their mastery of the
situation, run these tours on schedule, deep into former Jordanian
or Syrian or Egyptian areas. There is nothing quite as destructive
of Arab egos, I suspect, as a busload of gaudy, talkative, unprotected, camera-laden residents of Nassau County or the Bronx
climbing out of an Egged bus on the Golan Heights for a leisurely tour of the Syrian bunkers. No one is armed. No one is
worried. The guide tells jokes. He usually speaks Arabic. Maddening! It is all rather like that sequence in *War and Peace*
in which Pierre Bezuhov wanders around the front lines at the
Battle of Borodino, bespectacled, top-hatted, frock-coated, staring
at wounded Russian soldiers as puffs of smoke rise around his
dandyish boots. Bezuhov is preoccupied, unafraid. Cool, I
believe we'd say now. It is this audacious cool of the Israelis—and
their foreign guests, who, after all, are only following their
lead—that astonishes me.

The chief antiquities of Ashkelon are housed in the National
Park, a sprawling green shaded area at the edge of the sea. There
is no pattern to the way in which the ruins are displayed; they
seem to have been left *in situ* at some points, and at others,
moved about to make for attractive combinations of nature and
art.

At the entrance, a series of Roman columns form an impressive unfinished portal. They are smooth, massive, shorn off at the
top. To one side is the base of one of those curious heart-shaped
columns that one finds from time to time in late Roman sites.

Beyond these, across an undulant lawn, is a stone-lined pit that is reputed to be the sacred pool of Derketo. Derketo was the fish-goddess of the Philistines, a counterpart to Dagon. The pit holds a mixed bag of statues in bas-relief. One shows Nike, goddess of victory, perched on a globe that rests on the mighty shoulders of Atlas. It is a crude work. Atlas is small and simian-faced, a deformed dwarf. It seems doubtful that he could support the winged lady, let alone the world. Another stele depicts a goddess and a child, possibly Isis and Horus, mother and daughter. There are also some fragments of a mammoth Hercules, which, according to one of my guidebooks, was smashed up by the eccentric Lady Hester Stanhope. Apparently, at the beginning of the nineteenth century, this amateur archaeologist had a fling at Ashkelon in search of treasure. Like most of these early amateurs, she succeeded only in muddying ancient waters. She was a niece of William Pitt, at one time his private secretary, and was in the grand tradition of the high-born British nut. In 1810, around the time she played hell with the ruins of Ashkelon, she settled among the Druses of Lebanon near Sidon, where, according to the *Britannica*, "she wielded an almost absolute authority over the surrounding districts, mainly by her commanding character and by the belief that she possessed the gift of divination." In appearance and voice, the article states, "she resembled her grandfather, the first Lord Chatham." I have the feeling that Robert Benchley wrote that last sentence.

One follows the National Park paths down to the sea. There stands the great Crusader wall and the ruins of the ancient harbor. The wall slopes majestically down to a fine sand beach. Its facing has long since vanished, but the enormous boulders, locked together with cement, remain—forbidding, formidable, a challenge to any invader. Projecting from the gargantuan wall are innumerable Roman columns, felled by the Crusaders and inserted into the stonework for reinforcing. With the facing of the wall gone, these great granite pillars protrude from the rampart like batteries of coast artillery, mute cannon, unbored, silent, pointing adamantine fingers westward. Below, the turquoise and ultramarine waters pound at the submerged remains of the harbor, brown-gold-black boulders, moss-grown, slippery, nesting in the impacted sand. I looked at the gentle surf, the creamy white

foam, the sunken stones of old Philistia, and I thought that perhaps a lettered sign might be appropriate: "THE MEDITERRANEAN
ENDS HERE."

For there is truly a sense of finality, of geographical and cultural conclusion about this lovely coast. The Crusaders, I think,
must have sensed this: *so far, no further.* Where the warm sea of
Europe ended, so ended their dreams. Christianity could not successfully cross the Mediterranean, even in a series of bloody, pro-
tracted campaigns to reconquer the land of its birth. The dark
pagan world, the Greco-Roman-Levantine patterns—wine, silks,
spices, hot sun, women with perfumed flanks and oiled hair—all
were too rich and resilient for the dry faith of frustration, repres-
sion, and piety. All that spiritual loftiness, the obsession with
worlds beyond, were no match for the passionate sea of Homer
and Virgil.

Melons, soft thighs, ripeness, the invigorating waters, and the
inflaming sun, these blocked Christianity as it tried to turn east-
ward and kept it an essentially European affair, a religion of cold
cathedrals and bad consciences.

We swam off Ashkelon later. Dani, as was his custom, identified
the bathers. "Americans—the shorts are too long, hair too long,"
he would say. "Ai, some of my Moroccan girls, look, look, the way
they roll their eyes and hold their hands." Or: "Indians. The
bracelets, the color of the skin."

Two Yemeni women especially intrigued him. They wore long
dazzling dresses covered with multicolored needlepoint and
beneath them long ankle-hugging pantaloons of the same fabric.
Around their necks and dangling from their ears, silver jewelry
glittered and clanked. They did not swim, but they ventured to
the water's edge, wetting their dark feet, talking softly to one
another, flashing gold-toothed smiles. They did not respond to
Dani's attempts at conversation, apart from a word or two of whispered Hebrew. Finally their menfolk emerged from the crowded
sea, strange fellows, black-eyed, hawk-nosed, with shaved
crowns, long beards, twirled *payes.* Apparently there was no
interdiction against the men swimming. But the ladies, in their
hot, heavy costumes, were required to wait patiently at the shoreline.

"Marvelous people," Dani said later. "They speak a pure

Hebrew. And such a beautiful language. Hebrew is the most beautiful language in the world."

"There's no archaeology at Yad Mordekhai," Dani said as we sped south on the coastal road, "but it is worth seeing."

Yad Mordekhai is a kibbutz a few miles north of Gaza. Today it is flourishing, peaceful, secure. During the War of Independence it earned a name for itself as one of the most heroic of the undermanned, underarmed border kibbutzim that battled the invading Egyptians. In a war of miracles, the story of Yad Mordekhai was one of the most incredible. This small kibbutz, its fighting force amounting to a little over 100 men and boys, armed with thirty-seven antiquated rifles, six rickety machine guns, one antitank gun (with three shells), and four hundred hand grenades, held off the main invasion column of the Egyptian army, 2,500 men equipped with tanks and planes, for six days before falling! Eventually the kibbutz was recaptured by the Israelis. Any understanding of the Israeli army's morale, the national determination to resist, can only be realized in terms of isolated outposts like Yad Mordekhai.

The Six Days of Yad Mordekhai by Margaret Larkin gives a detailed account of the fighting around the kibbutz. One can picture the Egyptian tank shells smashing into chicken coops, egg-storage houses, fruit-packing plants; the Egyptian aerial bombs destroying the precious water tower, wrecking the flimsy barns and dormitories. There seems to have been a vulnerability about the place, a naked, exposed quality, that would have impelled these besieged Jews to surrender at once.

But from a summit ringed with a trench and studded with the ragbag collection of old rifles and machine guns, the farmers sent the Egyptians running for their lives time and time again. Tanks would almost get through the barbed wire. They would remain impaled there, the invaders frightened silly by the embattled farmers on the hill. One can understand the abandoned zeal with which the Israeli Army in 1967 sent the Egyptians reeling backward through the Sinai. The memories of places like Yad Mordekhai had been rankling for a long time. The moral: Do not bombard a man's water tower, or destroy his chicken coops, unless you are damned certain you kill him. He will remember.

All of this is memorialized at the kibbutz today. A heroic statue of Mordekhai Anelevitz, the man for whom the kibbutz is named, one of the Warsaw ghetto commanders, stands on a palm-fringed height, near a museum of the resistance. In the museum the history of the kibbutz and its days of glory are commemorated in photographs, letters, newspapers, and other memorabilia. There are photographs and pages from Egyptian newspapers recounting the glorious victory over the hundred-odd farmers. There are some superb faded pictures of Egyptian officers, pukka types, canes, brimmed caps, mustachios, posing in front of a ruined farm building. Was ever self-deception practiced on so grand a scale?

Again and again the enraged Egyptians stormed the kibbutz, only to be stopped in their tracks by a single grenade, a burst of Sten-gun fire, a fusillade from the old rifles. The entire battlefield has been preserved as a sort of alfresco museum.

On the summit of the hill the corrugated tin command post still stands, and around it runs the tin-lined trench in which the defenders took cover. At intervals along the trench stand the actual rifles and machine guns, painted black, clearly labeled: "POLISH MAUSER, 1936"; "ITALIAN MANNLICHER, 1927"; "GERMAN SPANDAU, 1940." They are objects of veneration.

The most astonishing feature of this outdoor memorial, however, are the Egyptians, who are immortalized in a mad horde of one-dimensional life-sized cutouts, detailed down to the web belts and flat helmets and leggings. They have been painted on thin plywood and have been planted on the hillside, helter-skelter, charging the lonely blackened rifles. It is one of the saddest attacking armies I have ever seen. And I felt a certain disgusted pity for these shoeless dupes of corrupt and vain rulers.

One reads in Miss Larkin's account how, after six days of incessant pounding, in which repeated Egyptian assaults were repulsed, the weary defenders were finally overwhelmed and withdrew. Some of the farmers were bitter. They felt they had not resisted long enough. What they did not realize at the time was that they had upset the entire timetable for the "conquest of the Jewish rabble," as the Egyptian High Command termed the enemy. Yad Mordekhai, a pitiful settlement of frame houses, barracks, and chicken coops, was to have been overrun in a few hours. The Egyptians would then roll triumphantly up the coast to Tel Aviv. Instead, 2,500 men and much armored equipment had been frozen just above Gaza. About 300 dead and wounded were left at the kibbutz. All momentum had evaporated. Even the most self-deceiving of the Egyptian officers knew that the kibbutzim would be tough to crack.

A change in strategy was indicated. The rifles and machine guns of Yad Mordekhai forced the Egyptians to understand that they could not afford any more glorious victories. They moved slowly now, hesitantly, up the coast. They got as far as Ashdod, fifteen miles north, and there the Israeli Air Force, consisting of four creaking Messerschmitts of dubious safety, attacked them. So stunned were the invaders that they ended their northern march at that point.

We took a final look at the shooting-gallery Egyptians charging across the sere field. Though not a very stylish or elevating memorial, it made its point. Many Jews are still sufficiently imbued with ghetto fears, with nervous jealousy of *goyishe* fists and toughness and muscle, with guilt feelings about our failure to be soldiers, so that these events of the recent past fill us with awe and gratitude. I was damned impressed.

"I have a confession to make," I said to Dani as we drove southeast for a look at Avdat. "It's about the way I reported the War of Independence. I was working for the International News Service, now defunct, the press association owned by Mr. Hearst. I was the night cable editor, which meant I received brief cabled information from a correspondent in Israel and then I had to rewrite these scattered words into exciting form so that our client newspapers would print them in preference to the Associated Press or United Press.

"I.N.S. was a poor outfit. We had no money. A.P. and U.P. men could file entire stories, rich in detail, quotes and so on. As a matter of fact, today their foreign bureaus send the *entire* story on leased wire, and the New York headquarters does no rewriting to speak of. But in those days, twenty years ago, all I would get would be a few words: 'Egyptians report advance all fronts' or 'Arabs enter outskirts Tel Aviv' or 'Jordanians claim capture three forts.' Now, these odd items would come to my desk, and I would buttress them with *The New York Times*—everyone in journalism steals from the Times—plus a *Britannica* and the stories of the past few days. Somehow, out of these scraps and shards of information from some underpaid fellow in Tel Aviv, I would concoct a story. And, I might add, I often beat the U.P. in the morning papers.

"One night I studied the accumulated dispatches. The Egyptians—those fellows commemorated in plywood figures at the kibbutz—claimed they were rolling up the coast. The Jordanians were outside Petah Tikvah (so they said) and the Syrians, led by the ferocious red-bearded Fawzi Al-Kawukji, the Desert Fox, were swooping down from the north. As I read these dispatches, I made notations on a map, and I discovered that Tel Aviv was obviously surrounded and doomed. I could not quite say this, so I wrote the following lead and I remember it word for word: 'Arab armies forged a ring of steel around Tel Aviv early today.' Isn't that beautiful? Doesn't it have a ring?"

Dani frowned. "Not terribly funny."

"I didn't mean to hurt the Israelis. I was scared stiff myself. But it was apparent that Tel Aviv was doomed. You know what happened? Everyone picked up my phrase. That goddamned Arab ring of steel around Tel Aviv turned up in *Time* and *Newsweek* and even in *The New York Times*. Staff artists were kept busy fashioning clever rings of steel, circles, arrows, chains, showing how Tel Aviv was being strangled by a cliché. The phrase itself became accepted usage in Middle East reporting. The Arab ring of steel forged around Tel Aviv. Of course, we all woke up one morning and discovered there was no ring of steel. Nothing."

"It hasn't changed," Dani said. "In fact the B.B.C. is still inventing stories."

"The British?"

"Very pro-Arab," he scoffed. "Full of misinformation. They are the worst. They're angry that we have done something with the land that they could never do. There are more frauds on a B.B.C. broadcast on Israel than in all your old I.N.S. junk." He leaned to Avram and told him to stop for two hitchhiking youngsters, a boy and a girl in uniform.

"As a matter of fact," I said, "I think—though I'm not certain—that I also invented the 'Arab triangle of terror.' You remember that one?"

"Up north?"

"Yes. The area bounded by the three cities of Nablus, Tulkarm, and Jenin. Fawzi Al-Kawukji's turf. I guess it's all yours now."

The hitchhikers got into the Dodge. The boy was tall, slender, pale-skinned, dark-haired, with an open and guileless face that reminded me of my older son. The girl had pleasant features, but the desert wind had disarrayed her hair. Immediately, she took out a mirror and a comb and went to work. Both wore shoulder patches depicting a sword and a sickle.

"They are with Nahal," Dani explained. "A militarized kibbutz unit. Part work, part defense. It's a three-year hitch. All volunteers."

They spoke no English. "Tell him," I said to Dani, "that he reminds me of my older son." Dani did so; there was no response from the boy.

Dani tried, without success, to engage them in conversation. I think they were youngsters with no time for small talk. They had their priorities: the land, a gun, a dedication.

"They are country kids, farm kids," Dani said. "They spend three years working at Mefalsim, that's down near Gaza. No pay. Guard duty. Anything near Gaza is no fun. They don't care about *talking*. They do things."

At a crossroads, where Israeli police had stopped three Arab cars with those formidable accordion spikes, we dropped the young people. We were heading south to Avdat, and they wanted a direct ride to Beersheba. *Shaloms* were exchanged, and they got out, to resume their hitching. The boy intrigued me—he was tall, laconic, calm, unimpressed. A new breed of Jew. All the color and loquaciousness and wit and intensity of the urban American-Jewish youngster had been leached out of him by the sun, the wind, the sand, and the mystique of his land. I admired him, of course. No one could help but admire him. But at the same time I also felt sorry for him, and for his uniformed girl friend, poignantly combing her desert-ravaged hair.

In the late afternoon sun, Avdat glows in an unearthly golden mist on its wind-blasted mountain top. This is the Desert of Zin, that part of the Negev where the fascinating Nabateans built their

stone cities. Although Avdat was a major Nabatean city, the ruins
one sees—sand-beige, gold, tawny yellow—are almost entirely
Byzantine. There are churches, monasteries, fortresses, and
attendant buildings of the fifth to the seventh century. If one
comes looking for Nabatean remains at Avdat, he will be disappointed. They are there, a handful of them, but the golden
stones of the acropolis are Byzantine.

The Israelis are intrigued by the Nabateans, and for a practical
reason. These early settlers in the Negev managed to develop,
with remarkable ingenuity and persistence, a system of water
supply that is a source of wonder and admiration to this day. To
the Israelis, who look upon the Negev as their frontier, the virgin
lands where with the blessings of water and the eventual migration of Russia's Jews a new Eden will flourish, the Nabateans
are models of intelligence and courage.

Nabatean cities grew largely as a result of the spice trade with
the East. After Alexander the Great reached India, knowledge of
these tantalizing powders, dried leaves, roots, herbs, and pastes
traveled westward. The people on the Mediterranean littoral,
Greeks, Italians, North Africans, developed an appetite, almost a
craving for condiments. Getting them to the Mediterranean population centers, where high prices would be paid, was a problem
in logistics. Indian ships went as far as the ports of southern
Arabia. But in the third century B.C. navigational techniques
were inadequate to cope with the capricious winds of the Red
Sea, and the precious cargoes of pepper, coriander, osmarin, frank-
incense, and myrrh, the pungent and piquant powders of the
East, were transported overland in tinkling caravans. Across
Arabia Deserta and Arabia Felix, into Jordan and the Negev,
went the caravans, and thence to the ports on the Palestine coast.
And that is where the Nabateans came in.

Nabatean cities were founded as stops along the trade route.
From Arabia northward each tribe staked out its zone of influence, where it participated in the trade, moving the aromatic
goods to the seacoast. The Nabateans were the last in the chain; as
nomads they had already wandered into the hills of Transjordan,
establishing temporary encampments at about the time of Alexander's march into India.

It was as clear a case of economic determinism as one can find. There was money to be made in the spice trade. From tent-dwelling, impoverished wanderers, the Nabateans became builders of mighty cities in desert-like Avdat. As wealth and treasure and stores built up in their tents, they began to use the sandstone caves of the Negev for warehouses. And as bridges between the East and the Hellenic cultures, they became sophisticated and settled, progressing in a short space of time from their primitive tribal state—they were an Arabic people—into a nation of mighty cities. By the beginning of the third century B.C. these busy traders and middlemen, caravan suppliers and spice jobbers, had set up way stations which expanded to become the desert cities of Mampsis, Halutza, Nitzana, and the acropolis on which we now walked, Avdat. Located at the junction of two major routes of the spice caravans, the road north from Eilat and the road west from Petra, Avdat became the most important community in the central Negev.

How does a large, busy city survive without water? This is the question that faced the ancient Nabateans and the one that obsesses the Israelis to this day. Rainfall is negligible in this part of the Negev. Underground springs, especially in the area of Avdat, are virtually unknown. The solution was an underground system of huge cisterns, tunnels, channels, and dams, to store every drop of water available during the brief rains. Not a drop fell in the Negev that they did not catch, divert, and hold. In the second century B.C. the Romans, like modern *mafiosi*, sensed a good thing and decided they wanted to run it. They took over road franchises from the Nabateans. But the ingenious water-supply system saved the Nabateans for several centuries: they used the water to develop agriculture and became farmers. In the vicinity of Avdat alone, according to Professor Abraham Negev, twenty large cisterns were built. One may still see one of them, a great dark pit, inside the Byzantine fortress on the acropolis.

The three of us were alone on the acropolis. Avram had seen enough old stones driving for the Ministry of Tourism, and he napped in the car below. An insistent wind, edged with a chill, blew across the yellow wasteland. The setting sun worked a delicate magic on the Byzantine stones, turning them gold to orange

to a ruddy brown. We explored underground caves, curious arch-
ways, the well-preserved apses and naves of the two Byzantine
churches, St. Theodorus and North Church. On the southern
corner of the fortress, which adjoins the complex of religious
buildings, we climbed the watchtower. The wind was brisk, carrying with it a sense of withering dryness, of acrid dust. To the
south lay the clearly defined walls of an old Roman quarter, to
the east a pile of rough stones which, Dani said, were among the
few Nabatean remains at the site—an ancient kiln.

"The Nabateans were in and out of this area for several centuries," he said as we walked single file along the high battlements
of the fortress. "About the second century they were finished for
good. The Romans got rid of them. Roman sailors learned how to
sail the Red Sea, so nobody needed the overland route for the
spice trade, and these cities no longer served any purpose."

"But they farmed. . . ."

"Yes, but there was no real *gelt* in farming. Not enough to support cities like Avdat. This place was deserted by the second half
of the first century. No more caravans, no more cities were
needed. Also there may have been a few years of bad drought."

I pointed to the huge black opening of the cistern below us in
the fortress courtyard. "You mean all that brilliant engineering
still didn't do the trick?"

"Possibly. We know there can be really bad years down here.
Maybe they had several in a row. From 1958 to 1963 there was
almost no rain, and the cisterns were not filled. If the kibbutzim
down here had to depend only on rainfall, it would have taken
only five years to dry everything up. We'd have ghost cities
again."

I thought of the kibbutzim we'd seen on the way down—Sde
Boker, Ben-Gurion's home, Mitzpeh Ramon, others. They would
not have made attractive ruins. The squat, blocklike buildings
would have crumbled and fallen, pitted, amorphous, graceless.
Whatever may be said of the old builders, they created structures destined to look impressive even in decay. Modern man, as
Professor Krutch points out, makes deplorable ruins.

"You see that patch of green down there?" Dani asked. He
pointed to an obvious settlement of square tan buildings, groves

of trees, cultivated fields, a green and flourishing surprise in the burned vastness. It was evidently not a kibbutz. The buildings were in one small group set off from the fields and orchards.

"It's bigger than a patch," I said.

"It's Professor Michael Evenari's place, the experimental farm for the agricultural development of the Negev. Evenari is our leading expert on Negev agriculture. He's the man who figured out how the Nabateans did it."

Evenari's name was to turn up frequently. Yaakov Morris's account of the Negev, *Masters of the Desert*, told me that Evenari was the man who came to the conclusion that the desert had been farmed centuries before the talented Nabateans. At Mitzpeh Ramon, ten miles south of Avdat, Evenari found evidence of Jewish agriculture dating back to the period of the Kings, 900 B.C. Previously, the desert was believed to have been farmed only as far south as eighteen to twenty-four miles below Beersheba. Here, the experts concluded, was proof that the Negev had been cultivated—by Israelis—long before the Nabateans, Romans, and Byzantines.

Today, at the Nabatean experimental station, Evenari is still unlocking the secrets of desert irrigation. At the heart of the research is this question: How did the Nabateans trap a four-inch annual rainfall? How did they catch, hold, and utilize these brief winter flash floods, doling them out to the mineral-rich lowlands, the yellow loess of the valleys?

The ruins of the Nabatean farms, Evenari found, were all located in these loessial valleys. The surrounding slopes were used as catchments. It was calculated that about thirty acres of catchment slope (hillsides not used for farming) were needed to irrigate each acre of valley land. To make the slopes effective, to combat wastage through spillage, absorption, or vaporizing, stone conduits, walls, sluices, cisterns, and other devices were built. It amazed Evenari and his team to learn from old Nabatean records that these ancient farmers produced an eight-fold barley, and a seven-fold wheat yield from each seed. Modern Negev farmers, as of 1961, with the most modern methods of irrigation, produced no better than a nine- to eleven-fold yield!

Evenari then calculated that if the rain that fell on thirty acres

of desert—four inches or less annually—was gathered and
diverted along stone-lined slopes to a single acre of valley soil, that
acre would receive the equivalent of 124 inches of rain. Of course,
the vital engineering problem for the Nabateans was development of an effective system of controlling and directing the
waters. Evenari and his assistants discovered the answer. Yaakov
Morris writes:

> Nabatean construction started on the slopes of the hills
> where rainwater flowed down by way of tributary wadis
> into the broad main wadi in the valley. The water-
> courses of those of the feeder wadis which were not too
> narrow or steep were terraced by the construction of a
> series of stone shelves. Instead of rushing violently
> down, the floodwater became rainwater gently cascad-
> ing down the steplike shelves, part of it sinking into
> the ground at each shelf, depositing in the process some
> of its soil and organic debris. Shrubs were often left to
> grow on these shelves to help slow the rush of water and
> hold plant debris to enrich the soil. . . . Each of these ter-
> races in the tributary wadis, accumulating soil year after
> year, became a farming plot. . . .

Ingenious? Of course. Impressive? Indeed. But all I could think
of after reading Mr. Morris's account of Evenari's research was
that if the run-off from *thirty* acres of desert was needed to irrigate *one* acre, would I be correct in postulating that only one-
thirtieth of the Negev—using only rain water—could be rendered
arable? And since it is the aim of the Israelis to settle the Negev
with a considerable population, to create great cities and farming
communities there, was not a great deal more water than the
amounts harvested by the Nabateans needed?

High on the golden heights of Avdat, looking down at the
greenery of Professor Evenari's rebuilt Nabatean farm, and photo-
graphing the Byzantine pillars, churchly ruins, surrounding walls,
and cool cisterns, I kept my doubts unspoken. One does not
express doubt to Israelis. Pessimists and worriers are out of order.
If they are convinced that the bleak Negev will bloom with

perfumed orchards and billowing wheat fields some day, I am not the man to discourage them. Still, even a desert veteran like Abraham Negev was moved to write, in his *Cities in the Desert*:

> The struggle between civilization and the desert was a bitter one, and even when man succeeded, he had little reward other than the spiritual satisfaction of his victory. A study of desert art reveals that the struggle was social rather than technical, and that only those willing to live sparsely could ever succeed in conquering the wilderness.

The operative word, I suppose, is "was." As an old desert kibbutznik, warrior, and archaeologist, Negev would probably regard the current struggles against aridness in a different light. And perhaps he is right.

CHAPTER V

Masada, Arad, and Points North

After a restful night at the Desert Inn at Beersheba—it is quasi-luxurious, modern, and invariably full in the summer—we were ready for Masada.

"I'm putting you on the regular Egged tour," Dani said. "Avram and I will take a day off, and you're just as well off with the Egged guide. They're good, very good."

It seemed a reasonable arrangement. And as it turned out, the Masada trip produced a treasured bonus for me. (I am a greedy sightseer; every trip, I am convinced, opens up possibilities of a side trip. A major monument visited, ogled, photographed, surely means that there are several *minor* sights nearby that can be sopped up before calling it a day.)

En route to Masada we passed Bedouin settlements. The word "settlement" would appear to be paradoxical here, yet the tin shacks, schoolhouses, cemeteries, and patches of cultivated land were unmistakably settlements. I learned that many of the Bedouin have given up the nomadic life. "And they have bank

144

accounts in Beersheba," Dani said. "Also jeeps, and tractors instead of camels."

I watched two Bedouin women, graceful, lean in their black robes, gliding across the tawny wastes. They do not walk. They float. They skim the surface of the hot sand. I wanted them to walk in that lubricated, effortless manner forever. Corrugated tin shacks and concrete block schoolhouses, I prayed, would not convert them to tight slacks, wedgies, and bouffant hairdos in curlers.

At Arad, a town of ten thousand, and to me the perfect symbol of the absolute determination of Israel to break the desert, we met our guide, a dark, burly, mustachioed young man named Ari. He was a quiet, pensive type, not the ebullient, joking variety of guide, and I found his solemnity gratifying. I had the feeling that the desert bred these deliberate, laconic people, that perhaps a sparse land creates men sparing of word and gesture.

Arad is a pure fabrication, a small Brasilia, but without that artificial city's atmosphere of gloom and defeat amid the prize-winning Niemeyer buildings. Arad is much simpler and cruder, yet it exudes optimism. One rides across the parched wasteland, the eye deadened by the endless vistas of rocks, sand, burning sky, desolation. And suddenly—Arad. Without warning there appears a filling station with its adjunct restaurant, the inevitable tour buses parked in the shade. A road widens into a four-lane highway. High, arched street lights blossom at the sidewalk's edge. It is a strange sidewalk, begun at some arbitrary starting point amid the acrid emptiness and leading bravely to a city of ten thousand with apartments, a town square, office buildings, hotels. They all look as if they were built yesterday. Many are mere frameworks still under construction. Most are neutral gray, preshaped concrete, terribly cheerless, utilitarian in the extreme: blockish, rectangular, sharply angled. Arad is a city less built than poured. One gets the feeling that a series of huge molds were slapped together and the gray concrete sloshed in overnight from an enormous mixer. The city is a mere eight years old, a lusty sunburned baby built as a symbol of the potential of the Negev. It sits on top of valuable deposits of natural gas that will furnish the power for industry and habitation not only in Arad but also in much of the Negev.

Yet for all its stark geometry, its bleached grayness, its formidable plainness, there is something encouraging and pleasant about Arad. Perhaps it is the tanned vigor of its residents. Or the clean dry air (how long, with natural gas underground?). Or the sense of limits, the ever-present sensation that man will not be able to alter irretrievably or conclusively the inhospitable desert.

When the bus stopped at the new hotels in Arad to pick up tourists, I experienced the unnerving notion of a civilization on the edge of nothingness. Arad is considered a resort area; it is a high, dry place, reputedly rich in therapeutic air and healing heat. Israeli doctors send asthmatics there. The hotels—the two I remember are the Masada and the Nof Arad—are perched on the edge of nowhere, buildings thrown up in oblivion, deep in the heart of a vacuum. There they stood—three-story buildings of rough concrete, swimming pools as blue as cobalt flame, a few sad red and yellow beach chairs and umbrellas, a Peugeot or a Fiat roasting outside. The paved road leading to the hotels seemed to end right in their driveways. It was as if the American pioneers had hacked a road into Death Valley, built a hotel, and stopped. The bleak terrible finality of those roads bothered me. They went nowhere. They ended at the hotels. Beyond were hills, rocks, the burned-out, rust-brown wastes, the inhospitable Judean desert.

As we waited, the tourists emerged from their air-conditioned sanctuary on the edge of the void. Two young couples were Americans. I took them to be shy honeymooners.

The other tourists included an attractive young Israeli couple with little children, squirts no more than four or five in red playsuits, cute white shoes, and floppy red sunhats; a fat American man, oyster-skinned, bald, bespectacled, in black trousers and black pointed shoes, who appeared a likely candidate for a coronary; two gray-haired complaining Jewish grandmothers; and an overweight teen-age American boy, with a huge rump, doughy thighs, white hands, and a musical whine that could be heard all over the bus: "It's not air-conditioned. . . . How come we didn't get the air-conditioned bus? I'm hot, I'm suffocating. . . ." Oh, pioneers!

I describe some of the tour group to make a point. Much has been written about the terrors and rigors of the climb up

Masada. Like a great deal of travel writing, it is nonsense, designed to prove to the reader that the writer is an intrepid adventurer; or that the particular feat is something that the traveler must be wary of or take credit for attempting. They wants to make yer flesh creep.

The ascent of Masada via the bank path on the northwestern side takes no more than twenty minutes. The slope is not severe. There are many sections where steps have been hewn in the rock. A hand railing is also available, and there are frequent small plateaus and sheltering overhangs where one may rest. I watched our group—the toddlers in playsuits, the fat man in his citified black shoes, the gray-haired grandmothers, and the unmanly boy—and I did not notice that any of them appeared to be suffering. In short, the exhausting climb up Masada is one of these exaggerated *bubba mayses* dear to professional travelers devoted to scaring innocents out of their wits. (I had such a friend in the army. He was known as Bad News Baumeister. Bad News could be counted on for a ghost story a day, a chiller to make you sleepless and trembling. Once it was the deadly nature of the infiltration course, where men were gunned down daily; then it was our imminent shipment to Guadalcanal. He invented everything. He was a gaudy, voluble liar, and after a while nobody believed anything he told us. He would have made a good travel writer.)

From the heights of Masada the outlines of the camps of the besieging Romans are dramatically clear, as is the great circumvallation of the Roman siege wall. The Cyclopean stones are almost too neatly lined up. I assumed that recent archaeological workers had restored them. But they are a terrifying presence. They do not seem two thousand years old. One expects to see Roman eagles and burnished helmets rising from behind the boulders.

The plateau of Masada, where we rested in the shade of a Byzantine wall, is over 600 yards long—six football fields!—and 250 yards wide. Across this compacted yellow surface of sand and pulverized rock are the ruins of several civilizations.

The most curious are Herod's three pleasure palaces at the northern end of the plateau. Taken together, these "hanging villas" of the builder-king resemble nothing so much as the prow of some luxurious ocean liner. There are three different recessed

"deck" levels, the highest of which is a rectangle fronted by a
semicircle, the next one a broken circle, the third and lowest a
double square circumscribed by columns. Why Herod needed
three pleasure domes, and how one differed from the other, I am
not certain.

Ari, our soft-spoken, laconic guide, offered some typical sabra
advice about Masada as we gawked at the crumbling ruins of the
hanging palaces. "When you come here, it is all right to look at
these palaces of Herod, his country club, his Turkish bath. But
that is the least important part of Masada. What is important is
that it is the place where Jews fought back and resisted. It is a
national symbol of courage. To us the Zealots are a lot more
important than Herod with his villas."

I wanted to ask him whether some Israelis regarded Masada as
not all that inspirational a symbol. I am forever aware that,
except for two women, every last Jew there died. According to
Flavius Josephus, 960 of them put themselves to the sword in
A.D. 73 to foil the Roman besiegers. The two women hid; they
emerged after the Romans entered, and related the story of the
suicide pact to the conquerors and possibly at a later date to Josephus himself. Masada, with all the bravery and determination of
the Zealots, grimly gripping their sunbaked plateau, frustrating
the Romans for seven years, outwitting the battering rams, sneak-
ing in water and food, and finally depriving the legions of victory
through mass suicide, has some cruel hold on Israeli imagination.
Its symbolism prevails, and I find the obsession with it less than
inspirational. That waterless, bleached rock in the middle of some
of the most desolate terrain in the world, looking out on the choking salty stew of the Dead Sea, did not inspire me. I suppose one
must be a bred-in-the-bone sabra to take heart from Masada. I'm
told some American-Jewish writers and intellectuals have made
the ascent and then all but swooned with mystic identification.
That did not happen to me. I was interested. I wanted to know
more. I was awed by the structures, the sheer logistics of getting
food and water and arms into the isolated dry mesa, but I was not
elevated. No eternal thoughts sprang from the eternal rocks.

It is a leisurely and instructive walk around the dusty surface
of Masada. Unlike some sites, everything is accurately described
in the guidebooks, and carefully mapped. This is probably a

result of Professor Yigael Yadin's meticulous work. (Professor Yadin's work, *Masada*, published by Random House, and illustrated with splendid color photographs, will make a trip to Israel infinitely richer.)

One proceeds from the Herodian villas on the north promontory, those trilevel patios of sin and hedonism, to a large bathhouse, where the stunted pillars that created a hollow floor for steam are clearly visible. There are numerous Herodian storerooms, used years later by the Zealots under their leader, Eliezer ben Yair. When Eliezer seized Masada from the Romans in A.D. 66 at the outbreak of the Jewish revolt, he found the rooms bursting with wine, oil, corn, grain, and dates—ample to withstand a long siege. When the Romans again took possession of the fort, there was still food remaining, after seven years of cruel isolation! Looking out on the waterless wasteland, the absence of green things, of animal life, I am unable to conceive of men existing there for any length of time, even with generous stores. The food had to be brought in, didn't it? People had to grow it somewhere. Then it had to be harvested, prepared, packaged, and dragged up the serpentine paths (impossible once the Romans besieged Masada) and then doled out with militant efficiency. Looking at Herod's huge storerooms, I understood better the kibbutz mentality. Those disavowers of personal property and monetary reward knew about scarcity, and abundance, and sharing.

A synagogue was unearthed along the southern casemate wall. We sat there on the stone benches, unprotected from the merciless sun, as Ari explained how the Zealots had modified the original building erected by Herod. They added a small corner room, under which two important scrolls were found. The original Herodian synagogue—Yadin seems convinced that the building was a house of worship even in Herod's day—is one of the oldest in Israel. Up until it was unearthed, most ancient synagogues discovered dated from the end of the second century A.D.

"Why did Professor Yadin conclude that this building was a synagogue in Herod's day as well as during the Zealot period?" Ari asked. "It would have been logical for Herod to have had a place of worship for his family and the Jews of his court. Also, the architecture is similar to the architecture of Galilean synagogues. And it was built in the direction of Jerusalem."

Someone asked what the building had served as in the period between Herod and the Zealots, when it was occupied by the Romans.

"Probably a stable," he said. "They found layers of animal dung between the original floor and the later floor. Such a gesture by the Romans would further support the notion that it had been a house of worship under Herod."

"*Formidable*," the man seated next to me on the baking stone bench muttered. He was a Negro, ebony-black, fat, with a short beard. He was wearing a maroon yarmulke embroidered with gold. I had seen him at the Desert Inn the night before, engaging in Hebraic debate with some Israelis. French? A Falasha, one of the black Jews of Ethiopia?

As we followed Ari out of the synagogue toward the casemate wall, I asked him in French what country he was from.

"Cameroun, m'sieu," he said politely.

"You are . . . a Jew?"

"*Mais non. Presbyterien.*"

"But you speak Hebrew . . . and the skull cap . . ."

"Ah. I am a professor of biblical exegesis at the Presbyterian Seminary in Cameroun."

"So you practice the rule . . . when in Israel do as the Israelis?"

"Spiritually, m'sieu, I am a Hebrew."

I nodded, because I could think of nothing to say. A gray-haired gentleman in a blue suit who spoke excellent French appeared to be the Hebrew-speaking Camerounian Presbyterian's traveling companion. He had a tired and tolerant look, as do many Israeli officials.

"Are you from the Cameroun also?" I asked, sure he was not.

"I'm from the Foreign Ministry. He's our guest."

We entered Herod's Western Palace, the largest structure on Masada. There were apartments, servant' quarters, an elaborate bath, and in the entrance to the throne room, one of the most beautiful mosaic floors of the period.

"I'm impressed by the way you treat your guests," I said to the official.

I got an Israeli shrug. "We need friends."

Sub-Saharan Africa looms large in Israeli foreign policy. I knew about the Israeli Peace Corps and the army officers working in black Africa. The strategy was to keep the traditionally anti-Arab blacks of Africa on Israeli's side. Nothing had changed much since Herod's time. He had had to do a tremendous amount of diplomatic maneuvering and scheming to stay on his feet. Hadn't he fortified Masada and retreated there because he feared Cleopatra?

In the corridor leading to Herod's bathroom, Ari halted us. "Another mosaic," he said. "From Herod's day." It was a large square enclosing a circle divided into segments of browns, reds, tans.

"Alongside you will see a crude stone structure, maybe a stove or the remains of a cupboard. It is from the time of the Zealots. Professor Yadin left it as it is, alongside Herod's mosaic, to show the contrast between the two styles of life. Herod lived in luxury. The Zealots barely got by, and at the end they all died."

We wandered through the smaller structures to the east of the main palace. These were probably villas built by Herod for favored wives and brothers. The one nearest the main palace is adjacent to a large swimming pool, a superb engineering feat complete with plastered steps and niches in which to store clothing while taking a dip.

"Another comparison between Herod's day and the Zealots'," Ari said. We paused, wilting in the murderous heat, at one of the satellite homes. "You see the walls? Beautiful frescoes. Imitation marble with red, brown, and green borders. But if you look in the corner you'll see some stones heaped together. The Zealots kept a stove in this room. They had other worries besides fancy wall paintings."

The heat now struck us with an insistent, malignant intensity. I noticed that everyone in our group walked slowly and spoke very little—the young couple with the infants, the paunchy man in black shoes, the grandmothers, the fat boy, the black Presbyterian Bible exegete from French West Africa. Was it the heat? Or was it the oppressive weight of history? For my own part, I kept coming back to the problems of ordinary day-to-day existence on this bare, burning height. It did not seem to me to be much of a place for a vacation, as Herod used it, or as a place to make a last stand, even though its geographical situation and rocky inaccessibility proved to be efficient impediments to the Roman legions. But it did fall. And surely the Zealots, those cantankerous puritanical descendants of the Maccabees, must have known that there was no hope of rescue once they were locked into the desolate heights. Yes, it was the burden of history, not the heat, that was wearing me down.

"This is the *mikveh*, the ritual bath," Ari explained. A group of three rooms were clearly visible, formed by crude stone partitions built into the southern wall. He explained the traditional structure—three chambers, one for collecting rainwater through a conduit, then the actual bath, and a small room for the washing of hands and feet before entering the *mikveh*.

In his book on Masada, Professor Yadin tells the story of how the discovery of the *mikveh* spread excitement among the Orthodox communities in Israel. One broiling summer day, two Hasidic rabbis, authorities on the properties of your true *mikveh* (mikvologists?), climbed the snakelike path. Bearded, cocooned in their traditional hot garments, followed by a retinue of Hasidic devotees, the two learned men then proceeded to the bath, and with tape measures and the accumulated wisdom of centuries verified Yadin's discovery. The archaeologist writes that occasionally one of the rabbis "furrowed his brow as if in doubt as to whether the bath was kosher." But kosher it was. The *mikveh* experts rendered their momentous judgment: Yadin's find on Masada was most certainly a *mikveh*, "among the finest of the finest, seven times seven."

Ari told us that the building of the ritual bath within the casemate was an example of the bountiful nature of these thick double walls. Intended mainly for protection, the double wall also provided an enormous amount of space for rooms. Except for the hanging villas Masada is girdled completely with this massive wall. The continuous space between the walls had several functions. Partitioned, it afforded numerous rooms for habitation, storage, and for building battlements and firing positions. Yadin's discoveries to a great extent supported Flavius Josephus's descriptions of the Masada wall; it is 1,400 yards in length as it makes its irregular way around the perimeter of the plateau, with a space of about 4½ yards between the outer and inner walls. Yadin estimated that the area between the two walls contained 110 rooms.

One gets a clear picture of the ingenious structure as one walks along the eastern side. On the edge of the plateau is the outer wall, then a valley or depression with a mud-plastered floor, then an interior wall. It was within this space, in the rooms formed by the walls, that the Zealots had their living quarters, and where the pathetic remains of their doomed resistance were found: lamps, pots, cups, measuring vessels, combs, perfume vials, and even a box for a woman's eye paint, with sticks for applying eye shadow. These frivolous artifacts softened the notion I had been nurturing of the Zealots as hot-eyed, intransigent, puritanical, self-righteous militants. After all, their women had applied eye makeup, combed their hair, and perfumed themselves—even while living in the cavelike chambers of the great wall and fighting off the Romans. Such a people were not mere fanatics. Again the past was closer to the present. I recalled our kibbutz girl in uniform, the young lady visiting her wounded friend in Beersheba. Uniformed, dusty, in flat-heeled service shoes, as soon as she entered our car, she combed her hair. Just as her feminine ancestors on the scorched heights of Masada had done after stacking missiles or sharpening spears.

The tour concluded, we paused around a starved, stunted pomegranate tree, planted in the impacted yellow clay of the summit and protected by a wire fence. "There shall always be trees blooming on the top of Masada," Ari said. "They symbolize our determination to hold it forever: Masada will not fall again."

I understood now that they believe every word that they say, these descendants of Eliezer ben Yair. Masada is their Valley Forge. They do not intend to let anyone forget it, least of all their enemies. Nor do they make the next logical gloomy step (as I did) and assume that they will be wiped out again. The point of Masada is, *never again* . . .

We began our descent down the bank path. Going down was a joy, a relaxed pleasure. One had the feeling of having performed some virtuous and elevating labor. Unearned perhaps, but invigorating. We all seemed uplifted by the example of those unyielding Zealots—starved, parched, surrounded, hated. But they had kept the Roman armies at bay for seven years, forcing them into prolonged bloody siege, creating dissension among their generals, giving emperors, proconsuls, and tetrarchs fits.

I was not trying to cash in on the Zealots' bravery or attempting to associate myself with them by reason of blood. But spending a morning in the bosom of the past, studying the old stones, learning from a tolerant man like our guide, letting the evidence of history imprint itself on my consciousness, afforded me a sense of achievement and rectitude. I was no modern Eliezer, no Walter Mitty playing Zealot. I had merely learned something. That, usually, is sufficient for me.

"The trip down is worse," Ari said. "There is no breeze. I prefer climbing up any time."

"That's because you are an Israeli," I said, "and you are forever proving your toughness. Like the Zealots."

He nodded. "Like the Zealots."

Before entering the bus we turned for a last look at Masada—the protruding prowlike northern spur, the plateau above. Old Herod had treated himself well. The Zealots, living their painful existence in the detritus of his ruined apartments, must have resented him. In a small bathhouse in the lowest of the three palaces, three skeletons, assumed to be members of Eliezer ben Yair's band, had been found.

"Well, dear," I said to Marie, as we boarded the bus, "this is where your ancestors beat the hell out of mine."

On the return trip I arranged with Ari to take me to Tel Arad, which was not on any regular tours. It was reachable only by desert track, with a guide who knew the backlands.

"Of course," Ari said. "I'll borrow the hotel's Volkswagen combi. But we'll have to eat first."

As I sipped grapefruit juice, Ari (like Dani and Avram) settled down in the Arad Hotel dining room to a meal of salad, soup, bread, meat, potatoes, vegetables, dessert. I could barely watch him. The routine for me had become oatmeal for breakfast, grapefruit juice and *homos* at midday, a light supper. (I lost twelve pounds this way.)

"Tell me about yourself," I asked him.

"I am a kibbutznik. It is a great life. The best life in the world."

"But you left?"

"I wanted something else. I suppose I have found it. I like it in the desert. I like Arad. My wife has a shop here. But I miss the kibbutz sometimes."

"How is Israel going to survive?" I asked.

"We will survive. There is not the slightest doubt about it. It will mean some miracles. The Russians must stop arming and encouraging the Arabs. If they stopped, the Middle East problem would end in twenty-four hours."

"But they have no intention of stopping. They have always wanted to be a Middle East power, to control this end of the Mediterranean, and here's a tailor-made opportunity."

"Of course. They are behaving exactly the way they should. If I were Kosygin, I'd be doing the same."

"Then why do you think they'll change?"

"Because I have to think that way. We believe in our future. We intend to live. We cannot lose, because we have no place to go. When the Nazis conquered France, some Frenchmen went to North Africa, or England. But we have no place. That solves the problem. We stay here."

"But someday the Arabs may be strong and united and capable of wiping you out."

Ari snorted. He was a dark, sun-seared man, burly, soft-spoken. "Don't believe any of that Arab propaganda. They will never be able to beat us. Or that nonsense about a hundred million Arabs. The ones on our borders are about thirty million, and they all hate each other. Every Arab leader hates the next one, and even the guerrilla groups are split."

"Did you fight in the Six-Day War?"

"Yes. I was a reservist, like everyone. I was on the Golan Heights for a week."

I hesitated a minute before asking the next question. "I read somewhere that when the Six-Day War broke out, there was a considerable exodus of Israelis. Someone wrote that the Upper West Side of New York was filled with Israelis who had run away."

Ari's eyes turned hard. He rubbed his stubbled chin. "Good for them. Such Israeli citizens we don't need. We are better off without them. Come along, I'll see if our car is available."

At the back of the hotel a green VW bus was being unloaded by young men in what was the hotel uniform, a white shirt and dark pants. One youth was coal black and frizzy-haired.

"All Bedouin," Ari said. "They have jobs. No more herding."

"The Negro also?"

"Descendant of a slave. The Negev Bedouin had slaves for centuries. You see many of these black fellows around here."

The VW would not start. Something was wrong with the ignition. I had to give it a push down an incline, run frantically, and jump in beside my guide. "Is this safe?" I asked, as we rumbled down the blacktop, the main road to Beersheba. "I mean . . . a car that won't start in the middle of the desert?"

He laughed. "It will start, it will start."

On the way out he pointed out a grove of tall trees. "That is our forest," he said proudly. "It was an achievement getting that many trees to grow here. We have our Independence Day celebration there—parades, games, speeches."

I found myself wishing that it were a bigger, lusher forest. For the truth was, it had a terrifying loneliness about it, a vulnerable patch of green stuck in the impoverished tan soil.

"Those trees beyond," he said. "That is Achvar. In 1920 the British gave Ben-Zvi, who was later our President, permission to start a settlement. The British didn't care about farming, but they wanted a security point to protect the country from Arab raiders. But it failed. There was never enough water."

"Odd that the British should have encouraged them. I get the impression that they were opposed to Jewish settlements."

"They were. But this was a special case. Ben-Zvi and the others were veterans of the British Army in the first World War."

A mud bridge traversed a roadside irrigation ditch. Ari swung the VW over it, and we were on desert track, a wide, flat, sandy trail. Because of its hardness and breadth, he was able to make surprisingly good speed, and we bounced along without too much discomfort. "This is the track to Tel Arad," he said. "Probably in use since the Canaanites."

To the east rose the Judean hills, and beyond them the Dead Sea and Masada, where we had spent the morning. While Masada had by no means disappointed me, it was almost too much of a good thing: too loaded, too glaring, too intense. But here on the windy stretches of naked Negev I felt I was grasping history. As far as we could see, studying the horizon in all directions (the blacktop road had vanished in minutes, a slight change in elevation obliterating it as if it had been buried in sand) Ari and I were the only humans in sight.

"Not quite," he said, when I commented on our isolation. "To your right. Where the land rises."

"Black dots."

"Bedouin. They are all over the place. The little dots are the sheep. The bigger dots, the shepherds. They graze all around here."

"Graze? You mean things grow here?"

"A Bedouin sheep will find something. These are barley fields we are riding on. You would not know it, but the Bedouin grow crops here every year."

I did discern tawny wisps of straw, the parched remnants of some stunted crop.

"Yes, they manage," he said. "I am sorry we do not have more time, I would take you to visit a Bedouin sheikh. They are marvelous people. Many of them have become close friends of mine. They give us no trouble. The only thing they don't like is paying taxes. If you visit them, you must walk around the tent three times to signify you come as a friend. Then you are welcome. The sheikh will insist you have coffee with him."

Shading my eyes, I could see the specks on the distant slopes moving—the starved sheep foraging for dry barley leavings, the black-draped shepherds leading the interminable search for water.

"And there is the tel," Ari said. "You should be able to recognize them by now."

It was true. The flat-topped mounds were becoming easier to distinguish. I recalled Dani saying to me, "A tel is a tel, and it looks like nothing else." Now, seeing Tel Arad emerge from the treeless yellow wastes, I knew what he meant. The shape was crucial. It was not an entirely natural shape. Although the artifacts and structures of civilization lay buried, or barely unearthed, and were blunted, eroded, and misshapen, the stones reverting to natural forms, there was something unmistakably artificial about the tel. I had a mental image of the successive generations of desert people, revived for a day's work, patting, stroking, and molding the mound into its characteristic form. It spoke of man's work, his lusts and his bad temper, as much as his achievements.

Here were the bleached bones of civilization. I was filled with a delicious terror. Perhaps it was the dread silence. Or the fear that the tremulous Volkswagen, rattling to a stop on a rock-strewn wadi, would never get us home, or that the Bedouin band above us, drifting eerily, would decide to murder the infidel dog intruders. Arad was too old. Too white. Too sun-bleached and silent and isolated. Terribly old, and bleakly terrifying.

There appeared to be two sites on the slope of the tel. They were, Ari told me, a lower city and a citadel mound, considerably higher because of the accretion of settlements over six millennia.

"What period are these ruins from?" I asked.

"They are Israelite. Tenth to seventh century B.C. From the Solomonic period to the later kings."

"When was this excavated?"

"The work began in 1962, under Professor Aharoni. He is working at Tel Beersheba now. You can stop off and speak to him. Wonderful man, very friendly. The dig here was begun the same year that the first new buildings of the city of Arad were completed—the square where we had lunch today."

"Ah, typical Israeli symbolism. As the new buildings rise, the old ones are unearthed. To prove the continuity of the Jewish people in the land."

Ari frowned, removed his kibbutz hat, and scratched his head. "I suppose so. We are prone to symbolic acts."

They are forever seeking signs in the earth, sermons in stones, parables in dead cities, to assure themselves—and the world—that this place is unquestionably, in fact, and on the basis of historical truth, *their* land. Later, I read an article by Professor Aharoni on the excavations at Tel Arad. It contained this revealing comment (the italics are mine):

The Arad Development Project [to build modern Arad] regarded the excavations as *part of the preparations for*

the establishment of the modern town of Arad, and
therefore bore much of the expense, supplied the needs
of the expedition, such as the labor force, and made part
of their camp available throughout the seasons as headquarters for the excavations. . . .

Here was a faultless example of the national compulsion to
relate past to present. As new Arad arose from the dry sand, old
Arad would be revealed, stone by stone, proof positive of the
Israelis' hereditary rights.

The site proved rich in ostraca, shards of pottery with inscriptions or seal impressions on them. The alphabets used were
Arabic, Aramaic, and Hebrew. The collective evidence of these
ostraca fairly well established that the site was, indeed, Israelite
Arad. Professor Aharoni also found a seal showing a plan of the
temple at Arad, and using it as a guide, his diggers were able to
know in advance what they would find!

From Professor Aharoni's article I learned that Tel Arad was
the largest and most important tel in the eastern Negev. Part of
its importance was due to its location at the intersection of several
major roads, one a track running west to Beersheba, another going
north to Carmel and Hebron, a third diverging in a southeasterly
direction to the Dead Sea and Edom.

According to Aharoni, the work was extremely difficult, being
interrupted by rains and floods in the first week, then strong
winds and dust storms. As I studied the white bones of Arad I
felt, as in few other places in Israel, the sobering sense of antiquity. These are, quite simply, very old bones, very old stones.
They have an odd, smooth quality, probably a result of the winds
that Aharoni mentions. Yet from a distance they gleam and spar-
kle in the sunlight. The crudely hewn rocks take on a gemlike bril-
liance. Studying my photographs of Tel Arad, I am amazed to discover how chalky white the stones of the citadel are. It is this
whiteness, this eroded, pale quality, I think, that gives Arad its
ghostly, frightening quality. Chorazim, an equally deserted
place, is by comparison gay, with its rugged black boulders and
the yellow fields and blue waters of the Kinneret. But there is no
solace at Tel Arad. Just the bad news of desert triumphing over

six thousand years of human stubbornness. (The Israelis, of course, would not accept this gloomy interpretation for a minute; they would point to the concrete sturdiness, the casual cockiness of modern Arad, and tell you to be on your way with your pessimism.)

Ari and I toured the two ruins, the higher citadel and the lower city. He pointed out the circular foundations of old towers, remarkably well defined, the base of the outer wall, storerooms, stone silos, and a peculiar stone channel, set at an angle, which I assumed was a water conduit of some kind. The Jewish sanctuary, with its sacrificial altar from the ninth century B.C., was probably the most dramatic find.

"You know, this was originally a Canaanite city," he said. "It is mentioned in the Bible as a city that fought the Israelites. It says in Numbers that the Canaanite king of Arad fought Israel and took some of the people captive. Later Joshua took care of the king of Arad. Moses' relatives were said to have settled around Arad. Actually, they were the children of Moses' father-in-law, Jethro, who lived around Arad. So the place gets several mentions in the Bible."

"I'm troubled about all those Canaanites," I said. "They seem to have been regularly kicked out of their land by you folks. Our folks."

"That's the way it was in those days. But no more. It's ours forever." He squatted over a pile of rubble, and after digging a moment, he extracted a small gray stone that to my untrained eye appeared to have been flaked or chipped. "Here. Souvenir of Arad. It might be something."

"But suppose a Canaanite nation suddenly turned up. I mean, a Canaanite revival movement. Couldn't they claim they were here first, and start an irredentist movement to throw you out? A sort of Eretz Canaan group, or a Canaanite Agency, or the Canaanite Organization of America?"

"No chance of that. We are the only ones who survived. We alone possess a historical continuity with this land."

We walked along the ruins of the citadel walls. Ari told me they dated from the tenth century B.C.—Solomonic. The walls still standing, some of them three meters thick, were of the ninth century. They seemed much older.

"Were any Canaanite buildings found here?" I asked, still sticking up for those vanquished Bronze Age settlers.

"That is an interesting question, and Aharoni raises it. The fortresses found here are Israelite, with some of the upper strata showing Hellenistic and Roman occupation. Now there *was* an Early Bronze Age city here, and it was destroyed in the third millennium B.C. But from that time until the tenth century, almost fifteen hundred years, the site was uninhabited. Who, then, was the biblical Canaanite king of Arad who captured the Israelites and later was defeated by Joshua? Some think he was a nomad king, an ancestor of those Bedouin you see out there. So, Aharoni raises the possibility that the Canaanite Arad was in a different place than this, the Israeli Arad. He says it might have been south of here, at Tel el-Milh. This was probably the place occupied by Moses' in-laws."

"Sort of a Greater and a Lesser Arad."

"Yes. But these are continuing problems with archaeologists. You see, they have a written record to work with. The Bible keeps them on their toes."

I returned to Beersheba on a public bus. It was late afternoon, turning cool, and the traffic between Arad and Beersheba was heavy. Exhausted, sun-seared, my feet leaden with pain and my eyes thickened with dust, I stood wedged between two Bedouin men wearing ragged overcoats. I was vaguely afraid of them. They did not look at me. They did not respond when I said "Excuse me" and tried to edge by. They did not move, and I had to force my way through, pushing against their spare, hard bodies. I smiled. No response from their secretive, black-eyed, dark faces. I tried a few hesitant "*Salaam aleikems*" and was almost ready to touch my heart, my lips, and my forehead, the way they do in the movies. But their blank, isolated eyes deterred me. Apparently there is little small talk in the Negev wastes, and none at all with foreigners in hiking shorts and white hats.

There is a myth circulating in Israel that "everyone here speaks a little English." This is true perhaps of the older generation, of city-bred university types, of officials. But in the boondocks this assumption is a rash and perilous one. Staggering, stooped beneath the weight of two cameras, after a long day on Masada and Tel Arad, I debarked at the Beersheba bus station. Where could I get a taxi? No one understood me. A bus to the Desert Inn? Not a soul comprehended. I tried the information booth. The fellow shrugged. He spoke only *Ivrit*. No English. The sun was setting. It was chilly. I was as tired as I have ever been in my life. Soon I was reduced to grabbing frantically at passersby in the bus terminal. Speak English? *Parlez-vous français? Parl' italiano?*

Clearly I was in trouble. Nor did I find many taxis cruising the streets outside the terminal. Several that I flagged down were not going my way. They were apparently a *sherut* service, the cabs that take six or seven people in a fixed run. After a half dozen attempts I stood forlornly, my cameras dangling around my neck, my head lowering, my jaw slack.

A Fiat 500 pulled up. "Please? Can I help?" A middle-aged man, gray-haired, handsome, wearing a white shirt and a tie, leaned out the window. He had a *mittel-europaïsche* accent.

"I'm trying to get to the Desert Inn."

"Please. Come in."

He asked me what I was doing in Israel and I told him I was a writer gathering material for a book.

"Would I know any of your books?"

I mentioned *The Last Angry Man*. He beamed. "Yes, yes. About the old doctor in Brooklyn. I read it some years ago. It interested me very much. You see, I am a doctor also." He pointed to the black bag on the rear seat. "I am a pediatrician. Originally from Budapest. My name is Itzhak Kisch. I enjoyed your book, because I knew doctors who had such a practice in the slum neighborhoods of Budapest."

I thanked this Good Samaritan of Beersheba, and I sent him, at his request, a copy of *The Last Angry Man*. When I told Dani at dinner of my encounter, he approved of Dr. Kisch. "A good old Hungarian name. But he is an Israeli now."

What that cryptic comment meant I was not certain. But I found myself becoming, like Dani, endlessly interested in the origins and careers and odysseys of these people. Who were they? Where were they from? How had they gotten to Israel? It was a subject that never ended with Dani. Even German Jews, whom he liked least of all, fascinated him. "They are called *yeckes*," he said. "We have a saying here—*a yecke bleibt a yecke.*"

"A *yecke* remains a *yecke*." I said. "Germans at heart?"

"That's the idea. And they do."

The next morning Dani got into an embittered political argument with an Israeli journalist, a former Berliner. I gathered it had to do with public statements concerning occupied lands. Neither could convince the other.

When the journalist left, Dani winked at me. "*A yecke bleibt a yecke.*" Meaning, I supposed, that his Berlin-born antagonist was excessively Germanic in his arguments. But he said it with a wry affection, as if bragging to me, *See, we've got all kinds.*

We were on the road again, headed for Jerusalem by way of Hebron and Bethlehem. A short distance outside Beersheba I noticed an unmistakable prison—a long, low, gray affair with grim towers. It stood in deathly silence in the midst of the desert. It appeared to be unoccupied. It was not the first we had seen. In Galilee I had observed at least three other menacing, brooding buildings, circled with barbed wire, guards posted in the watch towers.

"You seem to have quite a few prisons for a small country." I said.

"Yes, for our citizens who break the law."

Marie and I exchanged astonished glances. "Look, I have read everywhere and observed for myself that Israelis are among the most law-abiding people in the world. How can you get enough criminals for these prisons?"

"You'd be surprised. A lot of nasty stuff goes on."

"You are quite sure they haven't been put up to accommodate the Al Fatah and the other guerrillas?"

He turned his palms upward. In Israel it is usually bad form to discuss in detail (at least with tourists and journalists) the guerrilla actions, the bombings and mortar attacks. "Perhaps. It doesn't bother me. That place over there isn't even being used." He stretched and said something to Avram in Hebrew. Subject closed.

"Yes," I said, "an awful lot of jails for burglars and check-forgers."

But it did no good to joke about it. Everywhere one sees barbed-wire enclosures, security roadblocks, vehicles being halted and searched. Soldiers off duty almost always carry their weapons. There is, simply, no fooling around. Israelis are intent on survival. And they will live this way as long as they are required to—ten, twenty, a hundred years. I hasten to add that Israel is one of the safest countries in the world. Nothing I have said about the quasigarrison condition of some areas should deter anyone from a visit. I felt safer in the Old City of Jerusalem, or in occupied Jordan, than I feel on West End Avenue.

We spied Tel Beersheba, a rounded, flat-topped mound, in the distance. It appeared to dangle suspended in the morning haze, a few kilometers south of the main road.

"Ari told me about this," I said. "Aharoni is digging there. Do you think we can visit him?"

"That is what I had planned," he said. No other guide, no Negev *maven* would ever get a jump on him.

I read later that the Tel Beersheba dig was short of volunteers. Aharoni had been forced to place an advertisement in the Jerusalem *Post* asking for help. I could understand why. The heat, the aridity, the oppressive air, were the worst I had yet encountered. We found ourselves walking at a slow pace. Our eyes squinted to deflect the intolerable glare of the sun on the pale brown hills.

Professor Yohanan Aharoni was a slender and muscular man dressed in an orange knitted shirt and a rakish straw sombrero. He spoke softly, patiently to everyone, but he was very much in charge.

We wandered amid the five-meter-square pits on the face of Abraham's old habitation, where the patriarch had sat in his tent in the heat of the day, and Aharoni talked about the excavation.

"We began here two and a half years ago. The main layer, the one that interests us the most, is of the Israelite period of the Judges and the Monarchy, beginning about 1200 B.C. Above that there is a Persian stratum, and a Hellenistic, and a Roman, and an Arabic. The site was occupied into the sixth and seventh centuries, the early Arabic period."

I asked if there were signs that the tel's habitation preceded the Israelite period. It seemed I had become a partisan of the

Canaanites, the Early Bronze people, and even the Copper-Stone Age people of the Chalcolithic.

"Oh, yes. We have found Chalcolithic remains on the river beds below. But for the longest period of its existence it was Israelite. From the thirteenth century B.C. right up to the time of the destruction of the Second Temple in 587 B.C."

Several large boulders had been unearthed at the front of the mound. I asked Aharoni what they were.

"It is a stone glacis, an artificial slope on the front of the citadel. This is late Hellenistic or early Roman. However, the main wall is much older, eighth or ninth century B.C. Somehow that old Israelite wall was destroyed. If you look carefully, you will see one red layer, which is earth from the wadi, brought in as fill."

Later, I read in the Jerusalem *Post* that subsequently the actual Israelite rampart, dating to the eighth century, was uncovered below the Hellenistic-Roman glacis.

"One of the things we are looking for," the professor said, "is a *mikdash,* a place of worship mentioned in the Book of Amos and dating to the First Temple Period. It is possible it bears some relation to the *mikdash* I found at Arad some years ago."

We walked on the borders of the pits. Aharoni said that he had 120 people working at the site, of whom about 20 were professional staff, the rest volunteers. They were a mixed bag—many Americans, some Scandinavians, Germans, few Israelis. Israeli youth are all in the army. For all the absorption in archaeology and the past, the present is of far greater import to the country. It is admirable to establish through digging that you have historic rights to the land; but none of that romantic scholarship is of value if your borders are not secure in the present. Logically, most Israeli young people are more familiar with Uzzi machine guns than with trowels.

"There is a bit of everything here," Aharoni said. "The fortress, the Roman part, is well preserved. That floor is of the Hellenistic period. The bathhouse is late Byzantine and early Arab. The granary is Roman."

I pointed to a clump of stones in the corner of one of the pits. A shirtless bearded young man and a stout-legged Nordic girl in a bikini were digging delicately around it.

"And that?" I asked.

"A Bedouin grave. There are many of them on the tel. Long after this place fell into disuse, the Bedouin buried their dead here."

As we started to leave, I asked Professor Aharoni why there was such a national compulsion to dig, why Israel was almost a nation of archaeologists.

"I would say," he said slowly, "that this country is the only place on earth where there are ancient remains that the local people, Israelis, can identify with thir own culture, language, literature, religion, and tradition. All these have been maintained over the centuries, and the evidence lies here in the earth. When we unearthed Tel Arad, the old Israeli city was of great significance to the people founding the new Arad. Today, if you are a resident of modern Beersheba, everything found on this tel must have equally great significance for you. There is a continuity of our history from early times to the present and we find it buried in this earth."

As we left Tel Beersheba we had our meeting (recounted earlier) with the three Baptist ministers, resting like Abraham from the heat of the day.

I wondered, as we trudged down the side of the tel, our feet slipping in the dust and pebbles of eternity, who had the greater claim on the infecund land: the mysterious Bedouin, the friendly Baptists, or the modern Israelis? Probably there was enough history to go around. Fundamentalist believers, tough young desert pioneers like Ari, scholars like Aharoni and Negev—history had room for all. The archaeological life, it appeared, was warm, embracing, and expansive. As Professor Weinberg had said to us a few days ago on Tel Anafa: "That's the nice thing about archaeology. Nobody ever died for it—or of it."

It had been a long, parched, extremely hot morning on Tel Beersheba. We were now en route to Jerusalem by way of Arad. Avram had a brother living there and wanted to visit him. We stopped for lunch at the restaurant–filling station on the edge of town.

The waitress had the darting dark eyes, miniskirt, sexy hairdo, and saucy manner which I had come to associate with Moroccan girls. Dani complimented me on my perspicacity. "Oh yes, she is *marocaine*. You are getting observant. Look, look how she moves her arms and turns her head. I know it so well. Israeli girls are the most beautiful in the world."

She was essentially feminine, an eminently watchable and well-favored girl. Her appearance—especially the miniskirt and shapely bare legs—was in sharp contrast to that of a group of young girls who had entered the restaurant and were buying soft drinks and souvenirs at the counter.

"Look at those girls," Marie said. "They must belong to some kind of sect."

"Why?" I asked.

"Their skirts. Way below the knee. And long sleeves in ninety-eight-degree heat?"

"Yes, they do look rather restrained. Seventh-Day Adventists or Jehovah's Witnesses."

"They're Jewish," Marie said.

"No, no. No modern Jewish girl would put up with those hot dresses in the desert." I nodded my head at our *chatelaine*. "There's your liberated Jewish woman. Smooth of skin, firm of thigh, and a sassy toss of her brown curls. Eyes like two crazed cockroaches. Temptress."

One of the girls walked by. "Excuse me," Marie said, "are you girls with a group . . . or a school?"

"Yes. We're from the Beth Jacob school in Cleveland."

Dani nodded solemnly. "Very, very Orthodox."

"It's the leading Orthodox school for girls," the young lady said. "There's thirty of us on tour."

I took her to be about seventeen. Some careful work on her hair and skin, less homely eyeglasses, and a minidress in place of the hot, long-sleeved, below-the-knee print dress would have helped immeasurably.

"How old are you?" Marie asked.

"Twenty-two."

It was hard to believe. I suppose a life of piety and denial has some advantages.

Dani chewed his steak thoughtfully. "Oh, so Orthodox," he said.

I could never be certain where he stood. He had approved of the attractive nun and had even tried to flirt with her. He was usually favorably disposed to Hasidic types and other Orthodox. But his attitude toward the Beth Jacob girls was obscurely tinged with hostility. Was it simply because they were Americans trying so desperately to be profoundly Jewish? Or was he resentful of the desexing?

"Are you allowed to go out with boys?" Marie asked.

The girl—she had curly brown hair and pert features—pushed the crosspiece of her stern steel-rimmed spectacles up on her nose. "*Never*." She did not seem sorry.

"Do you want to get married?" my wife pursued.

"Sure. All of us do."

"Will you?"

"Beth Jacob girls always find husbands."

"But how . . . if you can't date. . . ."

She raised her firm chin. "It will be *arranged*," she said firmly.

Their group leader called them. They left, indifferent to the heat, our puzzled stares. They were secure in the Spirit. Like the Baptists of Beersheba they were sustained by certainties beyond us.

Avram hurried in. He had visited his brother and was ready for his steak and potatoes and had brought us a treat from his sister-in-law: a small jar of aromatic green relish which he called "*skhug*." Dani smacked his lips and advised us to spread it on bread or on our *homos*. We did. It was like green fire, searing the roof of my mouth with a hot pungent amalgam of pepper, basil, parsley, garlic, and other rare indefinable aromas. For such joys the ancient Nabateans built Avdat. The best hot relish I have ever tasted.

Outside, in the shade of a parked bus, four Beth Jacob girls were observing their afternoon prayers. They faced Jerusalem, these holy ladies in shirtwaists buttoned to the throat, gray skirts well below the knee, and they *dovinned* with fierce energetic bobbings and weavings. Straight-backed, prayer books open in their small hands, they bowed from the waist, over and over, in rhythmic spasms, as the sacred words issued softly from their lips. Desert heat could not weaken their faith. The cool shade of the roasting Egged bus was solace enough. Up and down, up and down they bobbed and jerked, letting God know that they were there and they cared.

"It's a substitute for sex," Dani said gloomily.

We drove off, leaving the Beth Jacob girls in holy rapture, weaving, bending, full of divine spirit outside a gasoline station in Arad. I suddenly remembered something the wife of one of my friends had told me years ago. She was brought up in an observing family—kosher house, regular attendance at shul.

"My mother was very strict about one thing," she told me. "I wasn't allowed to date boys from Yeshiva. They were considered 'fast.'"

More roadblocks; more solemn Israeli police halting vehicles with Arab license plates. We were on the outskirts of Hebron, occupied Jordan, en route to the Cave of Machpelah, Abraham's tomb.

"Keep your windows rolled up and the doors locked," Dani said. "They sometimes throw stones here."

The Arabs looked no different from Arabs anywhere else. They seemed docile, mildly curious. Entering the city, I was impressed with the prosperous-looking homes and farms. This was an affluent region. The houses had a solid, yet attractive quality, like the homes in one of the better hill towns of Italy. Hillside gardens were terraced with vegetables and melons.

Avram made some comment in Hebrew.

"He says the fruits and vegetables from Arab farms taste better," Dani said, "because they use natural fertilizers. He always buys grapes and melons in Hebron or Bethlehem."

I said I thought Hebron and its outskirts looked peaceful.

"Mayor Jabri is a smart fellow," Dani explained. "In 1929, in the big Arab uprising, all the Jews in Hebron were murdered. So when we took over in 1967 Jabri was afraid, and he should have been. They expected a terrible bloody vengeance. Every house flew a white flag. Jabri saw to it there was no resistance. In spite of Hebron's bad reputation, we didn't punish anyone. Not a single reprisal. And not a shot was fired then, but every now and then. . . ."

The Cave of Machpelah is actually a huge ungainly mosque surrounded by a high wall with foundation stones from Herodian

days. Before Hebron was an Arabic shrine, it was sacred to the
Jews. The name was once—and the place is still sometimes so
called—Kiryat Arba, the "Town of the Four." The "four" alludes
to the biblical couples believed to be buried there: Abraham,
Isaac, and Jacob and their wives, and according to hard-lining
traditionalists, Adam and Eve. (I was told later that Adam's skull
is at the Church of the Holy Sepulchre in Jerusalem.) I knew of
course that Abraham is revered by Moslems as a great prophet;
hence the ecumenical holiness of the Machpelah.

We walked along a street swarming with peddlers, Hasidim,
noisy French and American tourists, Israeli soldiers, and Arabs.
The hawkers sold some of the most sordid gimcrackery I have
ever seen, *chazarei* of stunning tawdriness. One item, which I
found hard to believe anyone ever, ever bought, for there were
scores of them for sale at every stand, consisted of an empty pop
bottle, filled with colored sand in layers, and with a photograph
of Moshe Dayan pasted on the side. I found it hard to imagine
the most fervid Israeli patriot or proud Jewish tourist decorating
his mantelpiece with these reused Moxie bottles and their bil-
ious yellow, red, and green sands. As for Dayan, he never looked
more ill at ease.

The street approaching Abraham's tomb swarmed with khaki-
clad soldiers. They peeked from rooftops. They sat on a bench
outside the entrance. They checked you as you walked in. They
rested with their stubby Uzzis and automatic rifles in a small
open truck parked midway up the sloping street.

"Show of strength?" I asked.

"Some Arab threw a grenade here a week ago. A little security
never hurts." Dani frowned.

Just as I began to grow uneasy, a party of French-speaking
tourists, chattering frenetically, behaving in an annoying *Nous
sommes français!* manner, a compound of arrogance and naïveté,
approached the truck—it was what we called a "weapons carrier"
in army ordnance—and asked to take photos of the soldiers. The
boys agreed. At once two hefty French ladies—fat-humped, heavy-
thighed gorgons, hair piled high in bouffant clouds, one in a
pale-green frock, the other in pink—hiked up their skirts, and dis-
charging whiffs of Chanel or Ma Griffe, they climbed up the rear
of the truck to pose with the soldiers. I stared in astonishment at

their exposed pink panty girdles, those tight elasticized knickers, and so did the soldiers. Now we all enjoy a sneaky look now and then. But this *was* a shrine. And these soldiers were supposed to be guarding the place, on the alert for bomb throwers. It was less the trivial lewdness of the incident that had upset me than its utter incongruity. There we stood, presumably in danger of assassination by the Al Fatah, and there were these giggling French ladies exhibiting their *gotkes* and embracing our guardians.

Inside the mosque, which has a kind of garish innocence, my sense of disorientation was heightened. Tourists in pastel shirts and droopy shorts wandered about freely. A Moslem priest, a bearded imam in the strange high hat of his office, showed some pale Christians—English or American—the marble *mihrab*, the wooden pulpit, the walls and pillars of Byzantine and Crusader origin. At the alleged tomb of Abraham, a small barred room containing a memorial stone, two bearded Hasidic youths bent and jerked in holy abandon while a third paced up and down, reading from his prayer book, stroking his *payes*, in ecstasy almost unbearable. He strode like a caged lion—a man imprisoned in the secular world, yearning for the truths of eternity.

The casual rubbernecking of tourists seemed inappropriate. It did not sit well, for example, with the mystic trances and devotions of the Hasidim. Dani tried to explain it.

"For years Jews could not come here. You can imagine how the Orthodox felt after the Six-Day War, being able to come here and worship at the tombs of Abraham, Isaac, and Jacob. As well as Sarah and Leah."

"Not Rachel?" Marie asked.

"She is buried at Ramat Rachel, near Jerusalem."

"And now Israelis come and go as they please?" I asked.

"Look around. Those boys over there, praying like crazy, ride a bus here. No one bothers them. Just as easy as taking the subway from Brooklyn to the Bronx."

The youths looked to me like natural victims—defenseless, pasty-faced, doughy-handed waifs. I marveled at their adventurous souls. I knew that ninety-nine per cent of the extreme Orthodox refused to serve in the army. And here they were in terrible Hebron—sitting ducks, easy targets for the savage guerrillas. But of course they were not quite that. There was another Israel. It was the land also of the laconic young men with the Uzzis who ensured their security. It brought to mind George Orwell's observation: "British radicals are protected by the British Navy."

We looked at the rooms purporting to stand over the graves of Sarah, Jacob, Leah, and the stones in the center of the main hall of the mosque believed to stand above the bones of Isaac and Rebecca. It is not an overly impressive place, for all its holiness. It affords only a marginal and somewhat cracked sense of the past. It is too much a hodgepodge, and the emetic colors used —bloody maroons, poisonous greens—do not suggest antiquity so much as a commercialized and amateurish notion of ancient days. In Tel Beersheba I could see Abraham; not in the Machpelah. I could not commune with the patriarchs there. The founding fathers deserved something better. But I suppose it is ungenerous and pointless to apply esthetic judgments to holy places. The two attitudes, the artistic and the pious, are not necessarily related, although our minds have been prejudiced by those interminable Byzantine Madonnas, the Sistine Chapel, Duccio's Maestà, and thousands of other Renaissance works.

As we departed, Dani told me that in 1968 some Orthodox Jews had moved back to Hebron to be near Abraham's grave. They came, these wet-eyed, unmuscular, defenseless holy men, ignoring memories of the massacre of 1929 and the hostile population, and daily they march around the mosque, under the querulous eye of the imam, intoning their prayers. It is a reasonably good example of the interfaith spirit, I think, and it speaks well of Abraham's potential for uniting the two monotheistic religions. Of course, the ecumenicity is a direct outgrowth of the Israeli occupation of Hebron and its military conquest. Let us not be overtrusting on this subject. Naïve optimism is out of order in the Middle East. When the Jordanians held Hebron, no Jew got a foot inside the tomb.

Before returning to Jerusalem that night—we had reached the end of our week's orientation as arranged by the Ministry of Tourism—Dani suggested we stop in Bethlehem. It was getting dark, and it was quite cool. But he said that many of the shops would be open, and he and Avram wanted to buy fruit and vegetables.

"Prices are much lower in Bethlehem," he explained. "After the

Six-Day War all of us in Jerusalem came over here once a week to shop. Everything was cheaper: fruit, vegetables, canned goods, clothing, textiles. My wife and I did a great deal of shopping here and made friends with the Arab shopkeepers. Most of them are Christians, and they are fine people. Marvelous manners, educated, friendly to us. They did not care for Hussein, or for being ruled by his Bedouin. There is only one bad result of the occupation. Ever since the Israelis started coming here, the prices have gone up."

He insisted that we visit some brothers, friends of his, who ran a small dry-goods shop at the edge of Manger Square. They were charming people, Christian Arabs, with relatives in Pennsylvania. They had their own knitting mills outside Bethlehem and, in a tiny, cramped shop, stocked an incredible variety of towels, sheets, blankets, mattress covers, tablecloths, and bolts of stuff for curtains, bedspreads, seat covers, and clothing.

The conversation was trilingual, in English, Arabic (which Dani spoke reasonably well), and Hebrew. Marie and I sipped our coffee and watched. The proprietor was a young man, and he had that pleasing delicacy of face—blue eyes, beautifully smooth skin, sharp features—and gentleness of voice characteristic of many Jerusalem Arabs. We enjoyed the pause amid the bolts of cotton and nylon, were invigorated by the potent coffee, and proceeded to the Church of the Nativity.

"You must go with the official guide," Dani said. "They have a monopoly here, and even the Ministry of Tourism must respect it."

The church, built on the site of Christ's birth, is built over the cave of the manger. From the outside it has the appearance of a sturdy fortress, which is appropriate, because it is basically a Crusader structure, dating from the eleventh and twelfth centuries. Nothing remains of Constantine's original church.

I was impressed by the simplicity and honesty of the Church of the Nativity. The exterior lines, despite the squat citadel-like appearance, are congenial, the stones are warm in tone. The building sits in dignified solitude at the edge of Manger Square, and the aspect is of an uncluttered, massive, properly unadorned place of worship. (Across the square stands a new mosque. The textile merchant told us—in a whisper—that the Jordanians had

erected it opposite the Church of the Nativity as a deliberate act
of provocation. But Christian Arabs are a wisely diplomatic and
even-tempered lot, and they refused to be provoked.)

We descended the narrow steps to the Grotto of the Nativity
and were shown the large gold star set in the floor, marking the
exact site of His birth. The guide said something about the star
having been a cause of the Crimean War, and in Zev Vilnay's
guidebook, the only one that mentioned this perplexing fact, I
found this reference:

> In 1717 the Latins set up the star and the inscription
> [Here Jesus Christ was born of the Virgin Mary]. In
> 1847 it was removed by the Greeks; but the Turkish
> government compelled them to restore it in 1853. The
> quarrel about the star was one of the causes of the Cri-
> mean War (1853–1856) of Russia against Turkey, Brit-
> ain and France.

Imagine! The Charge of the Light Brigade, after all, was an
outgrowth of an argument over a gold star in a church! As the
guide showed us the Chapel of the Manger, where Mary placed
the infant, and we returned to the main level of the church to
study the red limestone columns with their dim paintings, I
thought of the Crimean War.

Months later, I picked up Winston Churchill's *History of the
English-Speaking Peoples*. I suspected the book would be helpful.
Churchill—an eccentric in the grand tradition—would appreciate
a war touched off by an argument over a religious decoration:

> The immediate source and origin of the conflict which
> now came to a head between Turkey and Russia lay in
> Jerusalem, where the Greek Orthodox and Roman Cath-
> olic Churches disputed the custody of certain shrines.
> The quarrel would have been unimportant had not the
> Czar supported the Greek pretensions and Louis Napo-
> leon, now the Emperor Napoleon III, been anxious to
> please French Catholics by championing the Latins.
> After long negotiation the Czar sent his envoy Menschi-
> koff to Constantinople to revive his claims for a general

protectorate over the Christians in the Turkish Empire. This, if granted, would have given Russia authority over the many millions of Rumanians, Serbs, Bulgarians, Greeks and Armenians within the Ottoman domains. The balance of power, for which British Governments always sought in the Near East, as elsewhere, would have been destroyed.

Churchill had cleared things up. The star was a Latin star, that is to say, a Roman Catholic adornment in the most holy of Christian places. The Greek churchmen removed it in 1847, an action presumably pleasing to the Czar, who considered himself protector of Orthodox Christianity in the Turkish Empire. But the Turks, importuned by the Roman Catholics, who were championed by the French, then restored the star. Clearly, this infuriated the Russians, who were sworn to protect the Orthodox faithful in Jerusalem. It was a heaven-sent opportunity to meddle in the Middle East.

We made a final stop en route to Jerusalem to look at King Solomon's pools. It was soothingly peaceful at the stone-lined reservoirs. We munched grapes purchased from Arab women squatting outside the pools and rested in a grove of pines and cypresses.

"These pools still supply us with water in Jerusalem," Dani said. "Wonderful, sweet water."

"I know," I said. "The best water in the world. What was good enough for Solomon is good enough for Moshe Dayan, is that the idea?"

"More or less. Except that these really aren't Solomon's pools. In Ecclesiastes, Solomon said, 'I made me pools of water, to water therewith the weed that bringeth forth trees.' But these are probably Roman pools, although it is possible the water supply was in use in Solomonic times."

We had passed a sign pointing to a kibbutz, Kfar Etzion. Dani told us its story. "In 1948 the Jordanians destroyed it and murdered almost everyone there. So in 1967, after the Six-Day War, we resettled it. And some of the people who came back to start Kfar Etzion all over were descendants of the people who were killed. So you see how we feel about giving these places back."

CHAPTER VI

Behind the
Turkish Walls

Dani wangled a few extra days from the Ministry in order to, in his words, "get us started properly" in his Jerusalem. Knowing how he felt about most Americans, Marie and I were flattered. And considering my ignorance of the Bible, I was amazed.

"That's just it," Marie said. "He's got an edge on you, and you sop everything up. He can't tell you enough, and you never stop making notes."

On the dot of nine, Avram pulled up to the Intercontinental in the Ministry's Dodge.

"The best thing about the Intercontinental is the view," Dani said. "See—all of Jerusalem, my golden Jerusalem."

From the esplanade in front of the hotel, where the road up the Mount of Olives comes to a frustrating end in a hairpin turn, one is afforded a fantastic vista of the holy city. It is an awesome sight, surely one of the most enthralling in the world. I think the Turks and the Moslems deserve most of the credit. There are certain works of man that are of such supreme harmony, such gentle

176

melding with their natural setting, as to endow the viewer with an esthetic peace, a pleasing inebriation of the senses. In such a category are the walls of Jerusalem. Between the Mount of Olives and the walls lies the Kidron Valley, a ribbon of bleached earth studded with dark-green olive trees. Between the valley and the summit where we now stood is the Jewish cemetery. Much of it is in disarray because of Hussein's cavalier attitude toward Jewish places. Many of the tombstones were used as the foundations for buildings in Jordanian-held Jerusalem, I was told over and over by Israelis.

Beyond the somber graveyard on the slopes, beyond the tree-dotted Kidron are those sublime walls, simple, strong, elegant. Behind them rise the two plangent domes that so emphatically tell the viewer: Jerusalem. These of course are the two great mosques of the holy city, the el-Aksa and the Dome of the Rock.

As with the walls, there is something about their proportions, the manner in which they are set within the total configuration of terrain and structure, that create beauty, orderliness, a familiarity on first sight. There is a delightful aptness in the way in which the smaller silver globe of el-Aksa Mosque, which stands to the left as one looks at Jerusalem from the Mount of Olives, appears to hang in orbit, a gleaming satellite of the larger Dome of the Rock, itself a glittering golden orb. Even the space between them is a source of pleasure. Space, enough of it to allow for tranquil contemplation, is what I think makes the two Moslem shrines so refreshingly lovely. By comparison, the Christian holy places of Jerusalem tend to be cramped and cluttered. But as we discovered later, the enclosed area of the Temple Mount, the "Noble Sanctuary" where stand el-Aksa and the Dome of the Rock, benefits endlessly from the joyous presence of empty plazas, isolated walks, unadorned stairways, and judiciously placed old trees.

"I'll take you on a fast tour of the best viewing points," Dani said. As we entered the car, our lovely nun in her handsome white habit, followed by the grim duenna, came out of the hotel. Dani tried his most charming sabra smile. This time he got only a faint response. Proximity to the mysteries, I suppose, had put her on her guard. Up in the Galilean hills, she had smiled more warmly.

Our first stop was Abu Tor, an Arab village on the old border, the no-man's-land between Jewish and Jordanian Jerusalem. Sev-

eral houses were in ruins. Three small black-eyed Arab children
ran away, one of them crying, as Avram parked the car at the
old demarcation line.

An Egged bus rumbled by, not a tour bus, but one of the regular city routes. "I still can't believe it," Dani said. "Egged bus
routes through Abu Tor. This was an Arab Legion strongpoint
until we knocked it out."

On the Israeli side of the now-defunct border we stopped at
the Abu Tor observation point run by "Aunt Susie" Schwartz.
Over coffee and grapefruit juice, Dani told us her sad story.

"Before the Six-Day War busloads of tourists came up here to
get one of the best views of the Old City, Mount Zion, the Hinnom Valley. This is a famous place, a landmark. Near here is the
camp from where Titus launched his attack on Jerusalem. Abu
Tor and Aunt Susie's stand were the places to go, and she did a
nice business. Then came the Six-Day War, and now Israelis and
tourists can go anyplace they want in Jerusalem for a good view.
So the poor lady's business has suffered badly. A lot of the
guides have a warm feeling toward her, and they still bring people
up to Abu Tor."

We looked out at the bell tower of the Dormition Abbey and
the complex of buildings on Mount Zion. Later the redoubtable
Zev Vilnay would take me on his personal tour of Jerusalem,
giving his private lesson in military strategy and describing how
the city was taken in the Six-Day War. I was to learn a great deal
more about the Dormition Abbey tower and its military importance. Now we had time to become familiar with only the most
striking aspects of the city's dramatic skyline—the Dormition
Abbey, the Tower of David, the Church of St. Peter in Gallicante,
and the shining spheres of the el-Aksa and the Dome of the
Rock.

As we left to visit Herod's family tomb Dani told me that
almost all the important sacred religious sites had been in
Jordanian-held, or East, Jerusalem. The modern, faintly shoddy,
cramped streets leading into Zion Square, one of the hubs of
Israeli Jerusalem, were hardly a match for the picturesque alleys
and crumbling churches of the Old City. As a result of the unifi-
cation of the two Jerusalems, the city is open to everyone now,
and at all hours. Hence, quite a few entrepreneurs like Aunt Susie

Schwartz have come upon hard times. In the pre-1967 days, they operated observation points, high locations where Jews had to come to peek into the other Jerusalem.

"There was a poor fellow who rented binoculars in the French Church," Dani said. "Did a nice business with people who wanted to take a look at the Old City. But he isn't needed anymore. Like you Americans would say, he was programmed out of a job by our soldiers."

Herod's family tomb was located alongside the King David Hotel in West Jerusalem, which has been Jewish since 1948. The underground chambers are on land owned and administered by the patriarchate of the Greek Orthodox Church. After a while I gave up trying to keep track of which branch of the Church ran what shrine. The parceling out of holy places and of pieces of holy places is endlessly confusing.

(For example, the Church of the Nativity in Bethlehem has various sections set aside for the different subdivisions of Christianity. The basilica itself, I was told, is the only purely Roman Catholic Church in the Holy Land, but parts of it apparently belong to the Greeks and the Armenians.)

"You should see this to understand the whole question of the stone rolling away," Dani said. He showed us the giant limestone wheel used to close the entrance to a tomb in a typical Roman mausoleum. "Now when you read that the stone rolled away, when Christ rose, you will understand."

"Who exactly was buried here?" I asked. It had become witheringly hot. We sat gratefully in the cool tombs, like the dead in Carl Sandburg's poem.

"It is believed Herod put his *meshpucheh* here, the ones he murdered and some he didn't. The old man himself is buried in the mountains near Bethlehem. But this is interesting because the round stone is so big and so perfect, almost two meters in diameter. The tomb is in the shape of a cross."

I followed him into the dark interior. We were in a square chamber. A short passage led to two more square chambers, almost identical in size. A small central foyer led to an elongated room in which were two stone coffins.

"There is no escaping Herod in this town," I said as we emerged blinking into the afternoon sunlight.

"Wait till you see the excavations at the Western Wall," Dani answered. "It's Herod's show."

We descended Mount Zion through silent, shuttered streets—it was early afternoon—and entered the Old City of Jerusalem through the Jaffa Gate. This sublime portal is set at an angle in the great walls, so that its elegant lines are not immediately visible.

"The Turks widened it in 1898 to let Kaiser Wilhelm ride through in his carriage with a bunch of Germans following him on horseback," Dani said. "Anyway, some good came of it. You can take an official car in now and park it. Avram will meet us back here later."

I had already admired the walls and entrances of Jerusalem from a distance. At closer range, the gates were even more impressive. The pale-brown stones, tinged with gold, have a restful, warm quality. It is the kind of robust, weathered architecture that accepts the environment, the people around it, and renders them (sometimes too generously) dignified and gentle. The Arab children hawking shoelaces and chewing gum did not fill me with pity—they looked healthy and happy. A man selling round salted bread and hard-boiled eggs did not seem out of sorts with the world, nor did the newspaper boys, aggressive guides, elderly Arab women with shopping bags, and the crowds of tourists. All of them appeared content and relaxed. The walls have this soothing, mothering effect. Far from suggesting the violent nature of man, they seem, to me at least, to be portals of peace and harmony.

Inside the Jaffa Gate the first edifice one notices is the Citadel, with the so-called Tower of David on the right, where the Israelis now stage a sound-and-light spectacle.

"There is the moat," Dani said. "Most of the walls and structures are from the medieval period forward—Arab, Crusader. But the legend says King David built a tower here, although the one you see is not it."

We walked inside the courtyard of the Citadel. Huge stage lights were set in the ground and on the walls for the evening spectacle. There were also several archaeological pits. "Are they digging here?" I asked.

"Oh, yes," he said. "They are finding remains from the Hasmonean period, first century B.C. They've found at least one room—which trench it is I am not sure—but it is the only Hasmonean structure so far discovered in Jerusalem, apart from some tombs. They found a lot of Herodian and Hasmonean coins also."

"Your archaeologists are determined to find evidence of your prior rights to the city wherever they can."

"Of course. But an army also helps."

Some months later my airmail edition of the Jerusalem *Post* informed me that the dig inside the Citadel had produced additional evidence of Jewish history there. The archaeological team which had found the Hasmonean room had now discovered part of a tower forming a section of the city wall, also from the first and second centuries B.C. But they had pushed the evidence back even further. At bedrock the diggers had unearthed a white lime floor which they dated as seventh century B.C., the period of the Judean monarchy.

Other interesting finds were a stone seal of the First Temple Period—tenth century B.C.—and jar handles inscribed "JERU-SALEM" and "YEHUD," the latter being the name for the province of Judea under Persian rule, in the fifth century B.C. It was a rich haul, and more evidence of Jewish roots.

(A later edition of the *Post* informed me that at the annual meeting of the Israel Exploration Society Professor Benjamin Mazar disclosed that "500 archaeological sites had been located in the Golan in a survey launched after the Six-Day War." The Israelis lose no time in finding their roots. The militarized kibbutz in occupied territory is no sooner built than the diggers appear, looking for stony evidence of their ancestors. Another speaker at the convention discussed "the Jewish settlement in the Golan in the period of the Mishna and the Talmud" and disclosed that twenty Jewish habitations of that period had already been located!)

"This was the site of Herod's palace," Dani said, as we walked around the upper ramparts of the Citadel. "He built it at the beginning of the first century, and there were three towers for defense: Phasael, named for his brother, Mariamne, for his wife, and Hippicus, for his friend. In A.D. 70, when Jerusalem fell to the Romans, it was destroyed along with the Temple and the rest of Jerusalem."

"And you are determined to prove now that it is yours by heritage, right?"

"We *have* proved it."

On the way out he pointed out a dry stone pool. "Some people claim that is the pool where David saw Bathsheba bathing, although I am inclined to doubt it. It's a nice *bubba meysa.*"

"But it's important. If David hadn't seen her and admired her, there'd have been no Solomon, and no Temple, and no grandeur."

"But that isn't the pool, I'm quite certain."

Who really knew? I looked back at the rampart of the old fort, and I tried to see King David, that dashing, audacious leader, lover, musician, warrior, empire-builder. There he stood, stroking his beard and ogling Bathsheba as she washed herself. "And the woman was very beautiful to look upon." Poor Uriah! He died for his wife's beauty and immodesty. As for David, I don't think the Lord punished him sufficiently. The bastard child died. Uriah was killed in a rigged battle at David's orders, Bathsheba probably suffered pangs of guilt, although the Book is silent on this. But David rolled on, impregnated Bathsheba again, and Solomon was born. David surely got the best of the whole affair. All he suffered was some fasting, and a night of contrition in the fields. Kings have always had a talent for repentance on a modest scale.

The Old City is irresistible, enchanting, all the old Hollywood movies about the Middle East thrown into one garish, crowded, noisy, malodorous place—all of it diverting. Yet I kept wondering how these legions of retail merchants survive. I don't mean the strategically located tourist shops, with the camel-skin bags and religious souvenirs and sheepskin jackets. I mean the innumerable holes in the wall dispensing watermelons, spices, baked goods, chickens, household items. It always seems to me that there are many more times the number of retail outlets than can possibly be sustained by the population in these Eastern countries, and that the majority of these merchants must have a dreadful time making the minutest of livings. I remember once in Old Delhi pushing my way through a morning crowd of shoppers and vendors. It had seemed to me that as many people were selling things—a man hawking four cucumbers from a banana leaf, a child selling a box of buttons, a woman with a small sack of grain—as were buying.

It is to the credit of the Old City, however, that one is not long depressed by Marx, Malthus, or Keynes while strolling through its gaudy confines. It has a tawdry vigor, a bustling, overripe ambience, that is most enjoyable. I suspect that its residents— many people live there as well as operate small shops—accept its minimal comfort and sanitation in exchange for this ferocious vitality, this constant drama.

And drama exists everywhere. Having decided earlier that the golden walls had a gentling, sedative effect on people, I now began to think differently. A good deal of scuffling and arguing takes place inside the Old City. It is by no means Arab-Jewish rivalry. Israeli tourists abound, as do Israelis on business and police, and the Arabs are perfectly polite. But they are unquestionably a subjugated people. One gets an uncomfortable feeling that they are biding their time, but doing so decorously and with a soft smile.

In the space of an hour we saw three angry outbreaks of violence. They were all brief and not terribly brutal. But they had a cutting edge of frustrated anger, of pent-up bitterness that was disturbing. Nor did anyone seem inclined to intervene. Just beyond the Citadel we saw two boys, about thirteen, tearing one another apart, hissing and choking and grabbing at each other's eyes. People watched. We watched. Finally an Israeli policeman broke them apart. The second incident was more frightening. A young Arab sharpie in tight-fitting black shirt and hip-hugging trousers started to kick and swing at another youth working in a shop, a fat, moronic-looking fellow who evidently had made some nasty remark to the dude's girl, a homely blonde, possibly a German or a Scandinavian. The flare-up didn't last long. The spiv in black kicked the fat boy once or twice, tossed a few blows, and then retired, gasping and satisfied. As for the presumed masher, he had lumpishly stood his ground, a placid, dim-witted sort, content merely to survive. The last quarrel was an adult-child encounter of a curious nature. Again, two boys, aged eleven or twelve, not dirty urchins but well-dressed kids (as are most children in the Old City) began to scuffle. Suddenly a gray-haired man in a dark suit, apparently not related to either child or known to them, appeared and yanked one boy aside and slapped his face wickedly three times. The humiliated child did not run, but

began to defy the man in a shaky voice. Tears clouded the youngster's eyes, as he and the man exchanged insults. For a minute I
thought the boy would strike the man; but the latter raised a
hand as if to slap him again, and then, abruptly, both youths vanished in the swarming mob.

"Why so many fights?" I asked Dani as we proceeded through
the alleys toward the Arab School, in whose courtyard the procession along the Way of the Cross was due to start.

"Who knows? A strange people."

We stood on an elevated patio and looked down on the courtyard as the Franciscans assembled in a semicircle. Behind them
an Arab official sat cross-legged as they chanted. Dani explained
that this was an honored custom: a Moslem functionary welcom-
ing the Christian pilgrims about to reenact Christ's passage down
the Via Dolorosa.

"This is the First Station," Dani said. The file of brown cassocks
began to march off. "The place where Pontius Pilate questioned
Jesus and condemned him."

Outside the court, in the shaded street, we paused at the First
Station. "The Santa Scala used to be here," Dani said.

"I've seen the original," I said. "It's in Rome, opposite the
Church of St. John Lateran. I could never figure out how Christ
got to Rome to climb those steps."

"St. Helena had them brought to Rome," Dani explained.

We followed the processional a few steps. Neither Marie nor
myself had the energy or the spiritual elevation to attempt all
fourteen Stations of the Cross. We had paid our respects to the
holy parade, and Dani suggested we drop in at the Church of the
Sisters of Zion, where one of the best tours in the Old City was
conducted daily by one of his friends, an English nun. Before we
entered, he pointed out the arch erected by the Emperor Hadrian
in A.D. 135, alleged to mark the spot where Pilate said, "*Ecce
homo.*" Part of the arch was embedded in the walls of the
Church of the Sisters of Zion, and as we studied it, the nun who
knew Dani came to the door and greeted him. She was an attractive middle-aged Englishwoman clad in apostolic white—a shortened skirt and a becoming wimple—and she welcomed us with
warmth and a lilting accent.

"This church stands on the site of the old Antonia Fortress," she said. Several other tourists joined us, and we proceeded down cool corridors toward the basement. "The fortress stood on the Northern Wall of the Temple Enclosure. We are also known as the Ecce Homo Convent. It is believed that the Praetorium from which Jesus was led was part of the old Antonia buildings, since the Antonia bordered the southern side of the Via Dolorosa."

Someone asked why Hadrian had built an arch to honor Jesus.

"Oh, it was not quite that," she said. "It was a *Roman* arch, to celebrate what the Emperor imagined to be his victory over the Jews, Jesus, and Jerusalem." Inside she pointed out a portion of the Roman arch behind the altar.

In the basement we were shown the smooth old flagstones—the Lithostratos—the pavement running north from the Antonia fortress. Here, presumably, both Jesus and Pilate stood when the later cried, "*Ecce homo.*" Suddenly the sister held her arms aloft as we studied the venerable slabs. Her voice was loud, dramatic. "'Then came Jesus forth, wearing the crown of thorns and the purple robe. And Pilate saith unto them, Behold the man!'"

She pointed out curious markings on some of the stones, squares and incised lines. What were they? Probably games. The very games that the Roman soldiers played when they gambled for Christ's garments.

"Is there a clergyman here who can lead us in prayer?" she asked unexpectedly.

I was rather taken back. I had no objection to someone praying, if they felt so moved. But it seemed strangely parochial to me, an odd bag of tourists dragooned into group prayer.

There must have been twenty people standing in the gloomy cellar, staring at the old stone slabs. Shiny and smooth, they clearly showed the traditional grooves to keep the horses from slipping.

No one had volunteered. "Very well, I shall lead a brief prayer myself."

I don't recall the exact wording, but it was simple and appropriate, and as far as I recall, no Jew or Moslem, or atheist for that matter, took umbrage, although I could swear Dani's eyebrows (like those of certain TV commentators) rose a fraction.

Midday devotions concluded, we were prepared to leave the underground chamber, but the English nun was not finished. "So you see how it all began. In *love*. In love, and suffering and charity. For that was the message of Jesus to the world. To love one another, to love God, to practice charity and good works. And all the Stations outside—a man suffering, and dying for his faith, but only to bring love and goodness and charity to the world, a world that needed these things so desperately. That is the message of the Stations and of the drama that took place here on the Lithostratos, the paving stones where Jesus stood. . . ."

Her voice was tremulous, inspirited. She had superb diction, each syllable enunciated, each sentence properly stressed and delivered in a dramatic cadence. She was more than a routine actress, and her fluty voice, U-accented, faintly haranguing, spiritually transported, demanded our attention. We stood around humbly—clods, interlopers, half comprehending—until she had concluded her sermon. One was almost tempted to applaud on her last coda: *Christian love, Christian hope, Christian faith, Christian charity* . . .

In the street, pausing to read the sign outside the Third Station, where Jesus fell, Marie said, "Your friend the sister is a marvelous actress. She reads those lines superbly. That rising of her voice at the end of a sentence, the extravagant gestures with her hands . . . she sounds just like Maggie Smith."

Yes, the nun of the Church of Zion did possess the same vibrant, forceful qualities. The Church is drama, I had read somewhere. Sister understood that; and her guided tours and exhilarating sermons are theater of a very high order. Miss Jean Brodie in a habit.

Behind ugly scaffolding and supports stands the Church of the Holy Sepulchre, on the site of the Crucifixion. The scaffolding was put up to buttress the basilica after the earthquake of 1927 and it is still there.

"I shall leave you here," Dani said. "The Holy Sepulchre doesn't intrigue me particularly. You can go in, and one of the monks or attendants will take over. What you are looking at is a Crusader church built on the old hill of Golgotha. The Hebrew word for skull is *gulgoleth*. Constantine's mother, St. Helena, decided that this was the place of the Crucifixion. It was a temple of Venus then, and underneath were caves, chambers, cisterns, tombs.

Nothing is left of Constantine's original basilica that stood here."

"Why place of the skull?" I asked. "Whose skull?"

"Adam's. Didn't you know that? Sure. Adam is supposed to be buried at the Machpelah, but his skull is here."

"That makes it a fairly old cemetery. Did Adam belong to a burial society? Who preached the sermon?"

"Laugh, laugh, my friend. You live in Jerusalem, you learn to accept. Adam's skull is here. Calvary—Calvaria—is from the Latin *calva*, meaning skull. The legend is that when Jesus was crucified, some of his blood dripped on Adam's skull and restored it to life for a little while. Anyway, that should get you started. Marie, cover your shoulders and go in. I may see you tomorrow, if I can get off again. There is one more place I want to show you personally, one of my favorites, after you have been through the Holy Sepulchre."

One enters the Holy Sepulchre through a courtyard cluttered with building stones, piles of sand, lumber. On the left is a niche in the wall reserved for the Moslem doorkeeper, a courtesy similar to the presence of the Islamic official at the start of the procession along the Via Dolorosa. In the midst of the lobby rests a large pink slab, the stone of unction, on which Jesus was anointed. Since I had no guide, I used my redoubtable Vilnay, following his instructions and maps. I enjoy this kind of sightseeing; matching diagrams to actuality gives me a sense of achievement.

"Here's the iron grille," I said to Marie, "where the three Marys watched when Christ was embalmed."

We started toward the rotunda where the Holy Sepulchre is located. It is a dark and gloomy place, barely lit by dozens of dangling lamps that give a sinister half-light. Suddenly I jumped. Someone had grabbed my elbow and was kneading my upper arm.

"Plizz. I am official guide. All religions. Greek Orthodox, Roman Catholic. Armenian, Syrian, Coptic. Also Abyssinians. I am guide."

I looked into a round face, smooth as white satin. The eyes were wide and moist. A short black beard. Thick red lips. He was a man of average height, but softly fat and faintly menacing in a billowing black robe. His name, his ranking in the hierarchy of the basilica, or his faith (I suspect he was an Armenian) I never learned.

"No, thank you," I said. "I have a book."

"Plizz. I be guide. Is here Greek Orthodox, Roman Catholic, Armenian. Speak very good English. I show you."

Surrendering, I let myself be dragged to the middle of the rotunda in which stands the Holy Sepulchre. A mob had gathered around the curtained entrance to the holiest of holy places in Christendom. My bearded guide—was he someone of importance?—pushed and elbowed his way through, dragging me with him. There were no protests. Evidently he had authority. A swift shove in the small of the back, and I was in the dark musty cell. It is a minuscule room, with space for no more than four people. Suspended lamps cast a dim glow in the enclosed space. An altar stone of marble, placed there in 1555, stands over the spot where Jesus was buried, a cavity cut into the ancient rock. We could not have been in the room more than thirty seconds when, somehow, we were wrestled out, and were back in the middle of the rotunda.

"Angel Chapel. Stone from tomb." My guide pointed to a slab standing in the middle of the floor. "Church is Greek Orthodox, Roman Catholic, Armenian."

This litany, I soon realized, was the extent of his English. I tried to steal a moment to study the rotunda—the guidebooks call it an architectural disaster, a deplorable mishmash whose main interest is the foundation, which dates to Constantine—but the bearded functionary was dragging me behind the Chapel of the Holy Sepulchre.

"Coptic chapel," he said. "Special for you."

Directly in back of the Holy Sepulchre, behind an ornate golden grille, was another tiny chapel. Apparently the Copts have been given a small corner of the stone to exhibit and venerate. If the actual Holy Sepulchre was small, this was Lilliputian. A bearded, grizzled Abyssinian priest, grinning, bowing, muttering, emerged. He wore a gray smock and a tall gray yarmulke. Marie and I were shoved into the Coptic niche with him. He knelt and lifted a drapery to reveal a corner of the altar stone. It was, I realized, the back of the Sepulchre.

"He wants you to do something," Marie said.

"I respect all religions," I said, "but I won't kiss the stone."

His desires were more practical. He lifted the curtain higher. There, lying at the base of the sacred stone, was an antipasto of currencies: a one-dollar bill, a ten-franc note, Israeli pounds, a German mark. They had a rumpled, yellowed look, as if they had been there a long, long time.

I don't know why, but I was seized with terror. I glanced about me. Our bearded guide, the silken-faced, wet-eyed one, was staring through the grille, watching me. Stupidly, I called to him: "Ah, is it all right to give . . . I mean . . . a donation. . . ."

"Plizz. Greek Orthodox, Roman Catholic, Armenian."

"But this is Coptic."

"Also Syrian, Coptic, Egyptian, Abyssinian."

In a frenzy, I reached into my pocket and pulled out a ten-pound Israeli note. I placed it, with trembling hand, at the foot of the stone. The Copt nodded vigorously, squeezed my hand, and ushered me out. There was no one waiting to visit his little corner, despite the crowd at the front of the chapel.

Our first guide led us upstairs to the site of Golgotha, an ornate chapel, lit with dozens of hanging lamps. The sanctuary is shared by the Roman Catholics and the Greeks. Presumably, here was the place of the highest drama of Christendom, the Crucifixion and the death of Christ, the descent from the cross, the Pietà.

Again, I was uneasy, obscurely troubled. We turned to leave, pausing to look at the Chapel of Adam which Dani had mentioned. Here rested—so it was believed by many—the frail skull of the first man. Of course, Professor Leakey and his bone-wielding ape-man would have had other ideas. And as an old anthropology student of Ralph Linton's, I am on their side. Nonetheless, I envied those who could believe.

We paid our respects to the tombs of two Crusader kings—Godfrey of Bouillon and Baudouin I—and descended the stairs. Our guide was tugging at my sleeve again. He had his hand out, which was understandable, although he had guided us very little, told us nothing, and rudely interfered in my attempts at self-guidance with the help of Vilnay's book.

"Man wants money," I said to Marie. There went another ten pounds.

"*Merci, merci,* thank you." We were standing alongside the red stone of unction. "Plizz. Remember. Greek Orthodox, Roman Catholic, Armenian. No Protestant. You are Protestant?"

"Jewish," I muttered. He rolled his eyes. The furry brown pupils disappeared. Signifying what?

Outside we wandered through the market. Marie frowned. "You were awful in there. Twenty pounds? Why?"

"I was scared."

"Scared?"

"Scared stiff. They psyched me out. I was wallowing in guilt because of the Crucifixion, and they knew it. That fat guy with the beard, the Ethiopian Copt. Oh, they had me sized up. Big rationalist humanist Jew with inferiority complex. Scared stiff of all that mystery and blood and incense and miracles. And full of guilt, drowning in guilt, because my people killed him."

"You can't be serious."

"But I was. Twenty pounds' worth."

Some months later, these memories of the Holy Sepulchre were revived by a headline in *The New York Times:*

COPTS AND ETHIOPIANS
CLASH IN JERUSALEM

Jerusalem, April 26 (AP)—Coptic and Ethiopian Christians hurled abuse at one another over the heads of Israeli policemen today during Orthodox Easter observances at the Church of the Holy Sepulcher. . . .

The meeting of the two sects at the church began in comparative peace. . . . Then, however, the 200 Ethiopians slammed the door on the 100 Copts and refused to let them out. . . . The Copts hammered on the door and shouted epithets. The Ethiopians shouted back.

I was truly sorry for their troubles, for I am not a man to mock the warfare of Big-enders and Little-enders. But in some irrational way, I felt a little more secure in my neuroses. The dark dervish and the moist monk who had so frightened me were people with their own *tsuris*—even in the comforting shadow of their most holy place.

CHAPTER VII

Chinese Gordon's Memorial

"I think I understand the sort of thing that really interests you,"
Dani said the next morning. Marie, who had decided to spend
the morning shopping, wasn't with us.

"What would that be?" I asked. We were strolling up a
deserted walled street north of the Damascus Gate.

"Anything eccentric, out of the ordinary. Something with a
little controversy. Or an angle."

"Very good. I'm a journalist at heart. An old Hearst writer, to
be exact."

"I know you well, *chaver*."

We paused at a wooden door in the stone wall. A sign said,
"THE GARDEN TOMB." To one side was a dangling bell. Dani
tinkled it. The door was opened by an elderly gray-haired lady. A
quick glance told me: English, Protestant, country house, rose
bushes.

"Is the Reverend in?"

"Well . . . he doesn't normally take tours on Sunday."

Dani told her his name and mentioned the Ministry of Tourism. She was impressed and said she would find the Reverend. We walked through an anteroom—souvenirs for sale, a great deal of religious literature, postcards—into a garden of unexpected beauty. Jerusalem in August is a parched and hot place. But now we stood in an English oasis, the garden of a country squire in Chipping Campden or Evesham. There were artfully placed cedars and cypresses and a tree resembling a willow. And there were trimmed hedges and flower beds. Across a quaint timber footbridge stood rustic benches. A group of tourists—white hair, print frocks, long honest faces, a decidedly Presbyterian or Baptist group—were attending a service. A minister in a black suit was reading from the Bible. Behind him rose a yellow-white cliff, part of it reinforced with white bricking. A dark door opened into the rock. I took this to be the Garden Tomb.

We strolled out to observe the pastoral scene. "Yesterday," Dani said, "you saw the Church of the Holy Sepulchre. It is mainly Roman Catholic, but the other Eastern churches have shares of it. This place, the Garden Tomb, is recognized by many Protestants as the site of Calvary and Christ's burial. It's a long story, and I'll let Mr. Vanden Hoeven tell you. But the idea is that a lot of Protestants didn't like the idea of not being allowed into the Holy Sepulchre for services—they can go as tourists, but not for religious business—so they started their own."

"You must be joking."

"*Chaver*, about such things they don't joke. You see, there has been an old argument whether the Holy Sepulchre could have been the site of Calvary because under Jewish law, no one could be executed or buried inside the walls of the Holy City. If that place that St. Helena picked *was* inside the walls, then it could be the wrong place. Well, the Catholics get around that by saying that in Christ's day that hill was *outside* the walls. The present church, the Basilica of the Holy Sepulchre, was built by the Crusaders, and by then, the city walls had been extended. But . . ."

Dani made the traditional Talmudic gesture, his right thumb rising, turning downward, describing a large "U," and I laughed softly.

"But, people like General Charles Gordon didn't agree, and

they went looking for a *new* Calvary, another Golgotha. Wait, here's the Reverend. He will explain it better than I can."

"How do you do," the minister said. "I am John William Vanden Hoeven, and my title is warden of the Garden Tomb. This site is supported by a British Inter-Church Association to maintain the Garden Tomb in Jerusalem. We have many Protestant faiths represented, Anglicans, Baptists, Methodists. I don't know how much our friend from the Ministry has told you, but I shall start with the question of the walls. It is a bewildering question. The Church of the Holy Sepulchre, the other Calvary, stands well within the Turkish walls of the sixteenth century, which in general follow the lines of the Roman walls. So the question is, were the walls the same in Roman times or more contracted. If the former is the case, then the Catholics' Sepulchre would be wrongly located, since we know that Jesus—Epistle to the Hebrews is quite clear on the matter—was crucified outside the city. Mind you, we of the Garden Tomb come to no hard and fast conclusions. But we feel that the weight of evidence supports the belief that the site chosen by the Empress Helena was within the walls, and hence a wrong choice. Of course, we have an open mind on the subject. When Constantine built his basilica, it was certainly inside the city wall. But at the time of the Crucifixion, well, no one can be sure."

"So this place," I said, "is a Protestant alternate."

"In a sense. But we do not like to regard it as a second choice. I must be frank and tell you that many Protestants accept the Holy Sepulchre inside the city. On the other hand, there are those like us who feel tradition can be broken when new facts are discovered. We feel that *this* hill is Golgotha, the true place of the skull, and that the evidence supports us."

"And it was General Gordon who made these discoveries?" I asked. Charles George "Chinese" Gordon—depicted in the film *Khartoum* by Charlton Heston and immortalized before Hollywood by Lytton Strachey—had long been one of my favorite British eccentrics. The hero of the Tai-Ping rebellion, the leader of the Ever-Victorious Army in China, the troubled, mystical, controversial blue-eyed Victorian, foe of the Sudanese fanatic, the Mahdi, Gordon was an original, a contentious and maddening man, one of those intriguing oddballs who pepper the history of

the British Empire. I had read two biographies of Gordon, but I
did not recall his discovery of the Garden Tomb. What I remembered best was a contemporary drawing of Gordon's severed
head being displayed on a pike after his death in Khartoum.

"Gordon was largely responsible," Dr. Vanden Hoeven said,
"but the tradition of a different Golgotha was an old one." We
strolled through the aromatic gardens. Dani plucked mustard
flowers and sniffed them. It was a lovely place, a restful and
serene oasis. The British did some things properly.

"There are records throughout the Middle Ages of pilgrims
doubting the veracity of the Holy Sepulchre, mainly because of
the argument over the city walls. Scholars began to look for a
Golgotha outside the Jaffa Gate or near the Zion Gate. In 1842 a
man named Thenius decided that a hill north of the Damascus
Gate, this hill on which we are now standing—it rests on the
Grotto of the prophet Jeremiah—was the site.

"General Gordon, on holiday in the Holy Land in 1882, came
to the same conclusion. He was a most religious man, a devout
Christian, and an expert on such matters as terrain, ancient construction techniques, and the Bible. He came to the conclusion
that this was Golgotha because, among other reasons, Christ is
quoted in Romans as saying, 'All day long I have stretched forth
my hands unto a disobedient and gainsaying people.' What
he meant was that if the cross of the Crucifixion was on the
summit of this hill, Christ's outstretched arms would embrace the
entire city and the Mount of Olives. He also had an argument
based on the angle at which the cross stood in reference to the
Jewish sacrificial altar on Mount Moriah. That is to say if you
drew a skeleton over Jerusalem with the skull here, the extended
arms could embrace the city."

"And that was all the evidence he had?"

"Oh, no. There was a local legend that the hill was accursed.
But more important, from a certain angle it looks like a skull." Dr.
Vanden Hoeven gave me a photograph to study. It showed the
lower cliff facing of Gordon's Calvary. The cavities in the white
limestone did approximate a skull with eye sockets, a dark space
for the nose and a gash for the mouth. But it was not completely
convincing. Later I studied the cliff from the Arab bus station
below, which sits at the base of the Protestant Golgotha, but I

found even less of a resemblance to a human skull than in the photograph.

"Incidentally," the minister said suddenly to Dani, "can't you get Teddy Kollek to do something about that dreadful bus station down below?" We stood on a small viewing platform, at the edge of the garden. Below us, ancient motors belched and coughed; gears and bearings screamed for oil. Noxious fumes rose about us, an effluvia hardly in keeping with the sacred garden.

"It is under consideration," Dani said.

"It's really a disgrace. A holy place like this having to put up with that. I suggested to the mayor that a library would be a good idea."

"Or an interfaith center," I blurted out.

"No," the warden of the Garden Tomb said crisply. "We are getting too much of that these days."

This comment impressed me. In an ecumenical age, a time when the faiths seem overeager to exchange revelations, to smile shyly at one another, to indulge in a kind of forced bonhomie, the warden's independent spirit was admirable. And I too wonder if this love-feast is entirely a boon. Let me cite two examples that disturb me not a little. First, I am not so sure about that recurrent expression "Judeo-Christian tradition." My vague understanding of the philosophical bases of these faiths is that they are rather different. As a Jew, I appreciate the advantages of being included—top billing at that!—with the more potent forces of the Cross. But I am not convinced that we share all that much. Secondly, I worry a good deal about diverse Christians getting together. Once you organize all the Catholics, Protestants, Orthodox, and others into one mighty united host, I begin to worry about what might happen to Jews and other non-Christians. And once you have *all* the faiths—Christian, Moslem, Hindu, Jewish— dining at one groaning table, then let the atheist and the non-conformist beware. A cynical friend, an old-fashioned atheist crank, once confided to me, "Our only hope is to keep them snarling at each other."

As we strolled through the garden of Gordon's Calvary, I found myself applauding the General's askew individuality. None of your established churches for Chinese Gordon, thank you. Like all good religious eccentrics, he was certain that the deck of revelation had not been fully dealt, and that a few more cards were available to him.

"If this were the place of the Crucifixion," Vanden Hoeven said, "it meant there was a tomb nearby."

"And Gordon found one," I said.

"Actually, a Greek who owned the land at the base of the cliff had discovered a tomb in 1867, but he had covered it up again. Gordon rediscovered it and sent sketches to influential friends in London. In 1894, nine years after Gordon's death in the Sudan, the Garden Tomb Association was formed, money was raised, and this site purchased and maintained—forever, we hope."

We paused at the entrance to the tomb. It was surely one of the most pleasant burial places in Israel. The pitted facing of the cliff had a warm golden tint. The shaped stones forming the entrance were appropriately aged. The three of us walked in. It was refreshingly cool in Gordon's tomb. Outside, the morning service continued and we spoke in low voices. Reverend Vanden Hoeven sat on a stone bench inside the white cave. He seemed at peace.

"Near the place where they crucified Him, there was a garden," he said. "This tomb meets all the requirements of a Jewish family tomb of the Roman period. There is the groove for the rolling stone, here the wide room and the slab. It is all as it should be. All this is further evidence that here is the true Calvary. When St. Helena came to Jerusalem in search of the place, there was tradition even then that this hill was Calvary. But she was unable to find a tomb. So the Holy Sepulchre site was selected. Many experts disagree with her choice. Sir Rider Haggard came here and was convinced that what he called 'these dread mysteries' were enacted here."

"Then Gordon did not live to see the formation of the Garden Tomb Association or the establishment of this as a shrine," I said. "A pity."

"Yes. He died in the fall of Khartoum."

I suddenly remembered the chilling shriek of the Mahdi's soldier who hurled the first spear at Chinese Gordon's breast, and I uttered it softly: " 'O cursed one, your time has come!' "

"I beg your pardon?" the warden asked.

"'O cursed one, your time has come.' The dervish who led the charge against Gordon is quoted as saying that. Probably apocryphal. Whether he said it or not, it fits the Gordon mystique. After all, he refused to be rescued and was determined to die a martyr in the Sudan. He had a notion that he wanted the sins of the people of the Sudan placed on him by God, so that these sins would crush him."

"He identified with Jesus," Dani said flatly.

"Hmmm," the warden said. "I am not so sure. Why not leave it that he was a devout Christian with an inquiring mind?"

We left it at that. Months later, rereading biographies of Gordon, I found that one of the General's correspondents, the Bishop of Newcastle, concluded that the leader of the Ever-Victorious Army had "wanted to die and wanted to die for the sins of the world." Was any man better equipped by nature and conviction to go in search of—and *find*—his own Calvary?

We walked into the blinding sunlight and circled the wooden benches at which sat the morning worshipers, a good, solid, elderly Protestant congregation. Two white-haired gentlemen passed among them, dispensing small pieces of bread and paper cups of wine.

"Look, look," Dani said, "there is an Orthodox Jew, a young Hasidic fellow, who comes here and prays. There he is."

On the rear bench sat a solitary worshiper in black round hat, black kaftan, with a black beard. He was a pale, slender man, reading silently from a prayer book. He accepted the bread and the wine.

"*Oi vay*, there he goes, partaking of the body and the blood," Dani muttered incredulously. "I used to argue with him, but it's no use. He can't be right in the head."

We paused at the small reception building and watched the service. The bearded young Hasid looked lost, adrift. His squinting eyes followed the text. His lips moved delicately.

"I have talked to him," the warden of the Garden Tomb said, "and I appreciate his coming here."

I watched Dani, the arching of the eyebrows, the stiffening of his back. One did not trifle with these sabras; they had small patience with converts and Christophiles.

"But what is he? A Jew? A Christian?" Dani's voice was sharp.

"No, he does not believe in Christ," the Reverend said. "I asked him once, 'When will you believe in Him?' "

"And what did he say?" I asked.

"He said, 'When all Christians have apologized to the Jews.' "

"He's not so crazy," I said to Dani as we walked north from the Garden Tomb. We were on our way to look at other tombs—it was a good day to walk into cool, lofty chambers and meditate. On our left was the Mea Shearim, the quarter of the extreme Orthodox. We would stop by on the way back from the tombs. At the twisted stump of a street barrier—one of those stripped poles—we paused.

"*Chaver*, here is what remains of the Mandelbaum Gate on the Jewish side. Up at the top of this street is the Jordanian end of it. The Musrara Quarter. Of course, it's all ours now."

There had been considerable destruction around us; we saw tumbled stones, empty lots littered with rubble, plaques commemorating the fighting. As we passed a deserted field, Dani suddenly sat down on a long, carved boulder and grinned at me.

"What am I sitting on?" he asked.

"Part of an old wall?"

"Correct. This stone has been identified as part of Agrippa's Wall, the Third Wall of Jerusalem. Notice how far north of the Old City it is."

"But if the Third Wall were this far north . . ."

"Yes, yes, you are catching on. If it *were*, and no one knows for sure if it were, or exactly when it was built, then neither Gordon's Calvary nor the Holy Sepulchre could have been the site of the Crucifixion. Remember the law against executions and burials inside the city wall?"

"Yes. Which means . . ."

"Maybe they haven't found the real Golgotha yet. Who knows, one of *our* archaeologists may dig it up some day for them."

We walked farther north to the Tomb of the Kings, at the corner of Nablus Road and St. George's Road. This curious mausoleum is the property of the French government, given to them by a wealthy family named Peireira.

Descending a long flight of stairs, one is greeted by two huge gouges in the face of the rock. These, however, are not the tombs, but water cisterns. To reach the tombs, one turns left into a vast courtyard, where a tremendously high facade, like the proscenium arch of a great stage, serves as the entrance-way to the tombs. And what an entrance it is! A Sherman tank could enter it with room to spare.

"What kings?" I asked. "Who merited such splendor?"

"Just a tradition. They used to think that the early kings of Judah were buried here. Wrong. It was built for Queen Helena, a lady from Mesopotamia, who came here in 45 C.E. and converted to Judaism. Back home, her subjects didn't want to follow her, so she brought her son Izates here, and their families. Her conversion is significant, a sign that a lot of Middle Eastern people were turning to monotheism. In 73 C.E., in the siege of Jerusalem, all of her grandchildren were killed."

We walked under the high carved facade of the vestibule, the carvings of wreaths and grapes and foliage still discernible, and into the catacombs. They seemed endless, room after room, two floors of funerary chambers.

"My goodness," I said. "That must have been quite a family Helena brought here from Mesopotamia."

"Oh, it was. Izates had forty-eight children."

The Tombs of the Sanhedrin were next on our schedule. It was a considerable walk, so we took a cab. The driver, who was a talkative type, sported a rakish straw hat, a chartreuse shirt, thick arms, a huge wristwatch.

"Do I know where the Sanhedriya are? Do I know?" he bellowed. "Sure I do. I'm a Bukharian. It's near the Bukharian quarter. Let me tell you, Bukharians are the best Jews. The best food. The best women. The best soldiers. We lived here under the Arab guns all these years and nobody moved out."

"So did the Orthodox in Mea Shearim," Dani said. He was unimpressed.

"Yeh, yeh." Suddenly he jerked a thumb at me, and they began to speak Hebrew. He was asking who I was, I gathered, if I were an American. Then he began talking Hebrew in an odd nasalized way, and I realized what he was doing. He was imitating the manner in which American Jews spoke the language. It was rather clever: harsh nasal sounds, sharp r's, flattened vowels.

"He doesn't speak any Hebrew," Dani said. "And he's with me, and I'm with the Ministry of Tourism."

Silence from the driver. I concluded that the rude intrusive cabbie is not only a phenomenon of New York City.

The Tombs of the Sanhedrin—sometimes called the Tombs of the Judges—are set in a charming park on the northern edge of Jerusalem. The suburb itself is residential, with many new apartment buildings and is adjacent to the Mea Shearim. At the northern end of Samuel Street, the main street in Sanhedriya, is the presumed tomb of the prophet Samuel, revered by Jews and Moslems.

The Garden of the Sanhedrin Catacombs is a rather remote place, thick with pines and cypresses, almost always deserted, and covered with winding paths and convenient rocks on which to sit, ruminate, and like Richard II, "tell sad stories of the death of kings."

But they were not kings who were buried in these caves hewn in the sandy rock, but judges, tribal elders. The Sanhedrin were on the order of a supreme court—a political and religious council consisting of seventy-one wise men. This high place, with its severe cliff, was selected as an honored burial place for these sages.

The entrance to the tombs is singularly impressive. A well-preserved lintel in the form of a flattened isosceles triangle spans the facade. On it are intricate carvings of pomegranates, citrons, and acanthus. Inside a small vestibule, the actual doorway to the catacombs has a smaller version of the triangular decoration.

A bearded gentleman in a quasimilitary uniform with campaign ribbons on his khaki tunic appeared. He was Rabbi Sharaga, he informed us, custodian of the Sanhedrin Tombs, a Persian. As he showed us through the trilevel cave in eerie candlelight, I realized that his short round beard and authoritarian Oriental face bore a striking resemblance to a distant relative of mine, long dead, a legendary Uncle Berrah who was known as "the Terrible Turk" because of a hot temper and hard fists. Rabbi Sharaga, however, was a gentle and polite fellow.

On the way out, he stopped to show us a small tomb cut in a corner of the cave. What was it? A child's? A place for second burial, to receive ossuaria containing the dry bones? The rabbi felt around, and with a pained expression on his face, extracted an empty beer bottle from the cavity.

"The workmen leave them there," Dani said when we were outside. "He's very upset. In olden times, they buried the old Torahs in those small tombs."

The finest *felafel* in Jerusalem, Dani said, was on a street in the Mea Shearim, not far from where he used to live. We took the taxicab driven by our loquacious Bukharian to the center of Mea Shearim and started to look for it. Dani's appetite was better than his memory. Jerusalem is a small city, and the Mea Shearim—the "Thousand Gates"—is a confined area, but we seemed to walk for an hour under the broiling sun. Around us paraded the Orthodox, the inspired, the elevated. I could not take my eyes off them. Of course I had seen Orthodox Jews before. I had been bar-mitzvahed in an Orthodox synagogue. When I said my last fare-well to Brooklyn, twenty years ago, at the time of my father's death, the Hasidim were well settled in Williamsburg and on Eastern Parkway. *Payes* and long cloaks and knee britches and those soft, unformed, bearded faces were no novelties to me.

Yet still I stared—at the *melameds*, the kids in yarmulkes, the Orthodox women in long-sleeved dresses, with kerchiefs covering their shaved heads, and the *shnorrers* (there are too many in Mea Shearim). I don't know why I was so moved. Perhaps it is because they seem to be satisfied with the answers they have found. They have their books, their God, their ritual, their unshakable belief. Everything has been explained to them. Does anyone else swim in such tranquil seas of certainty? Even the Roman Catholic Church is riven with disbelief and conten-tion these days. But the Orthodox of Mea Shearim appear to be untroubled by the modern world, its confusions, and its temp-tations.

"How do you feel about them?" I asked Dani. Many Israelis had told me they detested the extreme Orthodox. Parasites, hypo-crites, cowards, were some of the epithets I had heard used by otherwise mild-mannered Jews.

"I like them. They have preserved the traditions."

"But they don't fight in the army, and your army means every-thing to you."

"I'll forgive them."

A troop of residents went by, burly men in round-brimmed hats, striped, loosely belted cloaks, white stockings, black Oxfords. "Look at them," I said. "Filled with the eternal verities. Isn't it maddening how they've stopped the clock when this country's main article of belief is the future?"

"Maybe." He pointed to the holy men. "Notice the red beards. Red hair is common among a certain group here, which ones I can't be sure. I think they are Russians, big men. You know, they're all diversified. Look down any street, any alley, you'll see a sign for a school, a synagogue. Mostly from different parts of Eastern Europe. In this section it's the *Sieben Gebirgen*, the 'Seven Villages.' They're from Translyvania, the border between Hungary and Romania. The clothing sometimes tells you."

"And I suppose there are the usual sectarian rivalries. Who is holier than who, who gets the word more directly from God."

"Of course. There's one group here, the Naturei Karta, who are convinced they are the holiest. They're anti-Zionist. You should see some of the stuff they publish—Zionism is the enemy of the Jews, the Jews don't need a state, Israel is a militaristic state, a chauvinistic, nationalistic state which defies the Torah. Because it's secular. You can imagine how that kind of thing goes down with the Ministry of Defense. Personally, I don't think they're a real threat. I know, I know, lots of sabras hate them and call them names. Me, I'm tolerant. I like to listen to them argue and score points."

Most of the children on the bright street sported curly *payes*, twists of hair in front of their small ears. They all wore yarmul-kes, and despite the heat, I saw the fringes and knots of *tsitsis*, the Orthodox undervest, peeking from some shirttails. A boy of about eight, with no sideburns and no yarmulke, came running out of an alley.

"Ask him why he has no *payes*," I requested.

They conversed for a moment. Dani laughed. "You see, never a straight answer from them. He says he gave them as a present. I asked to whom, and he said, the barber."

A barefoot girl with eyes like black grapes walked up to us and begged. A few yards down the street a dirty-looking, unshaven man in a workman's cap approached us and asked for money. Dani was embarrassed. "It's bad, very bad. One of the few places in Israel you will find beggars. It's a rotten tradition, and the rabbis should crack down on them."

We turned down an alley. The area leading off the main street of Mea Shearim is a complex of neat apartments, synagogues, and schools. Clothes dried crisply in the torrid sun. Housewives scurried about doing their chores. An occasional bearded religious, lost in sacred thoughts, wandered by.

"Do they work?" I asked.

"Most of them. Many are excellent craftsmen."

I noticed bilingual posters stuck on buildings, storefronts. One protested the continuation of autopsies. In violent, threatening language, it promised to bring down the infidels who permitted them. "They have a talent for raising hell," I said.

"They are a tough bunch. They stopped the digging at the Western Wall a few weeks ago. Whenever you stop an archaeologist in this country, you are using a lot of muscle."

We walked into a school, a wide, ungainly, three-story stone building with a sign over the door. "Do they mind our just walking in like this?" I asked.

"The tourists come here all the time to look. They take your name and you'll get appeals for money from them the rest of your life."

In a peeling, dirty lobby—I was shivered by memories of Brownsville and the *kheydr* of Tiphereth Hagro—a circular washbasin stood in the midst of the floor. Several older boys in traditional uniform—flat black hat, knee britches, coats, stockings—were there washing hands. One was a grossly fat youth of about fifteen with orange hair and a squashed nose. His *payes* dangled like two thin carrots. At once I felt sorry for him. He was a grotesque, a sad clown.

"Can we go in?" Dani asked.

"Do I have a gun?" the fat redhead responded. (Dani translated the colloquy for me later.)

"Where is the rabbi?"

"Maybe in the classroom. Maybe not."

"What's the name of this school?"

"Read the sign over the door."

We walked up a flight of stairs. "Fresh kid," I said. "Why was he so snotty?"

"It's a game they play. Everything has a twist. I enjoyed it."

I found myself awed by the redheaded *yeshiva bukher*. Given a different career he would have become a natural butt, a scapegoat and a punching bag, a classical homely fat boy. But he had been endowed with a sharp tongue and a surefootedness that had to be respected. A slum-born child who probably could not fight or run, he had forged a superb armor for himself. In faith, he had found strength and guile.

We shook hands with some teachers and were allowed to peek into classrooms. I was surprised at the youthfulness and the vigorous mien of the *melameds*. They had clear eyes, strong chins (what was visible beneath the whiskers), and gave you a firm handshake. The air of Jerusalem, no doubt. And proximity to God. The students stared at us, giggled, whispered behind white hands. Once, a youth got up and walked up to the teacher, a lean, black-bearded, blue-eyed man wearing a striped kaftan. They discussed a fine point in the text, and the boy returned.

"What was that all about?" I whispered.

Dani frowned. "A subtle point about proper behavior to a neighbor. This is all legal stuff, you know. It's like going to law school."

Outside we wandered through the sun-flooded backyards of Mea Shearim. We passed three more schools, one of them still under construction, although we could hear the chanting from within. I felt like the character in the *Rubáiyát:* "Why nods the drowsy worshipper outside?" Suddenly I was unsteady on my feet. The vapors of sanctity, the heat of tradition, the sun of God's city were too much for me to bear. I was not staggering under a burden of guilt, or sorrow, or fear. Rather I was bemused, numbed, by these guardians of the Word.

"Look," I protested. "Why are they so avid, so eager? They lived in expectation of coming to Jerusalem, and they made it."

"That's just part of it. Now they await the Messiah."

Drifting through the streets, we stumbled on the select *felafel* stand and sat down at a small outdoor table. This was typical West Jerusalem—poorly stocked small shops, apartments suggesting the Brooklyn of my youth, dark cheeky kids. There was nothing terribly exotic or Oriental about it. It was closer to Howard Avenue of the 1930's than to my preconceptions about golden Jerusalem. But it was pleasant and *haimish*. The *felafel* sandwich, washed down with tart Jaffa grapefruit juice, was a treat. *Felafel* consists of deep-fried balls of chick-pea paste. They are served stuffed into a pocket of a split half-circle of Arab bread—*pita*—garnished with green salad, spices, and sometimes a dash of sesame paste, *techina*. It is immensely satisfying and forms a block of cement in one's stomach, a kind of nourishing blob, from which body and blood draw sustenance for many hours.

As we dined—I think our lunch cost sixty cents—we heard the shouts of an argument. A few black-eyed kids had gathered around two agitated people about fifty feet away. Finishing our grapefruit juice, we wandered down the street to observe what was shattering the afternoon stillness of Mea Shearim.

A woman—one can only describe her as stunning, with the kind of face that creates instantaneous desire—was giving hell to a young man. She was in her early twenties and she was hardly dressed like an Orthodox housewife from a Hasidic family. She wore her black hair in a ragged mod cut. Her pink blouse was form-fitting and her bright green bell-bottoms hung low on her blossoming hips, girdled with a dangly metallic belt. Her skin was dark, her lips (even as they hurled Hebraic imprecations at the man) were full and wet. But her eyes! They were out of some biblical tale of passion or terror: huge, flashing, hot, glinting with the light that illumined the eyes of Jezebel, Bath-sheba, Queen Esther, and Deborah.

The young man, by comparison, was a clod. Loutish, a variety of street wise-guy, the kind my father would have called a "cake eater," he wore a brimmed cap, a red kerchief, and sported elegant sideburns, which he stroked as the lady told him off. She shook her fist under his nose, she jabbed a finger at him. He remained silent.

"What's it all about?" I asked Dani.

"She's threatening to get her brothers after him if she ever sees

him again. Ah, now it comes out," Dani said. He whispered to
me. "He patted her *tuchas*. Right on the street."

"Who can blame him? It's gorgeous."

"I agree," Dani said. "But here? In Mea Shearim?"

I watched her swivel off. A woman brimming with mystery and
love and anger. "Return, O daughter of the Shulamite." But we
never saw her again.

It was Dani's last day with us. He had some American television people to look after. Although he would not be able to accom-
pany us, we would see him from time to time.

"Well, to wind it up," he said, "we'll pay our respects to King
David. His tomb is on Mount Zion."

The complex of buildings on Mount Zion is interesting as a
sample of the ecumenical spirit, although I found them esthetically less inspiring than I had hoped. Perhaps brotherhood breeds
indifference to art. Is it possible that a burning sense of exclusivity
makes for superior creative efforts?

On the way up to the cluster of holy places on Mount Zion, one
passes the famed windmill of the Yemin Moshe Colony. This
suburb, named for Sir Moses Montefiore, was the first Jewish
community in Jerusalem built outside the walls of the Old City.
It was begun in 1860 and financed largely by the American
Jewish millionaire, Judah Touro of New Orleans.

"You've heard of him?" Dani asked.

"Yes. There's a famous hospital named for him in New Orleans.
In fact, a great jazz trumpeter whom I used to hear when I was in
college, a man named Muggsy Spanier, once wrote and recorded
a song about his convalescence there. It was called 'Relaxin' at the
Touro.'"

My friend and guide studied me with aloof appreciation. "Ah,
you know a little bit about everything. You never forget a detail
when it interests you. You would have made a great Talmudical
scholar."

On Mount Zion the two main attractions are the Dormition
Monastery and a peculiar domed building—it was at one time a
mosque—shared in seeming tranquillity by Orthodox Jews and
devout Christians each in their own special way. Moslems also

participate in revering the Jewish section, since they, too, honor King David.

We wandered first through the Dormition Abbey, where, Christian tradition says, the Virgin Mary fell into her eternal sleep. Its official name is Dormition Sanctae Mariae—the "Sleep of St. Mary." It is a new work, early twentieth century, and the style is pseudo-Roman. Because it is relatively small, and rather simple, and because the modern mosaics have a bright innocence about them, it comes off rather well—more so than the Church of the Annunciation in Nazareth. The mosaic in the floor includes the signs of the zodiac, but as colorful as it is, it lacks the golden glow and simple charm of the zodiac at Hamath Tiberias. Age does wonders for stone and mosaic. In the crypt a work of sculpture shows Jesus calling to his mother in heaven. The inscription is from the Song of Songs: "Arise my love, my dove, my beautiful one and come." This seemed a blamelessly guileless application of Solomon's song.

The domelike building that is the other important site on Mount Zion is two things. On its ground floor is the tomb of King David; above is the purported Hall of the Last Supper, or Cénacle (in French), or Cenaculum (in Latin). This latter room is most impressive: clean, uncluttered, whitewashed, a Franciscan restoration with some of the original Crusader columns and wall decorations. The stones in the floor are worn and irregular. A Moslem *mihrab*, or prayer niche, forms a cheerful, ornate break in the stark Gothic lines and blends harmoniously with the vaulted arches. Whether it was actually the room where Jesus and his disciples celebrated the first seder of Passover, I am not certain, nor are the biblical experts. But it certainly *could* have been the room in which Jesus sat, and ate, and prayed. "And he will show you a large upper room furnished and prepared: there make ready for us."

Having seen the original of da Vinci's *Last Supper*, dishearteningly faded and cracked, in Milan, I was willing to believe. Jerusalem does this to skeptics. Most people I spoke to made wry faces at the mention of the Cénacle building. They were inclined to be dubious of both the room of the Last Supper and David's Tomb. I was now willing to be tolerant. Certainly the Last Supper took place in an upper room somewhere. Why not this wide, airy chamber?

Thus Christians venerate the upper story, while Jews and Moslems hold the downstairs to be sanctified. It seems a fair arrangement, even though I was dismayed by David's Tomb. I wish I could have been more generous. One entered it via a gloomy anteroom, then a prayer room in which several bearded old men were praying or resting on benches, then the small chamber, containing the tomb itself. This is a large stone sarcophagus covered with a toxic green cloth. Silver Torah crowns adorn the long stone coffin. Several elders were praying before the sepulchre where presumably the warrior-musician-king is buried. The room was somber, the stone coffin not quite convincing, the billiard-green coverlet not especially dignified.

"It lacks conviction," I said. "I'm not sold on David's Tomb."

"Because of the way it looks? That doesn't prove the case one way or the other. But I guess you're right. I don't know that it's ever been authenticated. Like many of these places, an old tradition keeps it going. The Arabs worshipped it as the sepulcher of Nawi Daud, the prophet David. Benjamin of Tudela, the rabbi who traveled here in the twelfth century, claimed that in 1158, when they were rebuilding a ruined church, the tomb was discovered. But there's no real evidence."

We exited through another dark room where I was required to sign a book and make a contribution: homage to David. "I know what's bothering me," I said. "It's not in keeping with David. Let's be honest. It isn't his kind of place. David was a singer, a dancer, a lover, a warrior. God's darling. He literally got away with murder. Think of poor Uriah the Hittite. David requires something happier and brighter, something reflecting his gay worldliness. If he really is under that sarcophagus in that dark hall, he can't be pleased."

"I suppose not. But a little fiction never hurt. And if *they* want to think the Last Supper took place upstairs, we should be permitted David's Tomb downstairs. After all, they're only tenants. We're the landlords."

CHAPTER VIII

Dr. Negev and
Dr. Glueck

Abraham Negev is a short muscular man with prematurely iron-gray hair, a thoughtful manner, and a hard-earned reputation as one of the great experts on the archaeology of the Negev. I met him at a cocktail party at the Hebrew Union College of Cincinnati building on King David Street. I had been anxious to talk to some of the archaeologists connected with the college, especially its director, Dr. Nelson Glueck.

Dr. Glueck agreed to meet with me the following day in his office. Then he pointed to Dr. Negev. "You might want to talk to Dr. Negev. He's doing some fascinating work at Mampsis."

For an embarrassing reason, but one that any Israeli would understand, I had assumed Dr. Negev was a journalist. His right hand is missing. In its place he wears an artificial hand encased in a black glove. Some years back, in Belgrade, I had met an

Israeli journalist who was similarly handicapped and wore a
gloved artificial hand also and, as nearly as I could recall, bore a
facial resemblance to the archaeologist.

"No, my only writing is on archaeological subjects," Dr. Negev
said in a gentle voice. "If you are an amateur, a man with no
training, get my books *Cities in the Desert,* which is mostly about
Avdat, and one called *Caesarea.* They are written for the general
public."

I told Dr. Negev how impressed I had been with Avdat, the
honey-brown stones on the windy heights.

"Yes, it is a beautiful place. But it is mainly a Byzantine city
built on top of a Nabatean city. Very little that is pure Nabatean
is still visible. Mampsis, on the other hand, is probably the best-
preserved Nabatean site in Israel. Will you be able to go down
again to see it?"

I said I would not, on this visit, but that I valued the luxury of
keeping some places unseen, so that my next visit to Israel I
would enjoy them even more, on a second round of archaeological delights.

He smiled. "Sometimes it's good to wait a while. You might be
interested in how I became an archaeologist. I was working at
Kibbutz Rivivim in the Negev. It is south of Beersheba. This was
in 1944, and the kibbutz was only a year old. I had been in Israel
eleven years, arriving in 1933 from Pinsk in Poland. My name then
was Eisenberg. But when I came to the Negev, I was enchanted
by it, and took the name for my underground work. Later I got
rid of Eisenberg for good. In any event, I had an interest in
archaeology, and Rabbi Magnus offered me a scholarship to come
to Jerusalem and study. It was a great opportunity for a young
man. As you probably know by now, kibbutz decisions are collective decisions. So a vote was taken on whether I could accept the
scholarship and give up farming for archaeology. I was turned
down."

"That seems rather short-sighted, in terms of the career you
had later. You'd think they would have let you go."

"They had a very good reason not to." Dr. Negev smiled tolerantly. After all these years, he could forgive, he could understand.
"There were only eight people on the whole kibbutz."

"When did you finally get a chance to study archaeology?"

"Not until after the war. In 1948, of course, we were at war. I became a desert commander, in charge of the defense of Rivivim. I had a huge army, fourteen girls and sixteen men, thirty people. We were under attack by a thousand Egyptians, and we held them off. In fairness I must say they did not try too hard to take us. Their main thrust was up the coast to Tel Aviv and they never quite got there. I lost my hand in the fighting."

I asked Dr. Negev how his career was advanced after the war.

"In 1954, I had begun my studies. With much encouragement from Dr. Glueck, I got my degrees at the Hebrew University in Jerusalem. I am senior lecturer in archaeology at the university. I did a great deal of work at Avdat in 1958, '59, and '60, and as you have seen, it is a beautiful place, but I suspect that Mampsis will be even more dramatic once it is accessible."

"Then you are finished digging there?"

"We began in 1965 and finished in 1967, but it will take us several years to sort out the find. For example, one of the most spectacular finds at Mampsis—or Kurnub, to use its Arab name—was a hoard of ten thousand Roman coins. Most are from the reigns of the emperors between Commodus and Diadumenianus. We believe that the large monetary value of these coins indicates extensive commercial or perhaps military activity in Mampsis. Mampsis was presumably a prosperous place. The presence of rich frescoes would also support this thesis. But why was the town so completely abandoned in the middle of the second century c.e.? So completely, incidentally, that no one even bothered to come back and claim the treasure! And I assure you it was a treasure. I estimate that the value of those coins in their time was forty thousand work days of a laborer, or equal in value to eleven hundred slaves. Well, that is the sort of thing we have facing us with the material we have discovered in Mampsis."

"You say Mampsis is a more truly Nabatean town than Avdat?" I was scribbling notes frantically.

"There is no question about it. At Avdat, perhaps ninety-five per cent of the Nabatean homes and other buildings were destroyed by the Byzantine Christians. At Mampsis, most of the buildings have remained intact. This is of great interest to us. You know, by 135 c.e., the Nabateans were replaced by some Semitic newcomers, we aren't sure who. And only thirty years earlier the

last Nabatean king had died, and the domain was annexed to
Rome. So anything that is of pure Nabatean origin is of great
importance. If you come to see me at the university, I'll give you
some of my articles on Mampsis, and, of course, when you have
occasion to visit the Negev again, you will go see it for yourself."

"What caused the decline of the Nabateans?" I asked. "I've
read about the way they made profits out of the spice trade, of
their way stations along the trade routes from the Orient. But why
the swift decline?"

"We are not certain. Their fall in 135 may be related to the Bar
Kochba revolt. They were, at many periods, rather close to the
Jews. Many wealthy Jews owned property in Nabatean lands.
There are records of palm plantations owned in Nabatean places,
by Jewish kings. And if you have read Dr. Glueck's book, *Rivers
in the Desert,* you know about their water systems, the catchments and cisterns and tunnels. All this enabled them to turn to
agriculture when the spice trade bypassed them."

"You know the Negev as a farmer, a soldier, and an archaeologist," I said. "Are you absolutely convinced it can sustain large
populations again? This seems to be an obsession with Israelis,
and I wonder, having seen the barrenness of the place, those
lonely patches of green, whether it is a dream with any substance.
I don't think you people indulge in self-deceit, but still . . ."

Dr. Negev smiled faintly. "Have you tasted the peaches at Sde
Boker?"

"That's Ben-Gurion's kibbutz. No. We passed it, but we didn't
have a chance to stop."

"They grow the best peaches in Israel. The soil of the Negev is
the richest, the most laden with good chemicals."

"But a single crop of juicy peaches, even if Ben-Gurion helped
grow them, is not the same as a whole new populated area."

"You saw Professor Evenari's agricultural station at Avdat. He
has grown trees, wheat, vegetables using Nabatean techniques.
They have learned that if you plant trees, they will need to be
watered the first and second years—and then natural rainfall will
do the trick, provided a proper catchment system is installed."

"Dr. Negev, forgive me, but I have read about the Avdat experiment, and I seem to recall that thirty acres of catch-basin
areas were needed to water one acre. I don't have to be an agron-

omist or a population expert to realize that such a ratio will not sustain a large community, in the Negev or anywhere else."

"Yes, you are right, and we are aware of it. But the example is an encouraging one. Actually, two things are needed to convert the Negev into a flourishing agricultural region. One is atomic power to produce desalinated seawater in large quantities."

"And the other?"

"The three million Jews in the Soviet Union."

"I can envision the first requirement. That is a technological problem, and with wit, and money, and energy it can be solved. But I can't imagine the Soviets with their attitude toward Jews and Israel, and their dirty games with the Arabs, letting the Jews migrate here. How can you even think that such an event will take place in our lifetime? Or any time in the near future?"

The stocky, one-handed man seemed dismayed by my pessimism. "Stranger things have happened, Mr. Green. Who can predict the course of history? Who could say that we would be here today, a strong nation, progressing, making our way, building? Some morning the men in the Kremlin may wake up, feel differently, and send us our three million brothers. Then, then you will see a Negev, a different Negev, more glorious than in Nabatean times."

"Your optimism is admirable. I wish it were grounded in hard facts. I have a feeling you are too hopeful, because I keep hearing about these Russian Jews all the time, and . . ."

"And you shall keep hearing about them, until they are with us."

Dr. Nelson Glueck agreed to meet with me the following afternoon in his office at the Hebrew Union College offices on King David Street. I had read *Rivers in the Desert* and some of his articles, and I had known about him ever since he had been on the cover of *Time* magazine some years ago. Glueck is a legendary figure, a man of such varied and awesome achievements that I was somewhat timid about approaching him. He is a rabbi, the spiritual leader of Reformed Judaism in America; a college president; a renowned archaeologist; a biblical scholar; a graceful writer; and above all, he is a presence, a commanding and luminous figure.

We met in his office, and I began awkardly apologizing. "I'm a hopeless amateur, Dr. Glueck. All I can offer is my enthusiasm, and a career as a professional writer."

This seemed to interest him; he asked about some of my novels, then showed me his latest book, *Deities and Dolphins*. "You should read this when you get back to the States. Farrar, Straus and Giroux brought it out in 1965, and I think they did an admirable job with it. These big picture books are questionable things, they told me, but this one did surprisingly well."

I glanced at the large handsome volume and said that it did seem a beautiful job of bookmaking, but that the editors and publishers had rather rich material to work with, and that the author brought considerable prestige and talent to the project. This touched off a discussion of book design, first printings, advertising, word-of-mouth, publishers' peculiarities, and other esoterica dear to the hearts of writers. Enthusiastically, I joined in the dialogue—which had nothing to do with archaeology—and I could see what Dr. Glueck had so graciously done. To set me at ease, we had begun our talk with a subject that I knew a little about: books.

"Yes, I'm rather proud of *Deities and Dolphins*," he said. "The thesis I developed is an intriguing one, and one which is being proven at this very moment. I saw you talking to Dr. Negev the other day, and the story involves him also."

I had my pen and pad out. The man had captivated me already. To begin with, Nelson Glueck is a singularly impressive-looking man. Gray-haired, handsome in a spare, masculine way, possessed of that high color which is a result of long hours out-of-doors, and a natural inclination to vigor and action, he has a face that commands attention. His manner of speaking is forceful and forensic, and suggests neither the classroom nor the pulpit nor the dig, but a happy amalgam of all three. When he speaks he can be heard as the voice of Ecclesiastes, or Harvard, or Tel Gezer. Moreover, his slender, muscular figure—he is seventy years old—dispenses with any of the conventional nonsense about the softness and lethargy of the clergyman or scholar. Dr. Glueck is trim and tough and supple, his body advertising that competent leanness we associate with quintessential Americans like Gary

Cooper (there is even a facial resemblance) or Mark Van Doren or, on the fictional level, Natty Bumppo.

Did I tell myself these things because I wanted so desperately that a distinguished rabbi, a Jewish scholar, a great friend of Israel, be closely identified in my mind with paradigmatic Americans? Perhaps. If so, I think it was an excusable act of identification. We all long for Jews who are lean and tough and competent. Good-bye forever to soft hands and fat cheeks and mumbled excuses!

Apparently I am not the only one who has been impressed with Dr. Glueck's commanding appearance. Back in Stamford months later, I was to hear of a story that reinforced my concept of him as a born leader. In the thirties, early in his digging career, I was told, Nelson Glueck and some of his party were captured by a band of Arab brigands, who threatened to kill them.

"You dare not lay a hand on me," he was reputed to have warned the chief bandit. "I am the Prince of Wales, and if so much as a hair of my head is touched, the entire British Empire will descend on you and seek vengeance."

Dr. Glueck showed me a photograph of a stone dolphin decoration in his book. "Why are there dolphins in Nabatean tombs? We think they adopted them through contact with Hellenistic and Roman peoples. The Nabateans were traders, and they went to Greece and Rome and North Africa, where dolphins were used as a motif. But still, they were a desert people, a land-based people, and we know that the dolphin is basically a symbol of pelagic peoples.

"Why, then, this use of the dolphin? We theorized thus: First, the dolphin has traditionally been honored by sailors as a benign creature that leads them to safe harbor. The Nabateans understood this, and adopted him as a talisman, a kindly animal that guided their caravans across the seas of the desert. But the dolphin also appears in Nabatean tombs. Why? Well, they extended the dolphin's symbolic powers and came to regard it as a guide through that journey which all mortals must take, the journey to the hereafter.

"These theories were all supported by Dr. Negev's finds at Kurnub-Mampsis. He found some marvelous gold Nabatean dolphins

there, and as further proof, a dolphin goddess, all of this backing
up the theories we had developed about dolphin symbolism
among a desert people. I daresay few discoveries by my colleagues have given me greater satisfaction over the years than
these substantiating discoveries of Abraham Negev."

I said that he seemed to look at archaeology in a somewhat
more romantic fashion than many archaeologists, that he had a
lively sense of drama.

"Oh, this work is filled with romance," Dr. Glueck said. "There
is romance and adventure in every spade of earth we turn
over. You can discuss it in plain scholarly language, or you can be
moved by it on a rather different level. I suppose the Nabateans
affect me strongly. When I began my work, we knew very little
about them. We thought of them as nomads, as marginal traders.
Soon we learned that they were great traders indeed. A new concept about them developed. No, they were not mere subsistence
wanderers. They were too sophisticated. Today, we have identified over five hundred Nabatean sites. As far back as 1938 I'd
looked at my first Nabatean ruins—and they were not remains of
nomadic settlements, but mountain-top villages. Byzantine at first
glance, but Nabatean below.

"What is the lure of this kind of discovery, of the challenge of
archaeology? I can tell you it is a great deal more than digging
into the ground and finding pottery and assigning a date to the
fragments. The lure of archaeology is this reaching back into the
past, which of course is a vital part of our present and our future,
and determining how the three are tied together. It involves
pushing back the horizons of knowledge. It seeks to re-create history, to breathe life into history, as Dr. Negev and I sought to do
with our dolphins. An archaeologist often has the same feelings as
a sculptor working in stone."

I asked Dr. Glueck if Arab-Israeli enmities could be better
understood or clarified in the light of archaeological discoveries.
He frowned, not in anger (I trust), but as if trying to formulate
his thoughts.

"Let's discuss the Arabs. They came from northern Arabia.
Around the fifth century B.C. they appear as an identifiable
group, at about the time when Aramaic became the *lingua franca*
of this region. They rose to significance at a time when a series
of disturbances—we aren't sure what they were, climatic, geolo-

gic—affected the cities. Simultaneously, the Israeli people were
coming to power in this area. Naturally, rivalries would develop.
Now I have long had a theory that the Bedu, the desert nomads,
are always hungry. When the central political figures, the more
complex societies, are weakened and cannot defend themselves, the Bedu begin to move on in search of food. I sometimes
have the feeling that the Bedu in the fullness of their weakness
will inherit the earth, simply because they can *wait*. They can
live on next to nothing. When the urban and societal centers are
debilitated, the Bedu seize the land. Gradually, they settle in, and
build up a new civilization. Then they vanish, and in turn new
Bedu move in and replace them. That has pretty much been the
history of many places in this part of the world."

In Dr. Glueck's white, modern, air-conditioned office, I became
afraid of those hungry Bedu, those black-shrouded gliding spec-
ters, those desert wanderers, drifting into the cities as the political
power diminished, the armies lost heart, the granaries emptied.
I did not like the idea. I wondered if the tough men in the Knesset and the Israeli Army shared his views. Or whether he himself
would extend his rather terrifying analysis of the ebb and flow of
Palestinian civilizations to the present day. Perhaps technology
would make the difference. The urban centers, the existing political forces, aided by some of the shrewdest minds of the age, and
armed with a dedication that transcended that of the Roman, or
Byzantine, or Nabatean elites, would repel those mysterious wanderers.

"This characteristic of patience, of the capacity to wait," I said,
"isn't the sole property of Bedouin. Anthropologists say the same
of Africans. John Masters told me the same thing in regard to
East Indians. And it's argued that we can't win the Vietnam war
because we'll be out-waited. Students of the American Indian
report the same thing—that the one thing an Indian can do better
than any white man is wait. Maybe it's a result of a simple hunting culture, in which there isn't much for the men to do, either in
the way of productive labor or pastime. Having nothing to do,
they cultivate the wasting of time. And perhaps it isn't the virtue
we say it is."

Dr. Glueck smiled. "Yes, I may overstate the power of waiting,
of sheer patience. It is simply that in his seeming resignation, the
Bedu possesses a powerful weapon for survival, if not for eventual

mastery of the land. You must keep in mind that this part of the world, this Palestine littoral, the Negev, the adjacent lands, has been a cockpit, an arena, a battlefield. Look at it as the meeting-ground of the two ancient powers of the East, the Egyptian and Mesopotamian. For centuries they kept moving in and out, fighting, killing, conquering, now one in ascendance, now the other. Then it became a testing ground for the Greeks and the Romans. And always some foreign power, some invader from East or West, asserting himself on this strip of land at the eastern edge of the Mediterranean, and then being challenged by another.

"There was an old notion that Jerusalem was the physical center of the world, the navel. It is almost true. One can view it quite naturally as the spiritual heartland of the world. That is self-evident. But I am almost convinced that it lies at a definite physical center, a point where the great land masses of Asia, Europe, and Africa converge. It is not only the religious capital of the universe but an actual one in terms of cultures and geography. Many have speculated thus. Men like Halford, McKinder, and Karl Haushofer, the father of *Geopolitik*, speculated on the possibility. It explains the German preoccupation with *Drang nach Osten*, the push to the east, this urge to dominate the Middle East. Palestine's blessing and its curse lie in its geographical position. It is truly a crossroads of East and West, even if one rejects the theory that it lies at the center of the earth. It stands between Asia, Africa, and Europe, and in that respect it is the center of this hemisphere."

It seemed to me, I commented, an awesome responsibility for the Jews of modern Israel, assuming the governorship of this crucial land, making themselves stewards of such a vital historical and geographical area.

"Their claims here are rather strong," Dr. Glueck said. "Look back to ancient times. Take the Edomites, the descendants of Esau. Or the Kenites, who supplied Moses with a wife. Or the Midianites, or the Judeans. Now in terms of culture, of language, there isn't a dime's worth of difference between any of them. And what were the Jews of ancient times? A handful of nomads, desert people, not even camel-nomads, as I've pointed out, but ass-nomads. Yet they survived down to present times. And made one of mankind's most glorious discoveries, the concept of a god of history. All the other ancient peoples vanished as entities, as cultures, but the Jews did not. Look at our friends the Nabateans—vanished, utterly, absorbed by the Romans, replaced by other Semites. Why? Well, they were good traders and builders, but they had no Greek philosophy, no Roman laws, no Hebrew religion. They had no enduring values."

"They had no poets, and they died," I said, feeling rather sorry for the Nabateans.

"That's quite accurate. But poetry in itself, or law, or art, isn't enough to guarantee a people's survival. Roman law has survived, but there is no modern Roman people who can identify with it, and most Italians would admit that. Mussolini wouldn't. He tried to concoct some kind of modern Roman man, but it didn't work."

"I can vouch for that, having lived in Italy. The Italians have many virtues, and one is frankness. They'd be the first to admit that there are no more emperors," I said.

"I don't mean to denigrate contemporary Italy," he continued. "Greek aesthetics remain a vital force in the world, and thank goodness they are. But modern Greece—her people, her culture, her philosophy—bears no relation to classical Greece. No large body of modern Greeks celebrate and maintain and nourish Aeschylus or Socrates. But among Jews, our religion, with its code of ethics and moral system, persists and thrives and grows in the hearts and minds of a living people. I have no hesitation about saying this."

I asked Dr. Glueck a question that had been bothering me ever since I had begun my travels: "Is it possible that some archaeologists and historians in Israel conveniently find what they are looking for because of this overwhelming sense of continuity? Does the need to justify the present in terms of the past sometimes result in a sort of high-level serendipity? Nothing to match St. Helena's convenient discoveries, but at least a tendency to *interpret* discoveries in terms of the Bible?"

"I imagine some of that goes on," Dr. Glueck said. "There are some—not many—archaeologists who let their emotional identification with the past color their scientific thinking. I like to think that I, and the men I have trained and worked with, utilize a strict scientific approach to all our digging." He smiled a wry rabbinical smile. "You know, I never occupied a pulpit. So perhaps that's why I am so devoted to the scientific method."

"But Dr. Glueck, quite frankly, I can't help feeling dubious when an archaeologist tells me that this particular tel is where Abraham pitched his tent, or that King David is actually buried in that building down the street from here."

"Let me refresh your memory," he said. He opened a copy of *Rivers in the Desert.* "I stated my beliefs rather clearly in this book: 'The purpose of the biblical historian and archaeologist is not to prove the correctness of the Bible. It is primarily a theological document, which can never be proved, because it is based on belief in God, whose being can be scientifically suggested but never scientifically demonstrated. . . . Saga and song, legend and myth, fact and folklore were woven into the text to illustrate and emphasize the central theme.' "

"But aren't archaeologists tempted sometimes?"

"Not if they are good ones." He read again: " 'Those people are essentially of little faith who seek through archaeological corroboration of historical source materials in the Bible to validate religious teachings and spiritual insights. The archaeological explorer in Bible lands must be aware of the fact that as important as the Bible is for historical information, it is definitely not primarily a chronicle of history, as we understand the term today. It is above all concerned with true religion and only secondarily with illustrative methods. Even if the latter had suffered through faulty transmission or embellishments, the purity and primacy of the Bible's innermost message would not be diminished.' "

"I understand that, but . . ."

"Listen to this. I can't make the point more clearly." He read again: " 'As a matter of fact, however, it may be stated categorically that no archaeological discovery has ever controverted a biblical reference. Scores of archaeological findings have been made which confirm in clear outline or in exact detail historical statements in the Bible. And by the same token, proper evaluation of biblical descriptions has often led to amazing discoveries. They form tesserae in the vast mosaic of the Bible's almost incredibly correct historical memory.' "

"But isn't the amorphous quality of the Bible one of the reasons

that's so?" I asked. "You mentioned song, legend, myth, folklore.
Doesn't that in effect give you greater leeway? You can date a
potsherd, interpret an inscription, decide whether a site is Middle
or Late Bronze, all with great accuracy. And when you match
these provable facts against the Bible, you are rarely in conflict
with it, because the Bible itself is a theological and literary document, possessing elasticity, a plastic quality. I don't mean that it
is malleable in a moral sense, but only in regard to names, places,
dates, and so on."

"That may be. But I would still insist that no archaeological
discovery to date has yet disproved a well-understood statement
of the Bible."

"I read recently about your discovery of Ezion Geber, King
Solomon's port city, and how you concluded that the Bible was
geographically correct in locating it where it was. Can you give
me another example?"

Dr. Glueck paused a moment. "I could give you scores. But
look at the work I did in Transjordan and the Negev for twenty
years. I began in 1932, dug there until 1947, then returned after
the War of Independence. We had been told for years that the
Negev was uninhabited and uninhabitable. I refused to believe it.
The Bible said it *was* inhabited. Abraham traveled through it.
You were at Tel Beersheba. Solomon had mines deep in the
Negev. That meant that the land had to sustain population. I
wanted to show that the Negev could support human life, entire
communities. In Ezekiel we read, 'This land that was desolate is
become like the Garden of Eden.' We proved that the Negev *had*
been inhabited for millennia. There was a stretch of five hundred
years when the Negev was continuously inhabited—from the time
of Solomon at the end of the tenth century B.C. down to the sixth
century, when Judah was destroyed by the Babylonians. Later
there is a stretch of almost eight hundred years, from the start of
the Nabatean period in the second century B.C. down to the end
of the Byzantine era, in the seventh century.

"Of course, it isn't all statistics and dating and mathematical
calculations. There is immense fun in this work: adventure,
romance, discovery. It is the most intoxicating work in the world.
I can't think of anything I would rather have done, or any part
of the world in which I would rather dig. This challenge of open-

ing the doors of the past, of locating and verifying the tangible remains of a past that is part of my heritage, and a part of my son's patrimony—it is something that has gratified me beyond measure."

"I gather many Israelis feel that way about archaeology."

"Indeed they do. There is a national infatuation with the stones of history. I do some lecturing here, and I never have any trouble drawing an audience of a thousand or two thousand. These people have an awareness of their identity—who they are, and where they originated, and what their contribution to history has been, that is most striking."

"What has been Judaism's greatest contribution?" I asked. "Is there a single moment, in the Bible, for example, that we can point to?"

Dr. Glueck pondered a moment. "I would say that the birth of human conscience stems from that moment when God stayed Abraham's hand as he was about to sacrifice Isaac. In that act the emphasis, for the first time in ancient days, was on the sanctity and beauty of life. Human sacrifice would be ended forever. Life was to be respected, to be treasured. Judaism is a religion of *this* world, of the problems of life in *this* world. And the awareness of this originates with God's testing of Abraham and the saving of Isaac. When Isaac asked Abraham where was the lamb for the burnt sacrifice, we can imagine Abraham's sorrow. But God provided the answer, and humanity was given a new direction."

"This matter of Mount Moriah," I said. "It's been bothering me. Ever since I was at Tel Beersheba, I've been wondering about that long trip Abraham had to make, north to Jerusalem, to sacrifice his son. Is there evidence that Mount Moriah in Jerusalem is actually the place where God sent the angel to stay Abraham's hand?"

"You're perceptive," Dr. Glueck said. "I went into this in *Rivers in the Desert*. The confusion stems from mixing up the biblical Land of Moriah, where God ordered Abraham to sacrifice Isaac, with Mount Moriah, where Solomon built his temple and where today the Dome of the Rock stands. The places are much too far apart. Your instincts were correct. Why should Abraham have to trudge with the boy for three days, hauling his kindling? Moriah means God's revelation, and it is depicted as a barren region. My own feeling is that the place where Abraham heard God's voice was in the Negev, somewhere near the Sinai border, perhaps at Bir Birein, and not Mount Moriah in Jerusalem.

"Thus we see that early in history the Negev and the Sinai were centers of divine revelation. It has never been any mystery to me why such was the case in ancient times. This part of the world is a place of extremes. There are extremes of light and of darkness. There are extremes of climate, withering heat, a cold that penetrates to the bone. And what extremes of behavior among men! From the most noble acts to the most appalling wickedness. The contrasts are omnipresent. The human spirit is alternately assailed and uplifted. There is an inevitability to the revelations that took place here, the truths revealed to Abraham as he wandered the Negev and the Sinai, the truths revealed to Moses. I believe with all my heart that the Spirit of God hovers over this land."

Wasn't there a danger, I asked, that this proprietary attitude, this conviction that God had given them the land, might harm modern Israel? And what about the furious pace of modernization in Israel, the factories, the highways, the new cities? Were these agents of debilitation and disbelief, producing generations who would not be able or willing to identify with Dr. Glueck's Abraham?

"I don't think so. The Rechabites tried to preserve the pristine simplicity of the desert, and they died. Look it up in Jeremiah. They refused to build houses, or plant vineyards, or sow seed. But they vanished. Much later the Nabateans tried to exist in the desert on the desert's terms, and they were overrun and absorbed. But the modern Israelis are using their minds to survive and flourish here. The art of the Jews is an art of the mind."

Dr. Glueck invited me out to the roof of the Hebrew Union building. He wanted to show me the new wing going up, and the view of the walls of the Old City. As we walked out of his office, I mentioned Professor Weinberg's dictum: The nice thing about archaeology was that nobody ever died for it.

"I'm not so sure. Have you been to Lachish? You must go. Fascinating site. It was excavated by an Englishman named Starkey, John Starkey. He was self-taught, had been a tailor most of his life. He was returning to Jerusalem from the dig in 1939 when he was waylaid and murdered by Arab terrorists."

"But his death had nothing to do with his archaeological work, did it?'

"I suppose not. He had made the mistake of talking to the British authorities about something he had heard about the Arab terror gangs. It was a fatal mistake. I made it my business to see and hear nothing back in the thirties when I was in Transjordan. You know, of course, I was later with the O.S.S. here. That was a rather different situation. I was a close friend of King Abdullah of Transjordan, the one who was murdered outside the Aksa mosque. He was Hussein's grandfather, and a good friend of ours. He was a man we could have reasoned with. I always had excellent contacts with the Arabs, especially the Bedouin."

I said that if circumstances ever changed, he, Dr. Glueck, might be the ideal man to start negotiations with King Hussein. We were on the roof of the building now, looking out at the pale-brown walls of Jerusalem, the Tower of David, the Jaffa Gate, the Dome of the Rock.

"No, I'm afraid we are long past that possibility," he said sadly, as if he wished he could turn the clock back to the time when a rabbi from Cincinnati could count an Arab king among his close friends.

"There's the new wing I'm building," Dr. Glueck said. "We need the space badly. And it is costing us a lot more than we planned. I have had to invest an extra fifty thousand dollars in a bomb shelter. The city officials insist on it, and perhaps they are right. If it means building it to get the work done, we will. You know, we have several campuses of the Hebrew Union College: the main one in Cincinnati, New York, Los Angeles, and this one. I like them all, but I am hopelessly in love with Jerusalem. I am never so relaxed, so vigorous, so hopeful, as I am in Jerusalem. Just look at that city! Look at those walls! Are there any walls like them in the world?"

I put in a good word for the Turks. Jews and Arabs and Christians may have had prior claims to the city. But the walls were built by Turks.

"All credit to them!" Dr. Glueck said. "The city inspired them also, as it must inspire anyone who looks at it, and thinks about its meaning. I am not ashamed to say it. My heart is in Jerusalem."

CHAPTER IX

Up and Down the Mount of Olives

Preparations for a vacation are as much fun for me as the actual trip. What kind of clothing? What sort of film? What kind of medicines? I think a lot of this has to do with a boyhood devoted to Paul DuChaillu, the old Congo gorilla man, Zane Grey (*Roping Lions in the Grand Canyon*), and Admiral Byrd. These intrepids never went forth unless well equipped. Much time was spent on assembling the proper gear. Garments and guns were selected with meticulous care. A man would no more venture forth into savage lands with the wrong boots, than he would with an obsolete map. It was DuChaillu, I think, who made my skin prickle at the age of twelve when he told me that a man must never go out into the African heat unless he wore beneath his outer clothing a *thick flannel band around his abdomen.* The medical basis for this eluded me—it still does—but the ghost of Paul DuChaillu and his flannel girdle haunts me yet when I prepare for a vacation.

So it was natural that an Abercrombie and Fitch advertisement for an ingenious new hiking shoe piqued my interest. I recall the ad well. It ran the length of a *New York Times* page and included a line drawing of the shoe in cross-section, revealing cunning liners, supports, cushioning, treads and fabrics. The shoe was French. Abercrombie had somehow gotten a corner on them, I gathered. Each feature of the shoe was so artfully designed as to make hiking painless. I got the feeling that the shoe was in the same category as those rare thousand-dollar shotguns prized by true sportsmen. A killer I am not, but a walker I am. I would own the most prestigious hiking boots in the world, and I would tread the stones of the Holy Land secure in my aristocratically shod feet, size 12-EE.

They were rather odd-looking shoes. Actually they were closer to what we call sneakers. Pale chocolate in color, they were cut high and made of canvas, reinforced with a rubber toe and a rubber rear. The heel and sole were a single piece of thick rubber, deeply ridged and erratically cut, so as to afford traction on slopes and rocky terrain. The inner sole was thickly cushioned, and I can report to Abercrombie and Fitch that their exotic sneakers performed as advertised. They got me over dry hills and slanted boulders, up mountainsides, and across wadis. But I am beginning to wonder where in blazes Abercrombie got them.

I had noticed that occasionally an Israeli, or more often an Arab, would stare at my feet. My feet are big and clumsy, but that is hardly cause for people to ogle them. And the shoes, while of rather odd design, were not *that* unusual. In a land full of tourists, footgear takes strange forms. The mystery was solved for me the day I began my ascent of the Mount of Olives, a solitary pilgrimage from the Old City upward, without guide or wife or companion, the kind of lonesome journey I often undertake out of sheer gratitude for being able to see history firsthand.

My day began in King Solomon's quarries, the cold, winding cave between Herod's Gate and the Damascus Gate. These caverns twist their way underneath the Old City and are reputed to be the source of the stones with which Solomon built the city. The very Temple stones were believed to have been hacked and split from the dark caves. The Masons regard these quarries as the birthplace of their order, and I mused, as I wandered through the eerily lit grottoes, whether the cave in *The Magic Flute* bears some relation to them. One can still see the niches for the stone-workers' oil lamps, as well as the vertical cuts into which wooden splints were hammered, soaked, then permitted to swell until they cracked the wall into neat blocks.

I came out into the punishing light and frightening heat of Jerusalem at two in the afternoon. The change-over from the cool interior of the quarries—it must have been twenty degrees colder in the labyrinth—to the merciless heat of the city was an affront, a challenge. More and more I was beginning to understand what Nelson Glueck meant when he talked of the terrible extremes of the land.

Across the Jaffa Road, above the East Jerusalem bus terminal, I could see Jeremiah's Grotto, the prison where the prophet died. It was part, I now realized, of General Gordon's Garden Tomb, where a few days ago I had discussed the problem of the rival Golgothas with the minister. Squinting through the glare, I tried to discern the skull in the eroded white stones. It wasn't there. Perhaps it was the heat, or the flooding light, or the fumes of the toxic Arab buses.

I proceeded down the street, past the Rockefeller Museum, to the Jericho Road. (I did not realize it at the time, but this inter-section was a crucial point in the battle for the Old City during the Six-Day War. On my last day in Jerusalem Zev Vilnay would reenact the event for me, and I would understand its impor-tance.)

An Esso filling station stands at the corner. I stopped to ask the attendants if I was on the right road for the Tomb of the Virgin, the Church of All Nations, and the path that climbs the Mount of Olives. These were, of course, Arabs, since we were in East Jeru-salem. None spoke English. One fellow spoke some French, and I asked him, "*Est-ce que je suis sur la route pour la Tombe de la Vierge?*"

Staring at my feet, he did not respond. Then he muttered some-thing in Arabic, and his colleagues, deserting an angry German at the wheel of his VW bus, came over to study my feet also.

"*Al Fatah,*" the fellow said, pointing at my expensive sneakers.

"*Comment?*" I asked.

"*Ces sont les souliers d'Al Fatah. Les mêmes choses.*" Stooping, all three began inspecting the Abercrombie and Fitch shoes. The first fellow tweaked the brown rubber toe, another pinched the back.

"*Oui. Sans doute, Al Fatah.*"

They were convinced I was wearing the same shoes issued to the Arab terrorists, the Al Fatah. I was stunned. Their shiny black eyes—they were handsome fellows, as are most Jerusalem Arabs—were studying me with a kind of sly admiration. How did I get a pair of Al Fatah sneakers? Had I garroted a guerrilla in the Judean hills? Had I spent time in an Al Fatah training camp as a journalist? Had I access to their supply corps? The mystery intrigued them, and the more they chattered in Arabic and studied my sneakers (by now three cars were waiting for gas), the more they were amused.

"*Gardez, m'sieu, vous avez des souliers dangereux,*" the man who made the identification said. He then gave me directions to the Tomb of the Virgin, but not before all three escorted me to the Jericho Road and sent me off, with warm good wishes and laughter.

As I walked down the road paralleling the Kidron Valley, I began wondering about those hiking shoes. Where in heaven's name did you get them, Abercrombie and Fitch? And are you aware you are selling—at fifteen dollars a pair—the standard shoes of Arab terrorists? In truth, I have always been a little afraid of Abercrombie and Fitch. Ever since I read about Hemingway going there with Jock Whitney to buy a topcoat, I have had the feeling that I don't bring enough class to the store. I don't sail or hunt or golf, and my wife looks awful in tweed and leather. So I had purchased the shoes with a sense of gratitude and achievement. At last I had come to them with a worthy request, had bought exactly what I wanted, and had, in a sense, not let *them* down.

But what had they done to *me*? After much analysis, I have concluded that some shrewd French manufacturer was stuck with several thousand pairs of hiking shoes. But how had part of the consignment come to the snobbiest store in the world (I remember that clever ad) and the other to the scruffy sneaks who lob mortar shells into kibbutzim? Later, I made it my business to inspect photographs of Al Fatah warriors. The filling-station attendant was right—they *are* wearing my snooty French boots. I leave the problem with Messrs. Abercrombie and Fitch. I think it proves one of Green's Laws—no matter how upper-crust you think you are, you are deceiving yourself.

As I have indicated, the shoes performed wonderfully, and on this blistering day they got me down the Jericho Road and up the Mount of Olives. I walked past St. Stephen's Gate—also known as the Lion Gate because of the two splendid lions in the masonry—which is the main entrance in the Eastern Wall of the Old City. It is smaller than the Damascus Gate, but it has a dignity and an elegance that befits its history. Through its portals Christ entered the city to walk the Via Dolorosa. It was also the gateway through which Israeli troops surged through the Old City in the six-day war. In early afternoon, it seemed remarkably placid. A camel and his Bedouin master, available for tourist photos, lolled in the archway. They were too artfully positioned—picture-postcard figures.

Beyond St. Stephen's Gate, continuing on the Jericho Road in an easterly direction, is the bricked-up Golden Gate. The double-arched portal is in the wall of the Temple Enclosure, the holy area which once housed Solomon's Temple and today is the "Noble Sanctuary" on which stand the el-Aksa Mosque and the Dome of the Rock. It is a splendid little gate, more modest than mighty Damascus or graceful St. Stephen's, and touching in its uselessness. The name Golden Gate is a mistranslation of the words "Beautiful Gate" in Acts (". . . at the Gate of the Temple which is called Beautiful") into the Latin *Porta Aurea*. The sealed double-domed entrance is of the seventh century A.D. and is thought to have been built for the Byzantine Emperor Heraclius on his return from a campaign against the Persians. A Herodian gate preceded it, and before the Herodian era the Eastern Wall contained the main entrance to the Temple. But for a long, long period, in later years, it was a sealed gate. The Arabs walled it up in 810 A.D. The Crusaders opened it, but only for special occasions such as Palm Sunday. The Turks, aware of the Moslem tradition that the city would be conquered through the

Golden Gate, bricked it up once more. During the British mandate, old-timers said they were convinced that the British would
not last because General Allenby failed to open the Golden Gate.
(It is pleasing to see these legends shattered. In 1967 the Old
City was conquered not through the impregnable Golden Gate,
but through the adjoining Lion Gate.)

I now had my bearings. Between the Virgin's Tomb and the
gaudy Church of All Nations, I saw the steep road that winds
up the Mount of Olives. But before crossing the street to make
my ascent, I continued on the Jericho Road to locate the three
mammoth rock tombs on the lower slopes of the mount, pictures
of which I had seen in all the guidebooks.

They loomed up suddenly after a turning of the road, uglv, ponderous mausoleums. Carved out of the native rock, they date from
Hasmonean times, and in their ungainliness they reflect some of
the destructive, bloody character of that period. In their gigantic
eccentricity, they speak of despair and defeat.

The first is Absalom's Tomb, or Absalom's Pillar, which does not
date to the time of King David's rebellious son but is associated
with him because of a biblical reference. It is a soaring, dead-gray
affair, crowned with a strange ornament shaped like a trumpet, a
flower, or a distributor cap, depending on one's interests. It is not
an agreeable building, and the stone spire, so outlandish in
design, inspires a vague discomfort. In the Middle Ages, parents
would bring naughty children there for a whipping, and show
them what a bad end Absalom came to. I suspect the ugliness of
the monument helped terrify the children.

A bit farther down the road is the Grotto of St. James, smaller
than Absalom's Pillar, and recessed in the base of the Mount.
Depending on whether you are a Jew or a Christian, you have a
choice of legends. St. James is said to have hidden in the cave at
the time of Jesus' arrest. Two thick pillars and a sturdy stone
portal frame the entrance to the grotto. The Jewish tradition states
that the cave is the family burial vault of the priestly house of
Hezir. This has a bit more substance. Above the stone porch is an
inscription with the names of some of the priests.

The third of these faintly menacing relics is the Tomb of
Zechariah, also carved from the rock *in situ*. A flight of crumbling

steps lead to three massive pillars, and atop them rests a pyramid, a heavy, dull, uninspiring piece of work.

When you stand at the site of the three tombs you are no longer in the Kidron Valley but in the legendary Valley of Jehoshaphat, separating the Mount of Olives and Mount Moriah. On the slopes of the Mount are visible the tombstones of the oldest and most sacred Jewish cemetery in the world. The site was chosen for burial in ancient times because of a prophecy by Zechariah that the rising of the dead would begin on the Mount of Olives.

I now retraced my footsteps back to the Tomb of the Virgin. The church is a Crusader work of the twelfth century and has the spare, well-proportioned lines of the old churches one finds in the French countryside. The entrance is a series of wide pointed arches, the exterior arch resting on single pillars. There is then a segment of brick wall, followed by three more pillars, each slightly recessed. It is dignified and unadorned, and it has the satisfying aspect of a building that has aged gracefully.

"Ah, I am official guide, sir," I heard a voice say as I took photographs of the facade of the Virgin's Tomb. A strikingly handsome Arab boy in a spotless white shirt was smiling at me.

"I don't want a guide."

"I am official guide. I belong to church."

"Oh, you are a Christian?"

"No. Moslem. My name is Michael. I am terrific guide."

"Michael is not a Moslem name."

"My real name is Mahmoud. Michael is for Americans."

"If you will call yourself Mahmoud, and let me call you that too, you can be my guide."

"Excellent, sir."

We entered the church and descended the forty-seven marble steps into the subterranean tomb. A Greek Orthodox priest appeared, a bearded youth who furnished us with candles. Although the Greeks are custodians of the church, the usual allocations have been made to other faiths. The Protestants, Mahmoud told me, have the Chapel of St. Anne, the Virgin's mother. The Roman Catholics worship at the Chapel of St. Joseph. The tomb of Joachim, the Virgin's father, is on the stairway, about

halfway down, but I was never clear as to who had prior rights
to it.

At the bottom of the stairs, on the right arm of the cruciform
church, is the Virgin's Tomb, although to Catholic believers
she has long ascended, body and soul, to heaven. The tomb
is flanked by an Armenian altar, and a Moslem *mihrab*.

"Nothing for the Jews?" I asked.

Mahmoud held his hands up. "They not want."

We emerged from the cool tomb. I shivered and blinked in the
light. The change from these underground chambers to the sun-
drenched exterior is almost painful. I could understand why the
Bedouin wrapped themselves in layers of loose black robes. They
were creating a private underground cave on their bodies.

Mahmoud led me to the Cave of Agony, a Franciscan shrine,
where Jesus hid himself from his Disciples, "and being in agony,
prayed more earnestly." Laboriously, Mahmoud tried to tell me
something about "jumping with the feets," presumably a reference
to the oil press, the Hebrew *gath shamna*, which gives us the
name Gethsemane.

We crossed the roadway that climbs the Mount of Olives, and
we entered the Garden of Gethsemane. The garden is small,
exquisite, and utterly captivating. It blazes with yellows and reds
and purples, flowers bursting with passion and intensity. Suffering and denial are not at all suggested here; Christ's agony must
have occurred elsewhere. Indeed the Garden of Gethsemane is
one of the brightest and most flamboyant spots in Jerusalem.
Even the gnarled olive trees, which are said to date back to the
very day when Judas betrayed Jesus in the garden, have a certain
gaiety about them. Lush of leaf, firm of limb, they do not seem
out of place amid the crimson roses and purple iris.

"I like you to meet gardener," Mahmoud said. I had been pho-
tographing the Golden Gate. Now I turned and was confronted
by a startlingly handsome Franciscan in a brown cassock. He was
a middle-aged man with serene forehead, aristocratic nose, curly
black hair turning gray, and the beard of a Venetian nobleman.

I assumed that he was Italian. "*Buon giorno, padre, buon
giorno, Signor Giardiniero.*"

He was overjoyed to find an Italian-speaking American and

even more ecstatic when he learned I was a Jew. The drama of the situation was not lost on me, and I had to keep reminding myself that I had met and won over the gardener of Gethsemane.

"*Ho un amico ebreo-americano,*" the gardener said. "*Chi m'ha mandato radici di dahlia. . . .*"

It seems he had a Jewish-American friend who had sent him dahlia tubers, and they were now among his prized blooms. He showed them to me—maroon, lemon yellow, pale lavender, giant blooms in those original dahlia shades. I was touched and I was grateful. My father, a bad-tempered Brooklyn physician, had grown prize dahlias in our backyard in Brownsville years ago. I have always had a sentimental attachment to the flowers. I complimented the priest on his excellent dahlias, and on the other flourishing flowers of his sacred domain, and we walked the earth where Christ found shelter after the Last Supper.

The gardener's name was Salvatore de Siato. He came from the city of Lecce, deep in the Italian "heel," in the Apulia region. People from the Apulia tend to be courteous and soft-spoken, and Father de Siato was no exception. I had been to Lecce, an "art" city known as the Baroque Florence, and we discussed the Piazza and the Basilica of the Holy Cross. There was a gentleness and a warmth about the gardener, and whoever chooses the gardener of Gethsemane had selected wisely. In figure and face, in manner and in horticultural skills, he was a man for all faiths.

I asked him if I might take some photographs of him among his flowers. He was willing, provided I sent him some prints. Unfortunately I did not have my color camera with me, and I could not record the gardener amid the stunning hues of Gethsemane. But the black-and-white pictures I took show him in good light and reflect the sweet and tolerant quality of the man. I am partial to Italians.

"But you know," Mahmoud said after we left, "there is another Garden of Gethsemane."

"Really?"

"Across the road. Russian church. Saint Mary Magdalene. I show you. You speak very good Italian, sir. You speak Russian also?"

"No. Not a word."

We entered a wooden door set in a high masonry wall.

"I will teach you Arabic, sir."

"I don't think we have time today."

"Oh, no, sir. You take me to America and I will teach you. I will live with you. I will do anything you want. I can be your servant, your chauffeur. And if you so desire, I will marry your daughter."

"My daughter is only sixteen."

"She will learn to love me. I am certain."

Mahmoud told me that the Russian church was built in 1888 by Czar Alexander. "Inside, in crypt, are hearts of members of his family," he said, smiling. He was a gentle enough youth, but a bit forward and presumptuous. I found myself feeling sorry for him. Obviously he had been educated. He dressed well. He spoke pleasantly. And when he pleaded for me to take him to America and marry my daughter, it was not just in jest. It was worth a try; who could tell when he would meet some eccentric American Jew who wanted nothing more than to do a favor for an East Jerusalem Arab? I kept thinking about a line in a war novel I read many years ago about R.A.F. flyers in Greece who hire a sinister Greek youth as a guide. One of the Britons keeps saying, in post-Hemingwayesque style. "A nice boy if he doesn't kill us."

We entered the "other" Garden of Gethsemane; tourists have their choice of a Catholic or Orthodox site. The seven handsome domes of the Russian church rose above us, soaring over the pines and cypresses, glistening golden onions surmounted with crosses. Despite its ornate and new appearance, the church is among the few modern structures in the area which mesh with the surroundings. By contrast, I found the modern Church of All Nations, with its Byzantine facade, infelicitous and incongruous. Its newness is much too apparent. The mosaic depicting the weeping Christ is much too bright. Inside, a peculiar Spanish glass window sheds a purplish light over everything, including the Rock of Agony. The effect is too theatrical. Faith usually benefits from simplicity, from hard lines and innocent arrangements.

"Russian nuns here," Mahmoud said. "Not very friendly."

We walked around the side of the Church of Mary Magdalene, alongside a small graveyard. An angry female voice suddenly shouted at us to get out. "You have no business there," she called. "You want to come in church, come in here."

"You go. I stay." Mahmoud was in no mood for angry Christians.

Inside, an American couple, excessively polite Jews, were having their troubles with the sister who had just chased us out of the cemetery.

"You cannot go into the chapel dressed like that," she was telling the woman, whose skirt seemed sufficiently long. The nun began to wind a gray cloth around the woman's legs, draping part of it over her shoulders. "One must show respect for holy places."

The husband, a stout, glasses-wearing man, trying hard to get along with any Christian in the world, purchased postcards, and in the friendliest of manners asked the nun: "Where are you from, Sister?"

She fixed him with a basilisk's eye. What was her accent? Slavic? French? "I don't ask where *you* are from," she said, "don't you ask me where *I* am from."

I decided to ask her nothing, not even the price of a postcard. I turned my attention to the grim Slavic interior of the church. Huge modern frescoes decorated the wall. They have the look of calendar oleographs. The tourist who had just been insulted asked the sister what the paintings represented, and she gave him a mimeographed sheet, which he scanned and then handed to me.

Saint Mary Magdalene, I learned, was the patron saint of the Empress Mary of Russia, the mother of Czar Alexander III. The paintings depicted Mary Magdalene healed by Jesus, the apparition of St. James, and the largest, in the center of the wall above a handsome icon screen, Mary Magdalene before Tiberias in Rome. She is telling Tiberias that Pontius Pilate wronged Jesus, and as a result of her talebearing Pilate is sent into exile. She is offering the Roman Emperor an egg, according to the mimeographed sheet, a symbol of eternity.

Outside I told Mahmoud about the nun's rudeness.

"I tell you, sir, not very friendly."

"Nothing like the gardener of Gethsemane, which maybe is why the Roman Catholic Church is still in business in Italy and Spain and other places and will probably be around for a long time.

And you know what happened to the Russian Orthodox Church."

"I leave you here, sir," said Mahmoud. "If I walk to top with you, I cannot get another client. My station is at bottom, by entrance to garden. Is short walk to top of mount, and there are other guides there."

We stood in the narrow, winding path. A mixed aroma of hot pine tar and donkey droppings scented the air. It was not an unpleasant odor.

"I have no idea what to pay you."

"Ah, whatever you wish."

"I still have no idea."

"Five American dollars."

"Mahmoud," I said, "you will never get to America asking those prices. You know that is outrageous."

"Ah, but you like me, sir. You have shown it."

"I'll give you two dollars, which is more than generous for the hour you spent with me."

"Thank you, thank you, sir. I should still like to marry your daughter, if you will take me to America."

"That would be difficult, Mahmoud. My daughter has a boyfriend."

"Oh, oh, that is too bad." His beautiful olive face blanched, and his somber eyes fell. "Good-bye, sir. *Shalom.*"

Nearer the summit of the mount and overlooking the Russian Orthodox Church's onion domes is the small and charming Franciscan Church of Dominus Flevit; at the place where Jesus wept over Jerusalem. The church, original in design, is modern, built in 1955, and oddly shaped—a square rising to a dome with scalloped edges. An old tradition maintained that at this site Jesus "beheld the city and wept over it," and there are remains of a sixth-century Byzantine church within the tiny modern building. One approaches the church through a small garden, with a superb collection of old ossuaria, terra-cotta urns for second burial, carelessly heaped behind a wire fence.

Under a grape arbor, dozing in the shade, I found an ancient, trembling Franciscan monk. The scene could have been southern Italy—the perfume of pines and cypresses, the humming of insects, the soporific silence. But it was cool in the shade, and the old monk asked me to sit with him for a while when he heard me address him in Italian.

"Ah, yes, a very old place," he said. "They have found stones beneath this church, and the older church, going back to 1500 B.C., before David."

This seemed unlikely to me, but I said nothing. The oldest foundations discovered are usually Hasmonean or Herodian. A Solomonic layer is very rare indeed, and anything older virtually nonexistent.

He was from Sorrento, a gentle old Neapolitan with the soft speech and amiable manners of the south. "We found many coins and seals from the Hasmonean period, so this is truly an old place."

The Hasmoneans took over in 165 B.C. That sounded reasonable. Talking seemed to be an effort for the old man, so I thanked him and got up. The bells in the Russian Church of Mary Magdalene began to toll.

"A beautiful church," I said.

A look of gentle contempt turned his mouth, closed his eyes. "*Non mi piace quella chiesa,*" he said. "I don't like that church."

"You don't like its style?"

"I don't like *that*. I don't like where it is *from*." With delicate emphasis, he said, "*Muscovite. Muscovite. Non posso sentire quella parole . . .*"

He could not even bear to hear the word "Muscovite."

"It is even difficult for me to say it," the old monk said. "The word comes with great difficulty to my mouth."

We shook hands. I avoided any comment. Years ago my father told me to stay out of the quarrels of *goyim*. But it was clear where my own sentiments lay, and I think the custodian of Dominus Flevit knew it.

I passed the Jewish cemetery, on the upper slopes of the Mount of Olives, on the right as one ascends. Several people had told me that during their possession of East Jerusalem, Hussein's Arabs had looted the burial ground, using the stone slabs as the foundations for buildings. The cemetery is an ancient and a particularly sacred one, but no Christian protests were voiced over the desecration. In a mass grave near the path are buried a group of Israeli soldiers who fell near the spot during the Six-Day War.

Facing the path is an iron gate leading to the purported tombs of the prophets Haggai, Zechariah, and Malachi. An Arab custodian let me in. When I asked why there were so many burial niches in the circular underground chamber, he explained that in addition to the three prophets, forty-seven of their pupils were also interred there. Claims of great antiquity are frequent on the Mount. The old padre at Dominus Flevit talked about stones from 1500 B.C.; the guide here advised me that the place was twenty-five hundred years old. A book I consulted later said that the subterranean maze of niches and chambers is actually the work of an early Christian burial society, a fact proved by Greek inscriptions.

This matter of prior claims to ancient places is, of course, a puzzling and involved one in the Holy Land. At the summit of the Mount of Olives is a historical site called the Tomb of the Prophetess Huldah. (Nagel's guidebook advised me that "a dervish" had the key to the place, but I found no dervish, whirling or otherwise, and had to look at the tomb from the outside.) In any event, my friend Zev Vilnay later gave me some background information about Huldah's Tomb.

"All three faiths claim it as their own. Who knows the truth? The Jews pray to the prophetess Huldah there. She is mentioned in Second Chronicles as the daughter-in-law of a man named Hasrah, the keeper of King Josiah's wardrobe. They went to her for a prophecy, and she gave them one. About the eighth century B.C., the time of the prophets. The Christians regard it as the Tomb of St. Pelagia, a lady from Antioch who came to Jerusalem to repent about the fifth century C.E. Finally, the Moslems have what you Americans call a piece of the action, since they pray to Sitt El Adoui, a holy woman from the tribe of Adoui, very late, about ninth century. It's nice in a way. Everyone is allowed to worship his own holy lady."

As I looked through the locked gate at the stone exterior of the Tomb of Huldah—or St. Pelagia, or Sitt El Adoui—a bespectacled fat boy waddled up to me. "You want guide, sir? I am Charlie, very fine guide."

There were only a few more things to see on the summit of the

Mount of Olives, and I was weary. "No, thanks," I said.

Charlie was staring at my Abercrombie and Fitch hiking boots. "Why do you stare at my boots?"

His chubby face quivered. He did not know whether to smile or look grave. "They are Al Fatah shoes, sir. The same as the Al Fatah wear."

"Yes, I know. But I can't possibly tell you how I got them. It is a secret."

The hiking shoes had intrigued him. He would not leave. As I turned from the gate he waddled alongside me, a sad, overweight, unhappy boy. Three other youths, lean, noisy ruffians, came running down the street. They seemed to be shouting curses at him, and accusing him of stealing tourists. I cannot say how I divined this, but they seemed also to be making rude comments about his lack of masculinity.

"Oh, sir, I talk to you first, please let me be guide. They will beat me anyway."

"All right. You are my guide. But I will not call you Charlie, because that is not your name. What is your name?"

"Khalil."

"Much better." I chased the young hoods. One had tweaked Khalil's buttocks, another had whispered something in his ear. He took the abuse with laudable stoicism.

"He is not real guide, I am real guide," the tallest of the tormentors shouted at me.

"Beat it," I said. "Get lost. Khalil, you are my guide."

He was flattered, but he could not take his eyes off my Al Fatah feet.

"We see Chapel of Ascension, sir," Khalil said. "Where Jesus Christ go up into heaven. Very famous."

He led me to a courtyard behind a brick wall. The chapel proved to be a small circular building. It was deserted except for a stout old one-eyed Arab in a white robe who was selling olivewood beads and faded postcards from a table. I could identify the Crusader columns and capitals; the roof was clearly the dome of a mosque. It was a rather forlorn affair, and yet it had a minimal quality that had to be respected. Inside there was not a sign of decoration besides a few niches for candles. On a stone in the

floor, Khalil pointed to what was believed to be the footprint of
Jesus as he ascended to heaven. But there was no hole in the roof.

"Does anyone worship here?" I asked.

"Special masses sometimes, sir. Ascension Day. You see, sir, no
crosses allowed, no crescents. Christians and Moslems agree. Both
make it holy place. Jesus is prophet of Islam."

It seemed to me that the chapel, a site commemorating one of
the most wondrous and most momentous events in the history of
Christendom, was woefully underproduced. Moreover, I wondered about the absence of tourists. I visited it twice, and on both
occasions I was the only one present apart from the one-eyed souvenir vendor. After a while I began to wonder whether official
Christian circles, the learned doctors and divines who decide on
the veracity of shrines, had some doubts about the homely chapel-
mosque with its lonesome footprint. As an outsider, I found it
delightful. If an extra vote is ever needed to secure validation for
the Chapel of the Ascension, I will cast it.

Khalil took me next to the Church of the Pater Noster, where,
in modern tiles, one may read the Lord's Prayer in forty-four
different languages. I noticed one labeled "Chaldean," but the letters were Hebrew. The mystery was cleared up for me later by
the learned Dr. Vilnay, who explained that Chaldean referred to
the Aramaic language, and had I looked a bit harder I would
have found a Hebrew version also.

"I take you to Bethany, sir," Khalil said.

My feet felt like hot stones and my calf muscles were strips of
steel. I had been hiking around the city, up the Mount of Olives,
and around its summit for three hours. The temperature was in
the high nineties. The burning sky was cloudless. I longed for our
air-conditioned hotel room and a glass of lemonade.

"How far?"

"Not very far. A nice walk in back of Mount of Olives."

There are mad moments in my sight-seeing when I end the day
crawling on hands and knees to see one final church, one more
fresco. I become a huge blotter, absorbing experiences, motivated
by some Thomas Wolfian hunger I cannot rationalize. "On to
Bethany," I said.

We walked along the south slope of the Mount of Olives on the

Bethany Road, the old dirt road to Jericho. For a wide-hipped boy of questionable virility, Khalil had no trouble trudging along the dusty heights. He chattered gaily as we walked past Arab farms and homes. "Oh, sir, you are Jew?"

"Yes."

"Oh, I pray for peace, that we all live in peace. War terrible."

We never did make it to Bethany, the home of Mary and Martha, the place where Jesus raised Lazarus from the grave. I saw it in the distance, a church steeple, a small community. But by now, I myself was in need of resurrection.

We did get as far as the tiny church of the shrine of Beth Phage, the place where the disciples found the donkey on which Jesus rode into Jerusalem. The structure is nineteenth century, built on the ruins of a Crusader church. Inside I studied some partially restored early Gothic paintings. One showed "the bringing of the donkey," and the start of the Palm Sunday procession.

I liked the candor of the pamphlet that the shrine distributes. "Of all the Christian Shrines," it says, "that of Beth Phage certainly is not considered one of the principal ones." This modesty moved me. I left an offering and told Khalil I could not walk another step, to Bethany or anywhere else, and that I had to return to the hotel.

"Perhaps it is your boots," he said sadly.

"No, they are splendid boots. I am just very tired."

"Yes, yes. Al Fatah boots. The best."

CHAPTER X

At the Wall

In the pioneer kibbutzim, a determined and at times painful effort was made to crush the old ghetto habits of Vilna and Lodz and Budapest. Indeed, the revolutionary communal methods of child-rearing, which Bruno Bettelheim examines in *The Children of the Dream,* were designed to smash the traditional Jewish familial structure, to teach the sabra competence, loyalty to his peer group, and a confident attitude toward life.

Hence it is no mystery why the term "Wailing Wall" is frowned upon in Israel. It is the Western Wall, a precise translation of the Hebrew *Kotel Hama'aravi.* The attitude of the Israelis, religious and secular, seems to be, do your wailing in private, if at all. On half a dozen occasions when I visited the Wall, that great pile of Herodian stones on the western perimeter of the Temple Enclosure, I saw no crying. Where were all those old fellows tearing at their beards and flooding the narrow street with tears? Old men—yes. But weeping—decidedly no. And at the wall there were also children and soldiers with their machine guns, women—at a special separated area to the right—and a cross-section of tourists.

The Garden Tomb, or Gordon's Calvary. General Charles "Chinese" Gordon decided that this site was a more likely place for Christ's burial than was the Holy Sepulcher.

The Warden of the Garden Tomb points to the grotto of the Prophet
Jeremiah. Above it, Gordon believed, was the exact place of crucifixion.
At times the hill is said to resemble a skull.

Arab bus terminal below Gordon's Calvary. The Warden would like the buses elsewhere.

Mampsis, or Kurnub, the city in the Negev unearthed and studied by
Dr. Avraham Negev. It is the most complete and best preserved of all
Nabatean cities.

The gate with three names: St. Stephen's, Lion, Shechem. Israeli paratroopers fought their way through it during the Six-Day War and conquered the Old City.

The Golden Gate, sealed by the Arabs to keep out the Messiah; the paratroopers thus used the gate nearest to it.

Absalom's Pillar, a rock-cut tomb on the lower slopes of the Mount of Olives. It is of a much later date than King David's wayward son.

Near it the Grotto of St. James (to Christians); Jews call it the Tomb of Hezir.

The graceful Crusader facade of the Virgin's Tomb.

Father Salvatore di Siato, the Gardener of Gethsemane.

The nineteenth-century Russian Orthodox church of St. Mary Magdalene. Inside are preserved some hearts of the Romanov family.

Looking down at the Kidron Valley from the Mount of Olives. The modern building on the right is the interesting little Church of Dominus Flevit— where Jesus wept. Below, the onion domes of Mary Magdalene and, distantly, the eastern wall of the Old City.

A Jewish cemetery on the Mount of Olives. Some stones have been dese-
crated. Others were removed to make building foundations when Jordan
held East Jerusalem.

The Chapel of the Ascension on the grounds of a mosque. A modest and enigmatic shrine, considering its holiness. Nobody seems terribly interested in it.

At the *Kotel Hama'aravi*, the Western Wall. The stones are Herodian, the worshippers Orthodox.

Marie contemplates a mountain of pottery discards, leavings from the dig at the southwest corner of the wall of the Temple Enclosure.

Professor Mazar's dig. The trenches in the foreground have reached down to Herodian pavements at the base of the southern wall of the enclosure. The dome is that of el-Aksa Mosque, site of the tragic fire. Below it, the "double gate."

Herodian engineering at its most massive: the southwest corner of the Temple Enclosure Wall. The long stone in the fourth row from the bottom is the Wall's second biggest—more than eighty tons.

Inside the Haram el-Sharif, the Noble Sanctuary. The Dome of the Rock,
viewed from behind a Crusader arch.

"The Lord has given us the city." A tour at the site of biblical Jericho.

Distantly, towering above the ruins of Jericho, the Mount of Temptations, where Jesus fasted for forty days and forty nights.

A seventh-century Playboy Club: the Hisham Palace near Jericho, a winter resort of the Ommayid caliphs.

Plaster voluptuaries from the Hisham Palace: the lewd ladies of Hisham, now on duty in the austere corridors of the Rockefeller Museum.

A Yemenite jeweler.

Two views of Bar 'Am, a handsome second-century synagogue and one of Zev Vilnay's favorite sites.

The entrance to the tomb of Rabbis Simon and Eliezer, the great cab-
alists, in Meron. A beggar plies her trade at the door.

"This battered caravanserai." A Turkish khan, or inn, or caravanserai, in Akko (Acre). It has pleasing proportions, harmonious lines.

The Akko mosque of el-Jazzar, "the butcher." Pastel shades, a peaceful garden, and memories of murder.

A hidden treasure on the seacoast south of Haifa: Dor, called Tarentum by the Romans. Just above the beach are visible the honey-colored stones of the old harbor-fortress.

When nature takes over. A few eroded boulders are all that remain of ancient Apollonia, known to the Canaanites as Arsuf.

The great gate of biblical Lachish, where Starkey found the dramatic letters. My driver Reuven, a former Israeli-army tanker, studies the site of a tragic Jewish defeat and vows that there will never be another.

"And let my Lord know that we are watching for the signal of Lachish. . . ." Atop the so-called Governor's Residence of Lachish.

Praying is usually discreet, private, not excessively noisy, and rarely lachrymose.

But if there is agreement on nomenclature, there is abrasive conflict over other aspects of this holy place. I suppose it is in the nature of these sacred sites to invite argument. I had read about the dispute over the archaeological work at the Western Wall before I left for Israel. On Tishah b'Ab, the holiday marking the destruction of the Temple, hundreds of Orthodox Jews had broken into the site of the excavation at the southwestern corner of the Temple Enclosure and prayed amid the benches. According to the Jerusalem *Post*, the opening in the protective fence around the dig was made by someone from the Ministry of Religious Affairs. Quite naturally, the Department of Antiquities, Hebrew University, and other interested parties were furious. One does not trespass lightly on another fellow's dig.

I tried to ascertain why the religious should be so aroused against the diggers. According to a *New York Times* report: "The incursion by large numbers of Jews dressed in traditional black garb on the eve of Tishah b'Ab . . . was thought to be their reminder to scholars that the place is essentially a holy site, not an archaeological one."

But it seemed to me the evidence being unearthed by the archaeological team headed by Professor Benjamin Mazar could do nothing but bolster their faith. The work of the scholars would seem to strengthen the devotions of the faithful. But apparently they wanted to stake *their* claim to the new discoveries, and the Ministry of Religious Affairs appears to have worked with them.

Nathan Freedman, the learned director of public information for the Israel Government Tourist Office in New York, had told me about the work at the Western Wall: "It is probably the most exciting digging going on in Israel today, and one of the great archaeological undertakings anywhere in the world." He gave me the name of a friend at the Hebrew University who would make some introductions for me, since the site was overrun with journalists and photographers. Professor Mazar had to be approached carefully.

"I'll try," the gentleman at the university said, "but it's not that easy. Mazar has his problems. You read about the invasion by the Orthodox. It's got everyone's nose out of joint. A complicated and a messy business. They overturned a few baskets of potsherds."

I shuddered. This was terribly bad form. Classification, sorting, labeling—an orderly approach to confusion is essential in archaeological work.

"In addition," my contact said, "the Arabs are making noises. A few Arab houses were knocked down so the work could start, and that wasn't too bad. But the Moslem religious leaders claim that the digging is too close to the rear of the el-Aksa Mosque, and they aren't happy."

"I can see why Professor Mazar is concerned."

"And don't tell anyone I said this, but there are even some archaeologists, not Israelis, who think that our people are bypassing later strata—Persian, Arab, and so on—in their hurry to get down to Jewish periods. There's been some static over that. But the main issue is the religious one, and to put it bluntly, it's a contest to see who'll run things there, the true believers or the scientists. You can guess whose side I'm on."

After several days, I still had received no confirmation of an appointment with Professor Mazar. So being an old Hearst journalist, I decided to bluff my way in. Laden with two cameras, notebooks, and a smiling wife, I walked up to the barred entrance to the dig, to the left of the Dung Gate. A loose chain was draped across the roadway. Below stood a large modern building, the Rabbinical Courts of Appeal, one room of which was the excavation headquarters. To the left of this structure rose the southwestern corner of the wall, and around it were the new trenches, the pits of revelation, brimming with ancient evidence. Old Herod's works were being uncovered. The tyrant king was increasingly making his fearsome presence felt in new Jerusalem.

A bearded workman in a cap tried to stop me, but I tossed some names about and, walking in the dusty path—it was gray powder, pulverized building stones—I strolled past the trenches along the Turkish Wall and into the excavation office.

A lady secretary received me politely, listened to my needs, and said that Professor Mazar would be in shortly. It was now about ten in the morning and the heat was a physical force, a weight that lay on one's head and shoulders. A group of diggers, mostly foreigners, including some Americans, came in for their tea break. They looked utterly exhausted—sweaty, silent, coated with that dead powder—as they sipped their hot tea.

A few minutes later the professor walked in. Mazar is a short, wiry, gray-haired man with a sharply intelligent face. He looked harassed, angry, and very hot. At once he began to berate the volunteers sprawled on the benches and chairs. They cleared out. The professor then accepted a cup of tea and sat down wearily. For a few minutes he stared at the charts of the excavation. He looked like a man who had just completed a fifty-mile march in the desert, carrying a forty-pound pack.

Nervously, as gently as possible, I introduced myself and Marie, mentioned my contact at Hebrew University, and said I was doing a nonfiction work on archaeological sites in Israel. "I realize you are busy today, and that I've barged in without an appointment, sir," I said, "but all I would like to do is make an appointment for a later day this week, at your convenience . . ."

The professor seemed to be staring past me.

". . . I want this work to be as accurate as possible. I've already interviewed some of your colleagues—Dr. Glueck, Professor Weinberg, Professor Aharoni . . ."

Professor Mazar suddenly grasped my hand and gave it a sharp European shake. I wondered if my charm had captivated him. Then he rose. It dawned on me he was ushering me out, firmly, definitely, with terrible finality. I babbled on: ". . . any day at all, whenever you feel you can give me half an hour . . ."

He finally spoke. "Please, we are busy here. Good-bye." And he shoved me out.

With poor Marie beside me, I was suddenly standing on the porch of the Rabbinical Courts of Appeal, blinded by the sun, removed from the office and Professor Mazar's offended eyes. No one had ever faked me out of position more artfully. I wondered when the next confrontation with the Orthodox would take place. My money would be on Professor Mazar.

"You made your big mistake when you started reeling off those names of *other* archaeologists," Marie said. "Didn't you catch the expression on his face?"

"I don't know. The man is tired, hot, under pressure. I had no right to butt in the way I did."

"Maybe not. But you didn't help yourself with that name-dropping. I have a feeling that archaeologists are like movie directors. They don't want to hear anything—*anything*—about the competition."

The secretary had apparently watched us trudge like orphans back to the Dung Gate (an appropriate place to end up). She came after me. "You understand, it's very hard to get an interview," she said. "There is so much work here. But if you call me tomorrow, I shall see what I can do about arranging a meeting with the professor's assistant, Mr. Ben-Dov. He is authorized to talk to journalists."

I thanked her and studied the mysterious trenches at the base of the Southern Wall. In the Enclosure, I could see the silver dome of the el-Aksa Mosque, suggesting a radar globe. As we turned to take the path, an unbelievable sight loomed above us.

"Look at that mound," I said to Marie. "Next to the tar-paper shed."

"That pile of red stuff?"

"Red stuff. My God, those are potsherds, fragments." It was incredible. Baking in the sun was a mountain of fragments from the dig. It was about ten feet long, four feet in height, a mishmash of millennia: broken vessels, shattered dishes, enough old pottery to fill every museum in Israel. I wondered about those baskets that the Orthodox had up-ended. Suppose they had gone on a rampage, and attacked Mazar's mountain!

Rebuffed, I was by no means downhearted. In Israel there is always something else to see. There are no limits to the monuments and stones of antiquity. Equipped with a decent guidebook, the traveler never wants for diversion. We had not yet visited the Temple Enclosure, the sacred area within the Western Wall, and so we now crossed the ramp leading to the Bab-Al-Mughariba, the Gate of the Moors. On our left and below us was the Western Wall. Women prayed at the section nearest us. Along the main stretch of wall, a handful of men read their prayers. It was an odd time of day, late morning, and there were only a few worshipers. Facing the wall, a large modern esplanade has been built, replacing the old Arab houses and the narrow alley that existed before the Six-Day War. The pristine pavement and the modern stalls where prayer books, shawls, and skullcaps are available somehow do not mesh with the gargantuan old stones in the base of the Kotel Hama'aravi. Still, it is probably an improvement over the old arrangement.

We paused halfway up the ramp to the Gate of the Moors, and I read aloud from Zev Vilnay's guide:

> The tiers of large stones date from the Second Temple. In the course of centuries, however, debris of successive wars and destructions were thrown here, and ultimately a great part of the wall was covered with soil, so that a large portion of it is hidden beneath ground level. The lowest part may actually date from the time of Solomon's Temple. For generations the Jews have been making pilgrimages to the Wailing Wall, particularly on the eve of the ninth day of the month of Ab, Tishah b'Ab, in memory of the destruction of the Temple. Legend has it that in the dead of night a white dove—the Divine Presence —appears and coos sadly with the mourners.

I stopped and said to Marie: "White *dove?* Divine Presence? I thought that was a Christian notion."

"It had to start somewhere," she said.

"But . . . the dove . . . the Holy Spirit. There's that huge glass window in St. Peter's. And all those doves in paintings of the Annunciation. And now Vilnay tells me it was a Jewish symbol all along."

I was mulling over this Hebraic antecedent to the Holy Spirit as we entered the Moorish Gate and walked into the heated silence and tranquil beauty of the Enclosure, the parklike expanse known to Moslems as the Haram el-Sharif, the "Noble Sanctuary."

And it is noble. It is also restful, contemplative, a sanctuary both elevated and worldly, a tribute to the Arab caretakers who have maintained it. Just as one must give high marks to the Turks for the excellence of their walls, so must the Arabs be praised for the harmonious atmosphere within the Temple Enclosure. It is spacious. It is uncluttered. Trees and buildings maintain a proper distance from one another. And even when it is filled with tourists (it was not on this hot August morning, although on a later

visit it swarmed with them) it absorbs crowds and noise and
bustle and remains an oasis of calm and beauty. It is quite simply
different from other sites in Jerusalem, and it must be experienced to be understood.

Intoxicated, I fumbled with my exposure meter. Before me
loomed the golden Dome of the Rock, the misnamed Mosque of
Omar. Never mind that it has stood firmly on top of Mount
Moriah for twelve hundred years. Confronted with the majesty of
history, I sometimes cannot believe my good luck.

"You wish guide, sir?"

A middle-aged gentleman in a cocoa straw-hat and a green
sport shirt was smiling at me. On his breast pocket was a silver
badge. "I don't think so," I said. "I have several guidebooks."

"A guide is really necessary, sir. Mr. Nagel's book will tell you
as much. Look, sir, I have been guide for many Americans, and
they have no complaints. Here, sir, is one of my satisfied clients."
From his wallet he took out a card and gave it to me. I read:
"JACK PAAR, NBC, NEW YORK."

"Mr. Paar was most satisfied. Do you know him?"

During long years of service for N.B.C. I had met Mr. Paar
twice, and I had rather liked him. He was one of the few
"show-biz" people I had met who seemed genuinely interested in
other people and in foreign places. I knew about his travels and
had seen some of the films he had made. "I've met Mr. Paar," I
said, "and I know he is a demanding man. If he liked you, that's
good enough for me."

"Ah, sir, you will be satisfied, and madam too. First, sir, the
light is now too bright to take photographs of the Dome of the
Rock. You must take your picture at nine in the morning, No later
than ten. We will start with a general view of the Enclosure."

He had an engaging smile and a soft voice. I asked him his
name.

"My name is Moses."

"No, no. I have met a Michael who was Mahmoud, and a Charlie who was Khalil. Please tell me your name in Arabic, since
Arabic names have a pleasing sound."

"I see, sir, I see. My name is Mousa."

"Very fine, Mousa. Proceed."

"There are thirty acres in the Haram el-Sharif, sir. We are in the southeast corner of the Old City. This area is also called the Temple Mount, or Mount Moriah. Why Temple? Well, it was the place where stood the First and Second Temples of the ancient Jewish people. Orthodox Jews will not enter here, for fear they may walk on the holy places. Over there in the northwest corner is the Antonia Tower. Over on the Eastern Wall is the Golden Gate through which the Messiah will come. The golden dome, as you know, is the Dome of the Rock, and we shall visit it in a moment."

We walked across the smooth eroded stones of the immense courtyard. Two Israeli soldiers—older men with seamed faces, Home Guard reservists—lolled under a tree, cradling their rifles.

"The Second Temple was destroyed in the year 70. After that, many different structures were on this place. There was a Roman Temple of Jupiter. Then, in the seventh century, the Arabs built a mosque. Not the one you see, but one that preceded it. The Crusaders in the twelfth century put up a church. And then the Turks a new mosque. So all the religions have worshiped here."

As the sun rose the pavement of the enclosure turned white, becoming bleached and drained. The gleam of the giant golden dome was almost unbearable to the unprotected eye. The pines and cypresses, in contrast, underwent a pronounced darkening. They were now almost black.

"Now, sir, I shall direct you to the stables of King Solomon, in the southeast corner of the Haram el-Sharif."

"But I don't see anything there."

"Quite right, they are underground and locked. But I have the key."

We crossed the southern section of the Enclosure. The distance to the stable entrance was much farther than I had imagined. The sun not only discolored everything, it also played tricks with one's capacity to judge distance.

"Of course what you will see are not Solomon's stables, but Herod's, as used and reused by Romans and Crusaders. It is believed that Solomon's stables still exist below the ones now visible."

Underground, Mousa showed us the lintel of a Roman doorway that protruded several feet above the hard-packed gray earth, soil that had not seen daylight for several thousand years. In one

corner there was a Moslem *mihrab*, suggesting that the subterranean rooms—actually one vast room—had served various functions
in their long history. A hideaway? A sanctuary? In any event, I
was looking at the first underground parking complex in history.
Did the attendants slam the chariots into their niches with
screaming of brakes and denting of fenders?

"Now, sir," Mousa said, "we shall visit the el-Aksa, the second
holiest place in Islam."

I had read somewhere that Moslems regard el-Aksa as a place
that was holy even "in the days of ignorance" before the advent
of Mohammed, during the Abrahamic period. (I had to keep
reminding myself of Abraham's importance to Moslems; I had
always thought of him as ours and ours alone.) But the guidebooks informed me that the long domed building we now entered
was originally a church of the Virgin built by the Emperor Justi-
nian in A.D. 536. Thus it is an early Byzantine creation. Before
that, it was a Herodian building of some kind. Most of the guidebooks give the el-Aksa a low rating for beauty and architectural
style. It is something of a *fritto misto*, although it is not altogether unattractive. A restoration in 1938, according to Nagel's
guidebook, "disfigured" the interior with "sugary white Carrara
marble shafts." But to me the shiny white pillars were intriguing.
They suggested the old Hollywood Roman spectacles. Yet it is
easy to understand Nagel's claim that the restoration by Egyptian
architects was an attempt to obliterate the Byzantine and Crusader flavor.

"The pulpit, sir," Mousa said, "the most beautiful thing in
el-Aksa, a work of art, made by a craftsman from Aleppo for
Nureddin in 1168. It is carved wood with mother-of-pearl and an
ivory inlaid. Very, very beautiful."

(A few days later the pulpit was partially destroyed in the fire
set by the Australian Rohan. Although I saw no guards in the
el-Aksa—I am certain there were some, since the Israelis later
charged them with laxity—the defenselessness of so many sacred
places is a fact of life. One cannot expect the Israelis to post
armed guards at every stone. Considering the numerous holy
places they control, I think they acquit themselves very well. The
world, I fear, is filled with lunatics, and it is a wonder to me that
some idiot doesn't daily throw ink at the Western Wall or toss a

grenade at the Holy Sepulchre or paint "GORDON GO HOME" on the Garden Tomb. It is evident that the Israelis are doing a marvelous job of protecting shrines. Were they not, aggrieved parties would be wailing loud and long, with the French and the Vatican probably leading the chorus.)

I studied the diagram of the el-Aksa in my Vilnay guide. "That rear wall, Mousa," I said, "that is also the Southern Wall of the Temple Enclosure, where they are digging."

"That is correct, sir. Just behind the Huldah Gate."

"And the Moslem museum at the southwestern corner—its walls are the corner of the Western Wall, also an excavation site."

"That is accurate."

Orientation is always crucial to me. I want to know exactly where I am. What does the map tell me? Where does this road lead? What is at the end of that wall? In Jerusalem the proximity of historical places always astonished me. Here, in this one corner of the Enclosure, different religions, cultures, civilizations, millennia, stood cheek by jowl. One could climb to the roof of the museum or the el-Aksa and drop down into one of Professor Mazar's trenches, into Herodian pavements.

Mousa led us out of the el-Aksa and across the somnolent baking expanse of the Haram el-Sharif to the Dome of the Rock. Any panoramic photograph of Jerusalem must, perforce, include that aureate globe. It says Jerusalem the way the Eiffel Tower says Paris. It is a breathtaking creation, beautifully proportioned, dazzling with its colored mosaic facade, and altogether unlike any other holy place in the world. Most of the stones of the Holy Land are pale, burned out, worn down by that savage sun and the extremes of weather of which Dr. Glueck spoke. To give them their due, it is this aged, worn, irregular quality that enhances their charm. The doorway of the Virgin's Tomb, for example, or the fallen boulders of Chorazim comfort the eye with their noble plainness. They make for aesthetically satisfying if rather austere configurations.

Hence it is something of a gourmet feast, a holiday in a sweet shop, to confront the multicolored glory of the Dome of the Rock. The octagonal lower portion that supports the golden globe is a frenzied yet orderly bouillabaisse of tile, mosaic, glass, marble, and narrow Crusader columns. Behind the pale gray pillars on

the lowest level are extravagant marble plaques taken from old
Byzantine buildings. Above these are the arched windows, ornamented with exquisite square Armenian tiles. Above and between
the windows are mosaics, and running the length of the upper
part of the octagonal base is a frieze of verses from the Koran,
interlaced, delicate, graceful masterpieces of design. Without
being able to read a word, one is moved by the sense of motion,
of a continuum, of rhythm in these decorative figures.

It is difficult to convey the effect on the eye of all this
sensual color looming in the midst of the bleached stones of the
Temple Enclosure. The viewer almost feels guilty for enjoying it
so gluttonously. The predominating colors are green, yellow, and
blue, arranged to suggest variations on a single heavenly hue.
There must have been cunning trade secrets involving dyes,
designs, changes in color intensity brought on by age, to have
generated such a masterpiece. For the colors are not obvious or
blatant or vulgar. The blues tantalize, the greens mystify, the yellows soothe. I have wandered through the museums of Europe and
seen the French Impressionist, Italian Renaissance, and Flemish
paintings, and I doubt that the best of them—I am talking only
about *color*—ever achieved such magnificence in terms of subtle
hue, of consonant combinations, of startling contiguities, as did
the artists of the Dome of the Rock. Indeed, the more I studied
the tiles and mosaics around the eight-sided shrine, the more I
began to understand some of the arguments for abstract art. (Of
course, I am not won over. No modern abstractionist, to my way
of thinking, has ever come close to the work on the Dome of the
Rock.)

"Ah, sir. I see you are admiring the Dome," Mousa said.

"It is magnificent. It hypnotizes you, Mousa. It's a perfect unit.
It is impossible to study any of the segments, like that green and
yellow section over the windows, without relating it to the blue
and yellow squares above it. They lead your eyes on, and then
your heart and then your mind. My hat is off to the noble builders."

"Yes, it's a great source of pride to us. When you enter, you will
see the white rock of Mount Moriah, where Abraham your ancestor was ordered to sacrifice Isaac but was stopped by God. And
the same rock is the place from which Mohammed ascended to

heaven." (I did not mention Dr. Glueck's belief that the Moriah of the sacrifice was elsewhere, somewhere in the Negev.)

Talk about psychedelic lights and dayglo paints! No amount of Greenwich Village humbug, the gimcrackery of dingy light shows, could match the intense fantasy of the sides of the Dome of the Rock!

"Well, the history of the place, sir. It was built in the seventh century, after the Arab conquest. Perhaps you recall, sir, that the Caliph Omar was received in the year 638 in Jerusalem by the Byzantine emperor. But this building has no connection with Omar, and it is not a mosque, even though it is often wrongly called the 'Mosque of Omar.' It is like the Tower of David, which has nothing to do with David."

We paused to take off our shoes. I liked the ceremony, and I was finding that I liked the pace and the style of Islam. There is something to be said for slow, sleepy movements, unshod comfort, the ease of their religion.

Inside, it was the carpeting that struck me. It was bright red, unbelievably thick, and of such luxurious softness as to be positively sensual. It embraced one's tired feet, it caressed the toes and kissed the hot, calloused soles. However, it was too new, too ostentatious. It belonged in the Huntington Manor, not a shrine.

"Under Caliph Abd-al-Malik, Ommayad dynasty, the Dome was built to cover Mount Moriah at the same time that the el-Aksa was built. They say that this Dome of the Rock was the first great building of Islam." Mousa led us around the sanctuary.

I gazed up at the interior of the shrine. It is too rich, too gaudy, with its arabesques of gold, stained glass, and intricately carved and ornamental wood. Outside, the equalizing sun and the spacious surroundings of the Noble Sanctuary soften the bright mosaics. Within the great dome, despite the lofty ceiling and generous dimensions—it is seventy feet in diameter—the decor is almost stifling, repressive.

"The rock, sir," Mousa said, "very holy to all faiths. Where Abraham, our father, was going to sacrifice Isaac. Where Mohammed ascended to heaven. I shall show you his footprint."

The rock of Mount Moriah is a huge white-gray outcropping, pitted and cracked, surrounded by an iron railing and the monumental pillars that support the dome. I looked at the Prophet's footprint and wondered why the memorial to Jesus' ascension is so modest, so downright dingy, while that commemorating Mohammed's vertical rise is flamboyant beyond belief. A complicated theological matter, I felt, and one that I had best not pursue with Mousa.

"Here, sir and madam," he said, "if you put your hand in this box, you will touch the rock. A great opportunity. It is believed that Mount Moriah is the center of the universe."

Marie and I reached in and touched the stone.

"Now smell your fingers," he said.

We did. They were delicately perfumed. "Lovely," Marie said. "Jasmine, or lily of the valley."

"Oh, yes, madam. The priests put perfume on the rock, so that the memory of your contact with it will be a sweet one."

Mousa escorted us down a flight of stairs. Beneath the holy rock was a subterranean cave. We were in a small room with a few Arab tourists who were listening intently to an Arab guide. A glass partition blocked off part of the cave wall.

"This is the Bir El-Arweh," Mousa said. "The 'Well of the Souls.' It is thought the souls of the dead meet here to pray. Behind the glass, sir, is where the prophet Elijah prayed, also David and Solomon and Mohammed."

Mousa, with a look of annoyance, abruptly stopped his lecture and turned to the other guide. This fellow was pointing to a hole in the roof of the cave; his clients were staring up through it. Mousa spoke rather sternly to the guide, who shrugged, laughed, and resumed his explanation.

"So much misinformation is given out by those people who are not licensed," he said. "He was saying that Mohammed went up through that hole, that he made the hole in the rock on his way up. That is false. He ascended from the *top* of the rock, mounted on his horse Buraq, which had a woman's face, wings, and the tail of a peacock."

For some reason I didn't believe either version, but I kept my misgivings to myself. But after we had thanked Mousa, paid him, and resumed our wanderings in the Enclosure, I decided I liked the other guide's story better. Jerusalem is rich in sites where holy figures made their magical flight upward. Surely with all that divine backing the Messenger of Allah could have gone up anyway he wanted, and from any part of the rock. And why not by blasting his way through the rock, winged horse and all?

"What are you mumbling about?" my wife asked.

"I'm trying a countdown . . . seven, six, five, four, three . . . two . . . one . . . Prophet has lift-off . . ."

"Not too loud. You'll insult someone."

". . . right through the hole. I'm convinced that guide was right. Like a shot off a shovel, as Simon Dedalus used to say. This place was the Cape Kennedy of the ancient world, and the launch didn't cost nearly as much. I like the whole idea."

No summons came from the diggers at the Western Wall. It was not until the last week in August, after Marie had left to oversee our children's return from vacation and I was resting in my lonely room in the American Colony Hotel, that I at last made contact with Meir Ben-Dov, Mazar's assistant. "Yes, yes," he said, "why didn't you come out any day you wanted and talk to me?"

The truth was, Professor Mazar had scared me. The firm, imperious way in which he had shoved me out of his office had warned me off. I was not annoyed with him: I merely wallowed in guilt, shame, and self-consciousness. How could I possibly intrude again? How could I have the nerve to bother him, when he had Arab zealots, Orthodox intransigents, and rival archaeologists arrayed against him, not to mention the burdens of history? Moreover, in the weeks that had passed, the fire in the el-Aksa Mosque set by the addled Australian had exacerbated an already touchy situation vis-à-vis the Arab community.

"Come as early as you like," Ben-Dov said. "We start at seven in the morning and we finish at two in the afternoon."

As I trudged down the dusty path again, past the Rabbinical Court, I saw only a corporal's guard of workers. The 250 volunteers, all those tall, blond, bright American youths from Ambassador College in Pasadena (unmentioned in Barron's guide) were gone. Gone too were the bearded English boys, the Germans, Scandinavians, and Australians. (Odd that one never finds a Frenchman, Italian, or Spaniard volunteering for these jobs. Perhaps the link of their Latin heritage to the classical world makes them indifferent to it.)

On this ovenlike morning not more than a dozen people moved

about the square trenches. Silence, heat, the flooding light, had
settled over Professor Mazar's dig. The place was inert, lifeless,
the drama cooked out. It hardly seemed worth the fury of the
Orthodox.

Inside the office I saw Mr. Ben-Dov talking to Professor Mazar.
I stayed outside. Once chastised, I stay that way. Ever since the
archaeologist had sent me packing, I'd wondered what—apart
from name-dropping—I'd done to offend him. Was it my manner?
My face? My Al Fatah shoes?

After twenty minutes of lolling on the porch, snapping a few
photographs, I poked my long, anxious head in the door. Professor Mazar turned away. Mr. Ben-Dov, a pleasant ginger-bearded
young man with a gentle manner, came to my rescue.

"I am Mr. Green . . . the writer. You said yesterday . . ."

"Yes, yes," he said impatiently. "I remember. What is it you
want?"

"Some information, anything." I wanted to say, *a kind word*.
"You see, I'm working on this book on archaeology and I want to
say something about the dig at the Wall."

"I am afraid I am too busy to talk to you today."

My long features drooped. "You said yesterday I could come
out any time I wanted."

"Well, that was yesterday. I'll turn you over to somone. Come
along."

He led me across the site, across some wooden planks strad-
dling a depression, and up an incline to the tar-paper shack in
front of which stood the mountain of pottery fragments.

"Those buildings along the Turkish Wall . . . there . . ." I pointed
to them. "What are they?"

"Arab structures. From the Omayyad period, eighth century."

Inside the shack three women were sorting pottery fragments
and making notations. Ben-Dov introduced me to one of them, a
slender, dark girl in a yellow shift whom I shall call Yael.

"When Yael has taken you on a tour of the site," Ben-Dov said,
"drop by the office. I shall have a little free time."

He left. Yael kept sorting pottery. I stood in my tracks, a great
dumb ox, ignored. "Sit down," she said. "*Sit!*"

I sat.

"What do you want to know?" she asked.

"The basic facts about the dig. What its purpose is, what you are looking for."

"Can't you figure that out yourself?"

"In a general way, yes. I imagine it's to learn what Jerusalem was like in Herod's time. But I was hoping for something more specific."

"It's to learn about the pattern of settlements in this part of Jerusalem, to learn about topography, how the land was used."

"Ah . . . yes." I took out my notebook and started to sketch quickly. "I've read a great deal about the work and looked at some maps, and it would clarify matters for me if you could help me draw a rough map of the place, because I don't fully understand it." I started to sketch some lines on the notebook. She was glaring at me, furious.

"Now, let's make this the southwest corner of the Temple . . ."

"Temple *Enclosure.*"

"I meant the Enclosure. And this is the area just outside the Southern Wall. Here is Robinson's Arch; am I right? And the path that led to it was used by Herod and his court. Then there's the Tyropoen Valley, the Valley of the Cheesemakers, that ran north from the Siloam Pool, and continued to Wilson's Arch. And there was a bridge leading to that also, which was used by the priests. . . ."

As I made rough lines on the paper, I realized I knew more about the area than I had imagined.

"Why do you do this?" she asked angrily.

"I want it clear in my mind before you take me around. I have a weak sense of direction and terrain, and if you could clear this up for me I'd appreciate it. Okay, right below the Southern Wall of the Enclosure are those trenches. And along the southern wall of the city—the Turkish Wall—is the Omayyad Building. Now what I want to know is this: What is this area in the middle . . ."

Her suntanned fist slammed down on my drawing. The pen flew out of my hand.

"*No! No!*" she shouted. "*Stop that! You will do it my way!* If you keep up this nonsensical drawing we will be here all day, and I can't spend all day answering your questions!"

"I'm sorry," I said. "Just this one . . . if the Double Gate is here, then where was . . ."

"*No!*" She slammed her hand down on the notebook again. "You will not ask questions! You listen to me! Then we will go out, and *then* you may ask questions!"

I suppressed an urge to stuff my notes down Yael's lovely throat. After a while tolerance runs thin. What had I done that was so objectionable? My hastily sketched diagrams were pretty good—concise, accurate. Why was she so angry? Yet she was not passionately angry. Her mahogany eyes did not flash, her voice, though loud and peremptory, was not emotionally charged. Yael, I concluded, was hot and exhausted and sick of journalists.

Chastened, I folded my map and listened. The excavation of the area outside the Southern and Western Walls of the Temple Mount, or Enclosure, began in February of 1968, she told me. The greater part of the digging was taking place in an area bounded by the Turkish city walls on the south and east, the Southern Wall of the Temple Mount on the north, and the Rabbinical Courts building on the west. My pen dangled in midair—I was about to make a notation on my rough map—and she took it out of my hand.

"Listen to me and stop drawing," she said.

I listened. She discussed the question of topography. Herod the Great had altered the lay of the land, dumping tons of *milo*, earthen fill, into the Valley of the Cheesemakers, so as to extend greatly the sanctified area of the Temple Mount, that is, Mount Moriah. He thus created a broad plateau surrounding the Temple, buttressed with arches and columns and enclosed within mighty supporting walls. It was, Yael explained, a tremendous feat of engineering and imagination. Tons of *milo* were dumped into the eastern slope of Mount Moriah where it descended into the Kidron Valley. The valley bed on the west, the Tyropoen, likewise had to be brought up to the level of the Mount. The Southern Wall, at whose base they were now digging, was part of this Herodian urban renewal: giant stones placed on foundations resting in the bedrock. Above the Southern Wall, in the Temple Mount, Herod had built his royal stoa, according to Josephus "a structure more noteworthy than any under the sun."

"May I ask a question?" She frowned, but I charged on. "I'm not clear as to how far on either side Herod extended the Mount."

She snatched the pen from my hand again and began to sketch hurriedly on my notebook. In a few seconds she'd made the layout comprehensible to me. I still have her sketch, a souvenir of my communion with the great Temple.

Yael explained to me the significance of Robinson's Arch, the remains of which jut from the Western Wall. It was part of the bridge Herod built for himself and his court for access to the Temple. Farther north in the Western Wall is Wilson's Arch, the terminus of a parallel bridge used by the priests. The common people apparently entered the Temple Mount through the Huldah Gate in the Southern Wall, which can be seen today as the ruins of the rebuilt Roman portals, the Double Gate and the Triple Gate.

"What are the oldest levels you have reached?" I asked.

"Herodian. You must get over the idea, which amateurs always have, of Solomonic levels. The Western Wall and Southern Wall are Herodian. There is nothing left of the First Temple except possibly some material buried with the *milo* that was dumped into the valleys to support the expanded Mount. And that was nine hundred years after Solomon. The lowest stratum is Herodian, right down to bedrock."

Herod was very much around. I would have preferred Solomon, whose image is more distinguished and whose legacy is one we can honor. As for Herod, I had trouble relating to him, but I tried to be tolerant. "What kind of Herodian structures have you found?" I asked.

"Come, we'll take a walk around."

I followed her out. I could not help noticing her exchange a faint movement of the head with another girl. As if to say, *Oi, the shlemiels they send us.*

"I take it you are not too interested in the Omayyad Building," she said, as we walked past the terrifying pottery mound and crossed the plank bridge.

"I'm neutral on Omayyads."

"There are several theories as to what it was. Possibly a government house or a hostel for pilgrims. Most likely they were servants' quarters—the servants who worked for the Haram. It was destroyed in an earthquake in the eighth century."

We crossed the area in front of the Rabbinical Courts. Only a

few workmen, bearded, cap-wearing Israelis suggesting the ghet-
tos of Lodz and Vilna, wrestled wheelbarrows across the dusty
paths. It was not yet nine in the morning and their shirts were
drenched.

She led me to the base of the Southern Wall. "Look at the
stones in the bottom of the Wall," Yael said. "Have you ever seen
such stones?"

I admitted I had not.

"That one there. It is eleven meters long and weighs eighty
tons. And it is perfectly shaped. But it is not the biggest. The biggest you can't see from here, but it weighs a hundred and twenty
tons."

An edge of pride colored her voice. Some of the acerbity had
vanished. She was being softened by the sight of Herod's
gigantism.

"They are pretty big stones," I said.

"Now look down, all the way," she commanded. "And you will
see the original Herodian pavement, eleven meters down."

I stared into the pit and saw the great gray slabs. Something
was expected of me, but I didn't know what. "Eleven meters . . .
ah . . . that is down from where we are standing, or from . . ."

"Down? What means down? *Down*. From here!"

I decided to nod my head from now on and take photographs.

Four distinct periods were identified, she said. Arab, Byzantine,
Roman, and the native Herodian rock. In excavating, the archaeologists had to dig their way through an Omayyad street, then
the Byzantine and Roman strata, to the street of Herod.

"Look at those steps," she ordered me. "Those are from Herod's
time also. And do you see the big blocks lying on their side?"

"Yes. They . . ."

"They are from the destruction of the Second Temple. A lot of
the debris has been removed—parts of sundials, Corinthian
capitals."

The street ran parallel to the Southern Wall. The small flight of
steps was almost at the corner of the Southern and Western walls.
One could turn the corner and come upon the projecting pier of
Robinson's Arch. We were in Herod's bloody world.

Yael led me around the corner. Above were the projecting
stones of Robinson's Arch. Beneath were a series of boulders set

horizontally on giant ashlars, creating the effect of small booths. I was about to ask what they were—some digging and earth clearing was going on around them—when she told me.

"Shops," she said.

"Oh. For what? I mean, this was the Holy of Holies. What would they sell here?"

She tossed her dark hair. "Sacrifices. Pigeons. Animals. Grain. Oil. Incense. They sold them to the people. We have found measuring cups and stone bowls, so we assume they are shops."

This notion settled rather slowly; I had hoped for something else. Distantly I heard the bleat of a young lamb and the cooing of a white dove.

"Below them is an entrance to an aqueduct," she said. "It runs north and south. Charles Warren was the first to discover it. We are not certain where the water came from—maybe from some place to the north."

I shaded my eyes and stared at the protruding rocks and the projecting pier of Robinson's Arch. In my mind's eye I saw Herod—bearded, perfumed, with that hard, cold gleam in his eye —walking hurriedly over the bridge, his purple robes billowing, trailed by relatives and sycophants on his way to some bloody disembowelings. I was not moved by the vision. Solomon or David would have been more to my liking.

"And the king walked over the bridge," I muttered.

"We are not sure it was an actual bridge. It did not rest on arches, but probably on the roofs of buildings. They are digging across the Cheesemakers Valley looking for the opposite end of the king's way."

The stone kiosks seemed to me grim and morbid. Not a sentimentalist where vivisection is concerned, I am not reconciled to endless slittings of sheep's throats and eviscerations of pigeons as a means of reaching God. Oh, I am aware that religions are guilty of much grander bestialities than animal sacrifice; but what disturbed me as I gazed at the neat little booths where fluttering birds and defecating goats were once sold was the degree to which this cult was central to ancient Judaism. Jerusalem, I read somewhere, was once known as Ariel, the place where sacrifice is burned. And apparently it went on continually. To put it crudely, the Temple was a charnel house, an abattoir.

Wanting desperately to identify with the Temple, I found that all I could think of was the great horned altar, its four projections smeared with sheep's blood, the ashes of a pigeon's guts, the sizzling fat from a cow's intestines. *Mizbeah*, the Hebrew word for *altar*, means "place of slaughter." And evidently the slaughter was endless. At times the holy place ran with animal blood, burned bones, carcasses. Outside the Temple Wall, a mountain of ashes grew—the garbage from the altar.

As I studied the "shops," I tried to hear some rational voice telling me that the ritual killing of sheep and doves wasn't all that dreadful. Besides, this all took place several thousand years ago, and who are we, in our rationalistic modernity, to cast aspersions on our antecedents? I conceded that all this was true. What bothered me was the transported awe, the elevated respect, the unfathomable inspiration that observant Jews feel in the presence of the Wall and the Temple. It eluded me. I can understand the love for the *abstractions* of the faith—the Commandments, the laws, the codes, the binding sense of unity and community. But to stand outside these walls, bending, swaying, lost in unearthly devotions, enraptured with memories of the old Temple, when to a great extent this seat of faith was a place where blood-smeared priests slit the throats of cooing doves and disemboweled bleating sheep—all this I find so far beyond my experience that I cannot summon the remotest relationship to it. And I repeat, I am no hand-wringer about the killing of animals. But from what I have since read on the subject, sacrifice was central, continual, and obsessive with the old Yahweh cult of Jerusalem. In ancient days any free-association test would surely produce the response "sacrifice" to the word "temple."

Father Roland de Vaux's book *Ancient Israel* (published in two paperback volumes by McGraw-Hill) deals in fascinating detail with the history of sacrifice in Israel: "The altar was the place of sacrifice and sacrifice was the principal act in Israel's cult."

Father de Vaux explains that there were several varieties of sacrifice. First was the *holocaust*, in which the entire victim was burned and nothing was given back to the person offering it to the priest except the skin. A second type was *communion* sacrifice, in which the animal was shared between God, the priest, and the person making the offering, the last eating it as a holy object.

Yahweh's share—kidneys, liver, fat—was burned on the altar. The priest got the breast and the right leg. The rest went to the donor, who ate it, sharing it with his family and guests. *Expiatory* sacrifices were either for the remission of sin or for reparations. In these the blood of the victims had special potency. It was collected by the priest, who sprinkled it seven times against the veil that curtained the Holy of Holies, rubbed it on the corners of the altar in front of the veil, and poured it out at the foot of the big altar of holocausts. Father de Vaux cites several biblical references which explain these acts, notably: "Without the shedding of blood, there is no forgiveness at all." Finally, there were vegetable offerings. These appeal to me more. Flour, corn, first fruits, or bread were burned. The shewbread, which consisted of twelve loaves symbolizing God's covenant with the twelve tribes (these were not burned, but eaten), and offerings of incense, a practice common to all Oriental religions, were other variations.

Father de Vaux rejects out of hand the notion that Israel ever practiced human sacrifice. The story of Abraham, Father de Vaux argues (I gather he and Dr. Glueck differ on this) does *not* signify the replacement of human sacrifice with animal sacrifice by the people of patriarchal times. Rather, he states, it is a reassertion of what had always been the case. The Israelites did not offer children to Yahweh, as did the Canaanites, and Abraham, in obeying God's order, was rewarded by a renewal of the Lord's promise to his posterity to make them the select people. Father de Vaux states that the story has one meaning, *"namely, that the religion of Israel rejected human sacrifice."*

Father de Vaux sums up animal sacrifice as practiced by the ancients of Israel:

> Sacrifice is the essential act of external worship. It is a prayer which is acted, a symbolic action which expresses both the interior feelings of the person offering it, and God's response to this prayer. It is rather like the symbolic actions of the prophets. By sacrificial rites, the gift made to God *is* accepted, union with God *is* achieved, and the guilt of man *is* taken away. But these effects are not achieved by magic: it is essential that the external action should express the true inward feelings of man,

and that it should be favorably received by God. Failing
this, sacrifice is no longer a religious act.

Thus, sacrifice has three main functions: the gift to God, communion with God, and expiation. After discussing the denuncia-
tions of sacrifice by various prophets such as Jeremiah, Amos, and
Micah ("The sacrifice of the wicked is an abomination to
Yahweh, but the prayer of upright men is his delight"), Father de
Vaux comes to the Essenes, the Dead Sea separatists and reform-
ers who are often regarded as precursors of Christ. These desert
purists, the evidence indicates, did not reject the cult of sacrifice
altogether as is sometimes believed. What they did was to cut
themselves off from the priesthood which ran the ritual killings
in the Temple, regarding these men as unworthy. The sacrificial
cult thus became more inward and spiritual, an outward expression of an internal holiness and purity, of value only in terms of
the inner essence it symbolized.

Quite naturally, this brings Father de Vaux to Christianity, and
to this conclusion, a logical one for a history-oriented archaeologist who is also a Roman Catholic priest:

> The Temple could disappear, and animal sacrifices had
> to end, for they were merely the imperfect figure, indefi-
> nitely repeated, of the sacrifice of Christ who offered
> himself "once for all" in a "unique offering" for our
> redemption and our sanctification, as the Epistle to the
> Hebrews repeatedly insists. And the Church which
> Jesus has founded will continue, until the end of time, to
> commemorate this perfect sacrifice and live by its fruits.

I cannot help but feel that in this instance Father de Vaux's
faith clouds his historic judgment. It had seemed to me throughout the reading of his closely argued and felicitously written
account of sacrifice among the Hebrews that he was giving them
the benefit of all doubts. But I tended to side with the prophets
who denounced the endless killing of oxen and doves as abomina-
tions (Hosea 6:6: "For I desired mercy and not sacrifice; and the
knowledge of God more than burnt offerings"). Now, at the end
of the long exegesis, I realized where Father de Vaux's benign

logic led. Certainly I would not be the man to fault him on envisioning the slow change in sacrifice, from a primitive obsession to an inner spiritual ideal, a natural, preordained progression from early Judaism to the primacy of Jesus Christ. Indeed, if one is a devout Christian and entertains generous feelings about one's Judaic origins, it is comforting and reasonable to interpret the cult of sacrifice in that manner. But lacking any identification with "the Church which Jesus has founded," I found only minimal solace in Father de Vaux's argument. I say minimal, because as I recalled that hot August day at the Wall, and the sight of those stone kiosks where trussed pigeons and lambs were sold, I decided that if the priest-archaeologist could regard sacrifice in a compassionate light, so might I. On balance, though, I take my stand with Hosea, or the moralist of Proverbs who tells us (21:3) that "to do justice and judgment is more acceptable to the Lord than sacrifice."

I looked again at those mammoth Herodian blocks in the base of the Wall—flanged, shaped, ageless, immovable—and I tried to draw some inspiration, some sense of elevation from them. I failed. They are unquestionably very big stones, and it took engineering genius, lots of poor people and slaves, and organization to get them where they now stand, secure and eternal, after two thousand years. But they do not, I confess, fill me with faith or courage or confidence.

After Yael had shown me the smaller excavation across the Valley of the Cheesemakers (no one was at work there), where Professor Mazar is seeking the corresponding pier to Robinson's Arch, we returned to the office. I was hoping Mr. Ben-Dov would have a moment to talk to me. He was friendly but too busy.

"This business of Herod," I said, dust clotting my tongue, "how do the Jews of Israel regard him today?" We were standing on the porch of the office. The workmen had stopped. The site was deserted. Old Herod's stones were deserted—massive, pitted, pale-gray, unyielding. Beneath them, along the Southern Wall of the Temple Mount, I could see the long trench in which rested Herod's precious pavement and the three steps. Was it my imagination? Or had my guide and all the newspaper accounts I had read of the dig, all the talk I had heard about it in Israel, reflected an unseemly excitement, a controlled hysteria, over a

few gray steps, a sidewalk, and some purported shops—just
because they were Herod's?

Mr. Ben-Dov squinted in the morning sunlight. "The Orthodox
Jewish community is neutral on Herod," he said. "There is no
expressed opposition to him. Nothing serious."

"And the Christians, of course, hate him."

"But that is nothing new. He is a convenient villain."

"But he was a dreadful man, wasn't he?" I asked, gasping.
Herod's sins were sitting on my shoulders. "He murdered his
wife, his sons, countless others."

"So? That was the age he lived in. What about David? He killed
plenty of people also, but he's a hero."

"But Herod wasn't even born a Jew.".

"He was a *Jew*," Ben-Dov said. "Both parents had converted.
Antipatris was a convert, and so was Cypros. No getting around
it, he was Jewish, being the son of two converted parents. You
probably read it in one of those books that wants us to disown
Herod because Christians don't like him. Too bad."

The archaeologist had a point. I recalled a recent biography of
Nikolai Lenin in which the author went to great lengths to prove
that Lenin was not really a Russian, since he had a strong infusion
of Chuvash and German blood. It seemed like arrant nonsense to
me. If one wanted to discredit Lenin, there were better ways than
genealogy. Thus, like it or not, we would have to accept the fact
of Herod's Jewishness.

"Most of the rabbis," Ben-Dov said, "do not regard Herod as a
murderer or a killer. They look at him with a neutral and unemotional eye. Today, he is being revealed more and more as a great
builder of cities and of temples."

"Is it possible his character is being justified because of that?
That it's all right for him to have murdered people because he
built cities?"

Ben-Dov frowned. "I don't think so. This is an old estimate of
him, that he built well. It is just that archaeology is substantiating
what we knew of him from the sources, from Josephus and the
others."

"I have the feeling many people would like to be more than neutral where Herod is concerned," I said. "I don't think you are
quite ready to declare him a national hero, but I sense a kind of

grudging admiration. We have an old American expression. I think our generals used it in reference to Chiang Kai-shek during the war. 'He's a son-of-a-bitch, but he's our son-of-a-bitch.'"

"That may be true," the archaeologist said. "You must remember that Herod was a great politician also. It was not easy to rule in those days. The king had to strike a balance between many factions. He had to please the Jews, the Romans, the Arabs, all the new sects that were springing up. Herod did his best, considering the terrible times."

"But he was a stooge. He was a puppet of the Romans."

"What if he was? Every Jewish king of that period was, including the first Agrippas."

I thanked Mr. Ben-Dov and his assistant, Yael. She returned to her pottery shed, leaving me blinking in the heat of the forenoon.

Some months later, I discovered in the reliable Jerusalem *Post* that Herod was still making the headlines and arousing the admiration of archaeologists and journalists:

HEROD'S SPLENDID BUILDING REVEALED IN TEMPLE MOUNT EXCAVATIONS

The "magnificence" of Herodian engineering and construction in Jerusalem's Temple Mount area—during the century preceding the destruction of the sanctuary in 70 c.e.—has emerged in archaeological excavations at the site, Professor Benjamin Mazar, director of the dig, told the press Thursday.

The professor went on to discuss the twelve-meter-wide Herodian pavement I had viewed from above, some tombs from the ninth century b.c. found on the slopes opposite the Western Wall, and underground storage rooms below the pavements. He sounded optimistic in his report. There was no reference to interference from the Jewish Orthodox, protests from the Arabs (temporarily mollified after the sentencing of Rohan, the mosqueburner), or captious criticism by non-Israeli archaeologists. All was apparently going well.

CHAPTER XI

Who Are We Waiting For— Moshe Dayan?

We were on an Egged bus, becalmed outside the Egged office in Haifa. One tourist was late, the little blonde girl who was to be our guide informed us. So we waited—five minutes, ten, fifteen.

There was an American-Jewish family on the bus (I shall try to be objective about them) who, from the moment of boarding, acted as if they had invented Israel. The details pain me. They sang, they joked, they were loud, they applauded, they called to one another and they seemed to want the other tourists to notice them. *Look at us, how Jewish, how pro-Israeli we are!* They made me uncomfortable. They had built a fence around their Zionist pride. They talked to no one else—a mother and father, two sons, and a daughter—and there was something about their insular exhibitionism that did not invite participation.

300

After some loud complaints about delay, the woman—the most aggressive of the party, leader of songs, applause, cheers—walked up to the driver and spoke angrily to him. "What is going on here? Who are we waiting for—Moshe Dayan?"

He looked at her with the weary wisdom of a man who had run armored buses through the Latrun Pass. "Lady, in this country everybody is Moshe Dayan."

It silenced her, but not for long. The missing tourist arrived, we left a bit behind schedule, and spent an enjoyable day in western Galilee. I tell the story to indicate the informal nature of organized tours in Israel. I recommend them wholeheartedly to the tourist. The guides are superb: well-informed, friendly, multilingual. Many of them were trained by my redoubtable friend, Zev Vilnay. The drivers are skillful, patient, good-natured. Normally I am not a man for organized group tours, but strictures of time and schedule required us to do some of our sight-seeing by bus. It turned out to be a good decision.

One of the first tours we took was to Jericho. It had a marvelously ad-lib quality. To begin with, Jericho is occupied territory, a West Bank city that once housed a great many Arab refugees. Private cars still cannot drive through the West Bank area at night, but tours leave daily from the major cities. "Absolutely safe," the short, stout guide said. "I know all the Arabs in Jericho."

This did not thoroughly reassure me. But he did know his way around Jericho. A lady tourist, a New York schoolteacher, was having trouble with her shoe. Our guide had the bus stop in the heart of downtown Jericho, found a cobbler, and had it fixed. On the way back he bought dates from a pushcart and chatted with some elderly Arabs puffing *nargilehs* outside a coffee shop. (This compulsion to buy Arab fruits and vegetables is universal in Israel. The Jerusalem *Post* tells me that on Saturdays, when shops are closed in West Jerusalem, Jews go to the Arab section for produce, especially *koussa*, a variety of squash, and Jericho bananas, described as "very sweet and creamy." But real bargain-hunters spurn East Jerusalem. They go to Ramallah, a West Bank town, where fruit and vegetables are half the price one pays in Jerusalem.)

"We are in enemy territory," I said to Marie. "And I am not at all afraid." The guide, like Cinderella's prince, helped the schoolteacher put her shoe on. No charge, he said; the cobbler was his friend.

"These tour buses are psychological weapons," I said. "The Israelis run them into occupied areas to show the Arabs how little they fear them. And I think it is having a traumatic effect."

This, of course, was before the unfortunate Mr. Holtz, a tourist from Brooklyn, and a Christian woman from Michigan were killed in separate attacks. But the tours go on. Gaza is the only area that is off limits. Buses roll out of Tel Aviv and Jerusalem daily for the West Bank, the Golan Heights, the Sinai.

For my own part, I was less disturbed by fears of the Al Fatah than by the loquaciousness of tourists, Israeli, French, and American. Our guide to Jericho spoke in Hebrew, then English. As soon as he switched to English, the Israeli tourists would start chattering. There was a French couple aboard, and they were so enraged that he did not deliver a French version that they chattered through *both* the English and Hebrew. I daresay that the lady teacher, Marie, and I were the only ones who tried to listen to the poor man. Oddly, he did not seem to mind; he appeared inured to it.

We stood on the mound of old Jericho, the ancient tel, looking down on the deep, dismal pits as the guide tried to tell us something about the strata. I caught only three or four words. Everyone was talking at once.

"If Joshua had been in charge of this group," I said to him, "he'd never have gotten the children to shout. They'd all have been so busy talking to each other, they wouldn't have heard his order."

"Yes, probably. But maybe they would have talked the walls down."

In the distance, on the summit of a bleak, inhospitable mountain, I saw the Monastery of the Temptations. Tradition says this is the site where Jesus was brought to be tempted by the devil. It is known as the Mountain of the Forty (*Mons Quarantana* in Latin), to commemorate Christ's forty days and nights of fasting. It has an appropriately desolate look about it. And far from suggesting temptation it appears a place of denial, mortification and austerity.

Of course everything is not quite as serene in the occupied areas as I have indicated. We stopped at a police station near Jericho. The guide conversed briefly with one of those trim, mustachioed policemen. It developed that we would not be permitted to visit the site of Jesus' baptism on the Jordan River. Tours usually stop there for a swim. But this day it was off limits. No reason was given.

The main attraction of the Jericho tour is the Hisham Palace, an outrageously flamboyant pleasure dome of the Omayyad period. En route we halted to inspect the beautifully preserved mosaic floor of a small synagogue. It did not compare with the mosaics Dani had showed us at Hamath Tiberias, but it was worth seeing. "Proof that Jews lived in Jericho for a long time," the guide said to me. By now he had discovered that I was his main audience. "This is from the Byzantine era. Which proves Jews didn't listen to Joshua who told them not to live here, that it was a cursed city."

About a mile farther on we came to the Hisham Palace, so called because it was the seat of Caliph Hisham II. The Khirbet Mafjar, as it is also known, was a winter palace for the Omayyads, who had their capital in Damascus. Today a protective corrugated roof has been placed over the extensive ruins. But when the hedonistic Arab dynasts lolled there, oiled and scented and stroked by lissome, fawn-eyed maidens, it was roofless, a tribute to the sunny days of Jericho.

Even in a semirestored state, the pale-gold stones and pillars convey a sense of luxury, of Eastern sloth and indulgence, of heavy-lidded potentates, shifty eunuchs, and perfumed houris. It is a stunning ruin, an ornate and overproduced complex of colonnades, gateways, circular windows. A huge round decorative piece stands in the middle of one great hall. One expects Yvonne de Carlo, in harem pants and pointed slippers, to peek around it. Or Tony Curtis, announcing, "Yonder is the castle of my father." The mosaic pavement in the Caliph's bath, the work of Greeks from Syria, is particularly handsome, depicting a lion attacking a deer beneath the spreading branches of a huge shade tree.

"You can imagine this place when the Caliph came here," our guide said. "Tame animals, fruit trees, servants. Like the *Arabian Nights*. They knew how to treat themselves."

I asked him where the treasure of the Hisham Palace was located. He told me that some notable stucco decorations were in the Rockefeller Museum in Jerusalem, and were worth a look. We visited the museum a few days later, and the guide was right. Often one has difficulty placing a particular find with the site from which it originated. The vases and pottery and weapons, polished and cleaned and displayed behind glass cases, do not seem to relate to the bare, baking stones on some desolate hilltop. But in the case of the Hisham Palace treasure, the association is immediate. They have the look of opulent decadence, of crapulous sensuality, and they have a coarse, lewd humor about them that is absolutely beguiling. The works are in stucco, white-gray, and are well preserved. Some of the decorations are abstract designs; there is a series of balustrades, miniature courts, and colonnades. But the most fascinating are statues of women, Omayyad notions of ravishing beauty.

"That one winked at me," I said to Marie—and I was only half joking. (Actually one eye had been chipped away; but it appears a wink). It was a natural reaction.

The Hisham maidens stand in a large circular room in the museum. They seem to have taken over. Squat, broad-beamed, round-busted, it is their eyes that command. They stare like goiter sufferers. And they are crude, whorish ladies, without morals or scruples, intriguers and liars, each one eager to gain the Caliph's favors. Although their arms have been broken, they seem to be beckoning. There is in their attitudes a brazen, arrogant naïveté. They seem to be saying, *We will use our sex, our cunning, to get what we want.* What is most strange about this attitude—it is evident in the goggling eyes, the indecent rumps and fat bellies—is that they are singularly unattractive, although I am not prepared to sneer at whatever it was that intrigued Omayyad Caliphs of the eighth century. Dwarfism, steatopygia, and hyperthyroid eyes may have been widely admired.

"I thought that Moslems were forbidden to depict the human form in art," Marie said, after I had taken photos of the Hisham temptresses.

"I think that came later," I speculated. "Probably as a result of these statues."

Haifa, built on the slopes of Mount Carmel, proved to be a

good central point from which to take tours. We stayed there several days, enjoying the grand view from our balcony in the Dan Carmel Hotel, riding daily into the hinterlands on the Egged buses.

Haifa is spotless, a tribute to the indefatigable Mayor Aba Khoushy. (Jerusalem is also rather clean, but Tel Aviv is depressingly dirty.) Haifans, like San Franciscans, tend to exhibit an aggressive vanity about their city. Like them, they spend a good deal of time congratulating themselves on living in Haifa. An elderly tour guide, for example, as soon as the bus got under way, before he had even introduced himself, advised us: "Recently, travel writers of the world voted that Haifa was the third most beautiful city in the world. The first is Rio de Janeiro, the second San Francisco."

No one argued with him. He continued: "The Jewish people, because of Israel, are now living in their most fulfilled, most important period. Some tourists accuse me of speaking propaganda, but that does not bother me; I will say it anyway. All the prophecies about the Jewish people are being fulfilled at this moment. You can read it all in the last five chapters of Isaiah."

Unfortunately, no sooner had he elevated our thoughts with this pronouncement than the bus stopped at the Baha'i Shrine, or the "Shrine of the Bab." This gleaming gold-domed creation, visible amid its lush gardens from virtually every point in Haifa, is, I am afraid, a rude parody of religion, a Forest Lawn for the living, something out of a Peter Sellers film. Bronze peacocks and marble lilies abound in the formal gardens. The interior of the globular shrine is strangely middle-class—a carpet, flowers in a vase, a large mirror—and suggests Farenga's funeral parlor in the Bronx.

On the bus I read the pamphlet given to us by a black girl at the door of the temple to Bab—he was the founder of Baha'i or, more accurately, its herald, founding a precursor faith, Babism—and I realized that my thoughts were ungenerous. Architecturally the shrine may have left a lot to be desired. But as for Baha'i philosophy, it seemed to me as good as most religions, and better than some.

"The earth is but one country and mankind its citizens," a Baha'i devotee wrote. "Let not a man glory in this that he loves his country, let him rather glory in this that he loves his kind."

The original Bab was executed by the Persians in 1850, at the age of thirty-one, and it is fair to conclude that the man was ahead of his time. The actual founder of Baha'i was a successor, Baha-ullah, who was exiled to Acre, north of Haifa, in 1868.

The Persians killed the original Bab, the brochure said, because of his liberal religious teachings. As I read on, I could understand why—if the faith's modern philosophy was anything like its herald's. The man was a threat, a desperate revolutionary who had to be destroyed.

> It [Baha'i] enjoins upon its followers the primary duty of an unfettered search after truth, condemns all manner of prejudice and superstition, declares the purpose of religion to be promotion of amity and concord, proclaims its essential harmony with science, and recognizes it is the foremost agency for the pacification and the orderly progress of human society. It unequivocally maintains the principle of equal rights, opportunities and privileges for men and women, insists on compulsory education, prescribes monogamy, discourages divorce, emphasizes the necessity of strict obedience to one's government, exalts any work performed in the spirit of service to the level of worship, urges either the creation or selection of an auxiliary international language, and delineates the outlines of those institutions that must establish and perpetuate the general peace of mankind.

Now apart from a few fusty notions such as an antidivorce law, and the concept of unwavering obedience to the state, Baha'i seems to be a reasonably decent sort of religion. After all these notions were being entertained by a Persian sect (Babism was an offshoot of the Ismaili Moslems) in the middle of the nineteenth century, some years before Leo XIII began to consider the radical idea that labor unions might be permissible, and a century before John XXIII opened those windows. Although in its origins Baha'i, taking its cue from its earlier form, Babism, stressed the "divine presence" in its leader and was filled with mystico-authoritarian notions of a Supreme Intelligence and a Supreme Will, the modern faith sounds very much like the Society of Friends. It stresses humanitarianism, brotherhood, universal tolerance, social equality, and an end to sectarianism and denominationalism. Statistics on the faith are hard to come by, but there are believed to be two or three million members worldwide and several thousand in the United States. American headquarters are at the Baha'i Temple in Wilmette, Illinois. Interestingly, the faith does not require that its members withdraw from their former religious organizations, but prefers that they remain with them, the better to carry out missionizing in behalf of Baha'i. (Many of the organized churches might benefit from some small infusions of Baha'i tolerance.)

Later that day we were led up a dirt path in a scruffy park to the cave of the prophet Elijah. It was our first confrontation with a different aspect of Israel, and it was a sobering one. A family of swarthy Israelis—a lean, brown father, Indian in appearance, a shrouded mother, several runny-nosed children—were munching sandwiches under a tree.

"Orientals," our guide said. "They revere Elijah, and they come here to worship. You will see inside."

Two tall women, draped in billowing gray robes and white wimples, women with large features and vague, unformed faces, drifted by. "Druse ladies," he said. "They also worship at Elijah's cave."

As we turned the corner of a large whitewashed building, a stench of ripe garbage assailed us. To the right of the entrance to the holy aperture in the rock—it is a great gouge carved in the foot of Mount Carmel—was a kind of picnic area. Families were having their lunch under leafy trellises. People lolled about on dirty carpets and greasy mattresses. Children shouted; mothers grabbed at them; men spoke softly. Did they live there? Come for the day?

"These are Yemeni Jews," the guide explained. "They come for the day, for several days, to pray at Elijah's cave."

I looked at the people beneath the leafy bowers, and if I felt anything, it was pity. "Are they happy in Israel?" I asked him.

"Happier than anyone," the guide said. He was an older man, a brusque, vigorous type, an Italian Jew by way of Cyprus, Rhodes, and Turkey. "You see, they are the best Jews we have, better

than the Europeans. Why? Because they have preserved the old
traditions. They speak pure Hebrew. They know the Bible. And
they make the best soldiers in our army. You see how dark they
are?"

We moved slowly along the cement path into the cave of the
prophet. Inside, there were more dark-eyed, black-haired people.
Along one expanse of dirty white wall, two fat old ladies reclined
on shabby carpets. How long had they been there? It was insufferable in Elijah's cave—hot, breathless, malodorous.

"Dark? A genetic trait . . . intermarriage . . ." I was dizzy.

"No, no," the guide said, impatient with my denseness. "They
were turned dark by the sun. Generations of them were made
dark. That is why the Falasha Jews in Ethiopia are black. They
had even more sun."

Marie rolled her eyes. "He needs a new course in genetics," she
said. "He got his from Lysenko."

Candles flickered in the interior of the cave. Around them
stood the swarthy, gold-toothed Jews of the Yemen. To my astonishment a man holding a baby suddenly snipped off a lock of its
hair and threw it into a niche in the wall. This, I learned later,
was a standard ritual for Oriental Jews, giving the baby its first
haircut in the tomb of a holy man.

"Many people believe that nervous diseases can be cured here,"
the guide said. "Look here . . ." He pointed to a woman praying
at the wall of the airless cave, her arm around a starved boy with
the unfocused look of an imbecile. I had been through St. Anne
de Beaupré and Lourdes, those Coney Islands of Christianity,
with their abandoned corsets and artificial legs and trusses dangling like wurst from the rafters of a Yorkville delicatessen, and I
understood that this sort of belief was by no means the sole province of Jews. Faith-healing and mysticism of this nature are relatively rare in scientific Israel. I suppose it is the shock of confronting them in a land of Technions and experimental farms and
Hadassah hospitals that distress one more than their medieval
weirdness. In one niche, surrounded by candles and, to my bewil-
derment, half-filled soda bottles, was a gold-covered Torah. The
guide explained it had been in a concentration camp in Europe
and had been rescued and brought to Israel. There was a French
couple on the tour, haughty, rather handsome people, who on see-

ing the Torah walked up to it and gently, and with great solemnity, kissed its greasy covering.

By now the heat in the cave was unbearable, the odor an abomination. The two old ladies, reclining on their carpets like the silent voyeurs Kafka has in his stories, seemed not at all bothered by it. How long would they stay there? Why? I asked the guide.

"Oh, just overnight, usually. They are asking Elijah for help. They will pray, leave a candle, and go home."

I did not ask him about the soda bottles around the Torah.

It occurred to me on the bus that, the day before, in the Carmelite Monastery of Haifa, we had been shown a different cave of Elijah the Prophet, a dark, small hole below the main hall. I recalled a wood carving of Elijah over it.

The small cave in the Catholic monastery is believed to have been Elijah's residence (so the Carmelites say) and later the residence of his disciple, Elisha. But apparently Israelis have little to do with that one. Their main concern is with the large grotto below, the one now frequented by Oriental Jews. This place they regard as Elijah's school, where he taught his disciples. In fact the cavern is sometimes called the School of Prophets, and is said to be the place where Elijah fled from the king of Israel to resume his teachings. Later, various Christians—Orthodox hermits, Crusader monks, Catholic scholars—lived there. A Moslem tradition also adheres to the cave; a nearby mosque was called Al Khidr, which I presume is the same as the Hebrew word *kheydr*, or "religious school."

"I'm not sure that I'm satisfied with the two caves of Elijah," I said to my wife, "any more than I am with the two Golgothas and the two Gardens of Gethsemane."

The last stop on the Haifa tour was the kind of enforced sight-seeing that disturbs me. I understand that the economies of many countries benefit from the sale of handicrafts. But I am never happy when, under the guise of showing us quaint craftsmanship, we are marched into a factory showroom where we are expected to buy something. Moreover, the prices are usually higher than in the downtown department store.

The Haifa tour ended with a visit to a jewelry atelier where

Yemeni craftsmen—dark, elfin fellows—labored for a group of English Jews. The big attractions were the free refreshments the guide promised us. A bottle of grapefruit juice would have been fine, but I was deterred from accepting one because I knew I would stiffen and refuse to buy earrings or necklaces I didn't want. What I remember distinctly was that no sooner was our group of twenty-odd sweltering tourists inside the studio than the French couple had grapefruit juice bottles in their hands. How did they get them so fast? How did they know where the free drinks were being dispensed?

"They also got the best seats on the bus," Marie said petulantly as we rode back to the hotel.

"They always do."

"And when we went to the lecture in the Technion, everyone sat on folding chairs, but the French found a *sofa* at the side of the room."

"You can't lick 'em," I said. "Give up."

I report this with minimal malice and the assurance that this unflagging resourcefulness is not only noticeable in French-Jewish tourists—lest I be accused of anti-Franco-Semitism—but in all French travelers. Dozens of dazzling coups by these Gallic tourists come to mind, but the one I recall the best happened in Dubrovnik some years ago on a tour connected with a literary conference. All along the French had commandeered the best seats on the bus, in the dining room, in the conference hall. At official receptions they had eaten all the caviar and smoked salmon before anyone had a smell, absconded with all the souvenir portfolios and stationery, taken over the best positions on the beach, made a deal with the wine stewards for the rarest bottles, and driven everyone else into fits of envy and frustration.

But the paradigmatic example of French one-upmanship, of Gallic determination to get the jump on other tourists, occurred outside the Excelsior Hotel in Dubrovnik one morning as we gathered for a trip to Montenegro. As the bus door opened, one of the French delegates, a middle-aged, portly fellow in beret and glasses, began shouting from the hotel esplanade: *"Moment! Attention, attention!"*

All turned to look at him. He began skipping, bouncing *on one foot* up the steep incline from the hotel to the street above, where the bus waited. I realized that he was the man who, a few days before, had stepped on a sea urchin and had required first aid. His left foot was thickly wrapped in bandages, but he bounced along, a one-legged kangaroo, damned sure he would get on the bus first. And he did. As the rest of us goggled, this fifty-year-old athlete, bobbing up and down like a puppet on a string, bounded right into the open bus door, and into the best seat, in back of the driver. "*Alors,*" he said, barely puffing, "*les autres peuvent entrer maintenant.*"

We were aghast. "Nothing stops them," I said. "Crippled, poisoned by a sea urchin, suffering from septicemia. But, by God, he was going to get that seat."

"What I can't figure out," Marie said, "is how they folded up when the Germans hit them. All that determination!"

"But that's just it. It was all on an individual basis. Every man for himself. *Sauve qui peut.*"

One of the most worthwhile of the tours out of Haifa—I believe it can also be taken from Tel Aviv or Jerusalem, although Haifa is nearer to the area, and departure from there makes for less traveling—is the trip to Upper Galilee, taking in Meron, Safad, and Bar'am.

Zev Vilnay had told me about Bar'am when I had asked him to mention some of his favorite sites. "Absolutely beautiful, my boy. A gem. A facade you will never forget."

He was right. The old synagogue's ruins, dating from the second and third centuries A.D., stand isolated in a parklike setting on a hilltop. The stones are softly golden. Although the porch of the synagogue is gone, the front wall is well preserved, and the three doorways are virtually intact. Over the central doorway is a superb rounded arch, massive, graceful, full of years and dignity. The stones of the front wall are not nearly as large as Herod's boulders, but they are well formed and warm in color. Inside the building little remains except for some fallen columns and sections of the side and rear walls. But it is cool and restful, a good place to ruminate and watch the scurrying lizards.

The guide on this tour, a chubby little miniskirted blonde girl, was telling us about the Maronite Christian village nearby. We could see its ruins from Bar'am. "The town is now deserted. All the people ran away in 1948."

I wondered why. Arab Christians have been treated well in Israel. Generally better educated, more tractable than their Moslem brothers, they do well economically and have polite if distant relations with the Jews. But logic rarely dictates actions in the Middle East. They had left their village, probably for Lebanon.

While the guide was telling us this, the formidable American woman who earlier had inquired if the bus were waiting for Moshe Dayan kept up a cackling conversation with her family. The rudeness appalled me. I am a determined listener to guides, to anyone who knows more than I do. (Flattering myself, I suspect that was why Dani had enjoyed showing us around.) "I'd like to strangle that woman," I said to my wife.

We passed the memorial of Metsudah Koah—the stronghold of the twenty-eight—an old British fort that the Israelis had wrested from the Arabs in 1948, after bloody fighting in which twenty-eight young Palmach soldiers died. The guide said: "And on this height, our brave soldiers secured the road through the Huleh Valley that you see below. One of the twenty-eight, a boy named Dudu, strapped the dynamite to his back and raced up to the wall. He died in the explosion, but our boys could then run in and kill the Arabs."

That woman began to applaud, to cheer. Her family joined in. There were a few embarrassed looks from the other tourists. I suppose there was nothing wrong with her enthusiasm. But the story was a tragic one and called for silence. Moreover, her clapping, her grin, the feverish accolades, seemed to make a claim on the victory, to make them part of the Palmach. Why was I so irritated over their determination to identify with Dudu? Perhaps because—like me—they were soft, overweight, talky, citified people. They were not Palmach fighters. They were not of that breed of lean, taciturn, hard-handed Jews I had come to know in Israel. They made the identification too easily, too glibly.

The feeling that I was in a pressure cooker began settling over me that afternoon. It was one of the hottest days we had had.

High in the hills of Upper Galilee there was no escape from the unclouded sun. One felt closer than ever to the hot ball. The rays, the blinding light, the molten heat were overwhelming. But it was not merely the weather. It was the impact of history that was rendering me short of breath and unsteady. Bar'am, as beautiful as it was, had a blanched loneliness about it, not anywhere as cheerful as the black-gold-blue compatibilities of Chorazim. The Palmach memorial, high above the squared-off carp ponds of the Huleh, filled me with unsettling guilt: *I didn't help; I wasn't there.* I could never have been as brave as young Dudu (was he only nineteen?), who had strapped explosives to his back and blasted a hole in the citadel. Everything filled me with malaise.

Safad and Meron, which we visited in the afternoon, were no help. They are fascinating, full of surprises and unexpected sensations. But they made me mournful. I suppose it is because the mystic has never impressed me. These revelations, these occult mysteries—no matter what faith they adorn—seem to me conjurers' tricks, old wives' tales, stories told around a campfire. That they persist confounds me. I appreciate the impatience—and downright anger—of secular Israelis with the old arcana. No wonder that so many early kibbutzniks defiantly proclaimed themselves atheists.

Safad, which glitters in the sunlight from a distance, is the center of latter-day Jewish mysticism. It nestles high in the hills of Galilee, the biggest town in northern Israel. Its history is fairly recent. No mention of it appears in the Bible or the early writings, and it was evidently first heard of as Saphet, a Crusader town in the eleventh century. From Vilnay's guidebook I learned that it did not emerge as a Jewish community of consequence until the sixteenth century, when it became the hub of the Cabbalists, those mystical interpreters of Scripture, occult theosophists, who followed the teachings of Rabbi Shimon. It was a logical place for them to settle; Rabbi Shimon and his son Eliezer are entombed in nearby Meron. The mystics liked both the proximity of their departed sage and the bracing air of the mountain village, and they flourished. But natural and political disasters destroyed the Jews of Safad. An earthquake in 1738 killed 4,000 of them. A Druse attack in 1833 leveled what was left. Under the British mandate the Arabs moved in and made life miserable for the

1,700 Jews that remained. The old center of mysticism had an
Arab population of 12,000 when the War of Independence broke
out. Arab soldiers held the old British forts (like Metsudah
Koah) and were reinforced by Lebanese and Syrian units. Mirac-
ulously, 120 Jewish soldiers infiltrated the Arab lines, assaulted
the fortresses, and drove the defenders out. The garrisons fled; so
did the Arab population.

We walked through the winding clean streets of Safad. Old
ladies and importuning men accosted us with souvenirs and
postcards. When we refused to buy, they began battling among
themselves. One shrieking argument between an old crone and a
retarded fellow in a tattered cap took place outside the synagogue of Rabbi Itzhak Luria, better known as Ha'ari, the "Lion."

Luria, or Ha'ari, was born in Jerusalem in 1531 and died in
Safad in 1573. His students were known as the Lion Cubs. The
tiny shul was unlike any I have ever seen. The colors of the Ark
were as bright and as innocent as those in a child's coloring book.
The main room of the synagogue is the "Hall of Sacred Apples";
the Ark abounds in carved and cheerfully painted fruits: apples,
pears, bunches of fat grapes.

Farther down one of the narrow streets we were taken into the
Sephardic synagogue, where one of Ha'ari's notable successors,
Rabbi Joseph Caro, studied and preached. Caro was the great
legalist, the codifier of Jewish rituals and laws in his monumental
work, the *Shulhan Aruck,* the *Arranged Table.* Caro wrote this
work in Safad from 1555 to 1563. Inside there is an artlessness and
a sweetness about the Sephardic synagogue that is most appealing. The walls are a pale blue. Oriental couches are set alongside
the walls, which are simply covered in blue cotton. From the high
ceilings old-fashioned lamps depend. In the nearby cemetery are
buried Ha'ari, Joseph Caro, and other of Safad's revered sages,
mystics, and scholars.

We continued our lethargic progress through the town. The
ragbag retinue of beggars and vendors finally gave up. We
entered the artists' quarters and visited a disappointing exhibition
in the local museum. Most of the work seemed derivative and
strained, paintings and sculpture not without technical expertness
but constricted and confined.

Outside, as we awaited the bus, more begging children

appeared—barefoot, swarthy kids, Oriental Jews, dusty-faced, unutterably beautiful, with gleaming opal eyes. Guilt drenching us, ignoring the guide's admonition, we gave them all our loose change.

The last stop was Meron. At the hotel in Haifa, the woman in the travel bureau had said to me when I asked about Meron: "Meron is a dump. It's filthy. I don't know why they send tourists there. Either clean it up or stop telling people about it."

If the cave of the Prophet Elijah had perplexed me, Meron filled me with numb disbelief.

The tombs of Rabbi Shimon and his son Eliezer, second-century Talmudists, are in a large stone building. Shimon wrote the *Zohar*—the "Brightness"—the work on which the Cabbala is founded. The holy master is understandably honored. One of his predictions was that the Jews would, by suffering, win the land of Israel.

There is a courtyard in front of the tomb, and as we entered, an old man—a tall, ramrod-straight fellow wearing a filthy striped bathrobe, yarmulke, and sandals—approached us, cackling and begging. His eyes glinted with the angry righteousness of the cracked. I tried to ignore him; it wasn't easy. My father had had patients with that burning look in their eye. Within the court we stepped around goat droppings. Oriental families had taken up temporary residence there, and had brought their goats. Twitching, the animals dozed in the sun, surrounded by coronas of flies. A disheveled old woman had her hand out at the entrance to the tomb.

Inside there was the same stench, the same insufferable heat of Elijah's cave. Eliezer is buried in the center of the room, under a pale-blue stucco mound draped with a purple and gold cloth. On shelves around the grave are notes addressed to the departed sage. Again I saw those inexplicable half-filled soda bottles and thin tapers. A Yemeni woman in a beaded dress *dovinned* rapturously at the tomb, kissing the satin cover from time to time.

Shimon is buried in a corner of the room beneath a similar mound of plaster. Several women were praying at his tomb. I gathered these were prayers for fertility.

We filed out, intruders from modernity, slightly ashamed of our

pinched nostrils and affronted eyes. Was I expected to discover
virtue, value, lasting truth in this malodorous place? Surely I was
supposed to find common ground with Meron, and I had failed.

On the bus I told Marie, "I could never live in Israel. Not even
the way Meyer Levin does, a year here, a year in New York.
Wouldn't work."

My difficulty in Israel, I realized, was that I felt the need to
respond to everything. God knows I admired the people, and
found the land and the antiquities and the modern achievements
exhilarating. But my problem was that I tried to understand it
all, to react to it. It was this compulsion to *respond* that was agi-
tating me. If I lived there, I simply could not get from day to day
because I'd be ordering and arranging and refining my responses
every waking minute. I would never be neutral.

At Bar'am I had worried about the Maronite Christians who
were forced to flee. I've always thought well of Christian Arabs,
have known several, and at once I assumed the collective guilt of
the entire Palmach for having sent the Maronites packing. At
Metsudah Koah I was made miserable by the memorial. In a million years I could not be Dudu, with the explosives tied to his
back. More guilt, drenching guilt. Then at Safad I found myself
resenting the heat, the beggars, even the nursery colors in the
shuls. Was I missing the point? I kept telling myself gloomily that
this was the sixteenth century, when Europe was producing
Shakespeare and Rembrandt. I know cultural comparisons are
pointless. But I still get more inspiration out of a Pinturicchio
triptych, a Marlowe play, or a Mozart overture than I do out of
the Cabbala or the *Shulhan Aruck*. And I am afraid I always
will.

At the art gallery I had not liked the paintings. I found them
routine. But as soon as I had made that judgment, I began to
think that maybe those artists had survived the camps. Or helped
build kibbutzim or fought in the wars. Who was I, a well-fed and
smug American, to put them down? If it were a gallery filled
with inferior Yugoslav or Hungarian paintings, I'd reject them
and think nothing of it.

The guides know what they are doing when they shout at you,

"Don't we have a beautiful country, folks?" Then there was Meron. Frightening. Goat droppings, flies, and half-filled soda bottles, and Yemeni women kissing the purple coverlet. And all of it as alien to me as a Kaffir kraal. So I drowned in guilt for not being more generous in my reactions.

Of course, the Israelis themselves are very self-critical. They don't hesitate to knock one another, to criticize one another. They do it all the time. They raise hell with each other's art, politics, education. But I could not. I am, truthfully, an outsider, one who escaped Hitler and the building of Israel, the fat, insulated fellow who has no right to be critical of anything.

And even when my response was not specific—love, fear, disapproval, anger, puzzlement, whatever—there was always that menacing backdrop, the matter of survival, the endless war on the borders, the threats to exterminate them, the U.N. votes and Arab summits and B.B.C. reports telling them they are wrong and had better give it all up. So of course I respond to that, with a hundred times more fear and trembling than does the frailest old lady shopkeeper in the streets of Tel Aviv.

I worry for them. I wonder how they'll make it. That was the constant response, the eternal fear in my gut. That is why I could never live in Israel. I would be no help to them.

When I voiced these feelings to Marie, she suggested, "On tomorrow's tour try to throw out all these lunacies. Sit back and enjoy the scenery. Behave as if we were in Switzerland or Greece. Okay?"

The next day I tried to take my wife's advice. I slyly cast myself in the role of a sixty-two-year-old furniture manufacturer, a Missouri Synod Lutheran from Peru, Indiana, with a wife named Hazel, a son in Purdue Medical School, and a daughter married to a computer analyst with Merrill Lynch in Chicago. I'd be cool, observant, indifferent, blunt, and doggedly *goyish*.

"On the right," the guide said, "is Napoleon's Hill, where Napoleon sat in 1799 for two months, trying to capture Acre from el-Jazzar. But he failed, and it ended his eastern campaign. But in 1948, our General Moshe Carmel sat on that hill and captured Acre from the Arabs, doing what Napoleon could not do."

Several people cheered. I was silent. I tried to be indifferent and obtuse, a Rotarian and Lion and Kiwanis, only dimly concerned with Israel. Mighty strange folks, them Hebrews.

Acre, or Akko as it is called in Israel, has a markedly different flavor from the usual Christian site or ancient biblical place. It is the Crusaders who endowed it with this distinctive ambience: blockish, massive, ponderous, a bit frightening. Its location on the sea is beguiling, and a walk around the sea walls is a treat—the huge battlements and bastions are of regal proportions, the ancient gray stones contrasting happily with the white foam and undulant blue waters. It was a day of exceptional clarity, and the sea and the sky around Acre were notably bright and limpid. The sea wall, the Citadel, the mosque, the lovely old khans, all appeared sharply outlined, richly detailed.

The Citadel of Acre, of course, is part of the Israeli legend now. During the time of the Mandate, it was the British prison in which Jewish underground fighters were interned, and some were executed, among them Dov Gruner. Zev Jabotinsky was imprisoned there, and, in an earlier era, so was my friend Bahaullah, the founder of Baha'i, the successor to the Bab. (He was a prisoner of the Turks, not the British, in 1868.)

The Museum of Courage in the Citadel was closed for some reason. I was, to be candid, just as glad. In my role as a Hoosier Protestant, I was becoming relaxed. All I needed was to see the scaffold room in which Gruner died with "Hatikvah" on his lips, and the old guilts and fears would return.

The Crypt of St. John, near the Citadel, exudes Crusader gigantism. This was the headquarters of those bloody-handed, callous swordsmen, the Knights Hospitalers of St. John, a thirteenth-century structure. The great room, erroneously called a crypt, was probably the knights' dining hall, and it is appropriately cavernous, gloomy, and yet architecturally admirable, with its high cross-vaulted ceiling and the three great pillars that support it. It is a severe place, unrelieved by decoration except for a lonely fleur-de-lis on the wall facing the stairway. One thinks not of Akko, or Acre, in the chilled dark interior of the Crypt, but of the Crusader name: St. Jean d'Acre.

Sight-seeing in Acre is pleasantly jumbled. Israeli military memorials, the remnants of the Crusaders, and Moslem influence are all side by side and exist in artistic harmony. The mosque of Acre, the largest in Israel, is called el-Jazzar, and is named for the same fierce fellow who took Napoleon's measure in the last year of the eighteenth century. El-Jazzar means "the butcher." The man who bore that title proudly was an Albanian adventurer named Ahmed, who took over rule of Acre from the Bedouin Daher el-Omar and built many of Acre's imposing structures: the mosque, the bathhouse, the aqueduct. When I learned about el-Jazzar I wondered about the persistence of "Albanian adventurers." The founder of the last Egyptian dynasty, the one that ended with Farouk, was also an "Albanian adventurer," the cunning Mehmet Ali. For a scorched, barren, rocky country—I have seen it from the deck of a Yugoslav coastal cruiser and it is clearly the Hoboken of Eastern Europe—Albania seems to produce more than its quota of scheming scoundrels. The historical connection, however, is understandable. Albania was part of the Ottoman Empire, and many Albanians served in the Turkish armies. Why Albanians ("adventurers" at that) achieved such prominence is a bit of Middle Eastern curiosa that deserves further study.

The butcher's mosque is built over Crusader ruins, possibly Acre's old Cathedral Church of St. Cross. It is in an attractive pastel-colored compound, with a neat garden and a surrounding border of columned and domed cloisters in which live the mosque personnel and Koranic students. Nearby in a small double-domed building rest the bones of the horrid el-Jazzar, who had a wily Jew, one Haim Farhi of Damascus, as financial adviser. Later he had the adviser assassinated.

The interior of the mosque is modest by comparison with such overwhelming structures as the Blue Mosque of Istanbul or the Jumna in Delhi, and it cannot even be mentioned in the same breath as the Dome of the Rock. But its colors—wash blues and faded reds and thin greens—are gay, and the atmosphere is airy and fresh. For reasons never explained, one is not required to remove one's shoes on entering the el-Jazzar, provided one walks carefully on the wood planks and reed mats.

"Are you sufficiently detached?" Marie asked as we trudged through the back streets of old Acre in the wake of a garbage

"I think so. I didn't feel required to register any kind of emo-

truck redolent of rotten fish.

tional response to the el-Jazzar Mosque. As they say, I just dug it.
I was 'Against Interpretation' and accepted it as merely one more
sensual experience."

My new self—Lutheran businessman from Peru, Indiana—was
working. When we stopped in the Khan el-Umdan, I was grati-
fyingly neutral. Khan el-Umdan means "Inn of the Pillars." A
khan was a Turkish caravanserai, a stopping place, or *relais*. A
Turkish tower of recent vintage (1906) stands in the center of
the Khan, and around it are the three-tiered arcades that form the
apartments, the hotel rooms used by the travelers. The main part
of the inn dates from 1785, and the pillars for which it is named
were taken from the ruins of Caesarea. The apartments and the
walls form a hollow square, and presumably animals, servants,
and vehicles used the huge court below. Evidently some of the
flats were still occupied. We saw clothing drying and an occasional shrouded woman pass by in one of the cells above. In
design, I found the Inn of the Pillars singular, handsome, and not
without a certain warmth. It had a hospitably enclosed and self-
contained quality. The dimensions of the pointed arches, resting
on the Roman pillars, are not so huge as to intimidate and not so
small as to cramp the guest. The rooms of the inn are at a respectable distance behind the arches so that a great deal of cool
shade is provided. I wondered (as an efficient businessman from
Indiana would) if any thought had been given to converting one
of the old Turkish khans into a modern hotel. In Europe I had
stayed at ancient monasteries converted into modern hostelries,
notably the San Domenico in Taormina, Sicily, and L'Abbaye in
Talloires, France. They were marvels of comfort, peace, and convenience. As Edward FitzGerald's translation of the *Rubáiyát of
Omar Khayyám* puts it:

> *Think in this battered caravanserai*
> *Whose portals are alternate night and day,*
> *How Sultan after Sultan with his pomp*
> *Abode his destined hour and went his way.*

The word "caravanserai," I realized, had stuck in my mind for
many years. And now I stood in the court of one, a true khan, a

caravan stop along the spice and silk route. Omar, or FitzGerald, might have had the Inn of the Pillars in mind. But I shed no tears for the traveling Sultan. He probably had spent a good night at the Khan el-Umdan, enjoyed his morning coffee, said his prayers, and moved on happily, bells tinkling and camels snorting.

At lunch in the Dolphin Hotel in the resort town of Nahariya, I found that I was not only no longer reacting emotionally or responding with guilt, fear, confusion, enthusiasm, or pride to my experiences, but was accepting Israel and its people with stolid midwestern neutrality. I was even affecting a nasal Indiana drawl (or what I imagined to be one) and had begun to call my wife Mavis.

Seated opposite us in the dining room was a family of three that had been on the bus with us, and with whom we now chatted. The man was in his early fifties, darkly handsome with graying coal-black hair, and the kind of features—drooping, generous—that I have always associated with the word "Levantine." His wife was stout, less Jewish than Italian, and they had a frail, sallow son of about twelve.

"Where you folks from?" I asked.

"Brooklyn," the man said politely.

"Ah, but not originally."

The man sighed. "My wife and I were born in Istanbul, and then we went to Egypt. During the War of Independence, 1948, we moved to France, spent some time in Spain, and now live in Brooklyn, which is nice, but not as nice as Israel."

The woman smiled. "I love Israel better than any place in the world. We visit here whenever we can, and if my husband's business permitted it, we would live here."

"May I ask how many languages you speak?" I asked.

The man smiled tolerantly. "Of course, English, as you can tell. And Hebrew, which we learned in school as children. Turkish. Arabic. Spanish. French. Italian. And since we are Sephardic, Ladino. Just a few words of Yiddish."

"I make it eight," I said. "English, Hebrew, Turkish, Arabic, French, Spanish, Italian, and Ladino. Have trouble keeping them apart?"

The woman smiled. "Just the Romance languages. I mix up French and Italian verbs sometimes."

"And your son?"

"English. A little Hebrew. That's it. He is a Mets fan."

I absorbed this with appropriate middle-American appreciation. I felt no sympathy for this family and its odyssey, no identification, no emotional spillage—just healthy American interest.

On the bus again as we sped north to Rosh Hanikra and Kibbutz Hanita, I talked about them to Marie. "Marvelous poise and style, those Ladinos," I said to her. "Vivacious, interesting people. And juggling those languages like apples. No strain to them. That woman spoke Tuscan Italian. My heart goes out to them—"

"Watch it, Babbitt."

"Pretty coastline, Mother," I said to her. "Reminds a feller of parts of California."

Then at Rosh Hanikra I was again swept up in the mad casualness, that aloof attitude toward danger that is the hallmark of the Israeli. Rosh Hanikra is the northwestern tip of Israel, a rocky chalk cliff overlooking the Mediterranean, on the Lebanese border. Rosh Hanikra means "Grotto's Head." Along the cliff face are a series of caves, crevices, and grottoes. They are a major tourist attraction, and to facilitate entrance a funicular cable car has been built, anchored precariously into the rocky heights high above the breaking surf and jagged rocks. It is a spectacular eighty-second ride, and during the summer months Rosh Hanikra swarms with Israeli and foreign tourists. A long wait is often required before a seat on one of the swinging *télépheriques* is available.

Although low-keyed, an amusement park atmosphere has grown up around the funicular that takes tourists into the limestone caves. There is a self-service café, always crowded, soft-drink stands, souvenir kiosks, and quite a few guest houses in this northernmost outpost of Zion.

But what made the place memorable—indeed incredible—to me was the fact that this tourist complex is smack on the Lebanese border. A man steps out of the restaurant licking his ice cream cone, and he is face to face with the red-and-white-striped barrier that says: "BORDER—NO FURTHER." Just beyond is Lebanon and the

roving gunners of Al Fatah. I knew perfectly well that this area
of the border had been quiet, and that in general the Israelis
regard Arab guerrillas with contempt. But any skulking thug can
fire a mortar, and why not at easygoing, ice cream–eating,
photo-taking tourists (as they have done near Hebron)? I looked
at a soft drink stand where two ladies in summer frocks were
buying grapefruit drinks from large glass coolers for their youngsters. Then I permitted my eyes to rise above the kiosk (the one
next to it sold picture postcards) to the hill above. On this promontory was a squat tan fortress building. It was ringed with
barbed wire. A radar dish spun on its roof. I could not see them,
but I knew there were weapons inside—machine guns, automatic
rifles. Ahead, where the road ended at the border, Israeli soldiers
in sweaty tan uniforms kept coming and going. Apparently there
was a no-man's-land of some kind between the two barriers, for
the Israeli Army jeeps moved past the barrier freely and without
hesitation. To the left of the barrier was another fortresslike
building—more rings of barbed wire, another radar dish.

"You see," I said to my wife, "these people must survive. Here
they are smack on the frontier of a country in league with others
sworn to annihilate them. A country, if we are to believe the
American and British newspapers, full of violent, fearless, blood-
thirsty Arab terrorists, ready to die in the effort to subdue them.
And what do they do? They put up souvenir stands. Under threat
of mortar attack, they build a funicular railway for tourists. In
imminent danger of destruction, they sell soft drinks. Under the
guns of the Al Fatah they set up a cafeteria dispensing frozen
custard and sardine sandwiches. What can a man say about them,
beyond registering his disbelief? And this is a *healthy* response.
I'm trying to stand outside of my Jewishness and look at them
plain. Look, there is the ultimate truth about Israel."

A stout Israeli tourist in a red and white kibbutz hat, blue
shorts, yellow shirt, tan sandals, was focusing his camera on the
red and white sign that warned one not to transgress into enemy
territory. On either side of the placard stood two women, his wife
and daughter, I assumed, smiling for the camera. *Click-click.*

"They are saying to everyone," I said, "look, we're here. You
can't kill us. You can't scare us. You can't make us stop living."

The absurdities of history, ancient and recent, were with me all the way back to Haifa. In reading Vilnay, I learned that Rosh Hanikra was also known as the "Ladders of Tyre," and is so called in the Bible. Abraham, according to legend, wandered about Canaan, dissatisfied with much of what he saw because of the frivolity of the inhabitants. But when he looked into the land around the Rosh Hanikra he saw hard-working farmers and so decided "that this is the land that I would ask of God as my portion."

What, I mused, would a modern Abraham think, peering over into the limestone cliffs and the land below, if he saw those sunny, smiling tourists sipping orange soda and taking pictures of one another, while above them the soldiers watched and waited behind barbed wire?

Content that perhaps in my new guise as Protestant American I would adjust better to the land of my ancestors, I listened to the English language broadcast that night and heard of the fire in the el-Aksa Mosque. At the moment no one knew who had set it. But the Egyptians, the Syrians, and the Jordanians were certain the Jews had done it. Arabs rioted in the old city. Moshe Dayan was stoned when he visited the Temple Enclosure. Nasser threatened war. Syria swore to destroy Israel. The Russians said that this proved Israel wanted to conquer all the Arabs. The U.N. pursed its lips and rolled its eyes. For some time now the situation on the borders had been relatively calm. Now the Arab broadcasters and propagandists were at it again: Israel had to be annihilated. There were cries for jihad and the extermination of the Jewish aggressor.

"It's useless," I said to my wife. "I cannot look at any of this with a neutral eye. My Indiana doppelgänger is a fraud and a hoax. I am as disturbed over that damned fire as if I were the police chief of Jerusalem. To hell with disguises. I must take Israel on its terms, worry for her people, cheer them on, be on their side. If it demands emotional responses from me, I will give them. No one is ever a little bit Jewish."

CHAPTER XII

Half-Hidden
Treasures

He was a chunky, muscular fellow in a blue and red kibbutz hat, a knitted white shirt, dark trousers. Thick forearms, bristling black hair peeking from the yoke of his shirt, a paunch that suggested strength rather than sloth—the kind we called a *shtarker* back in Brooklyn.

"Mr. Green?" A central European accent, much more pronounced than Dani's. "I am your guide for the day. Yigal is my name."

We were to drive from Haifa to Tel Aviv in his car. But along the way I wanted to visit a half dozen obscure sites, places mentioned in the books but not on any tours.

"Did the lady in the office tell you what I wanted to see?"

Yigal held his hands up to stop me. "Please. Please."

"What do you mean, 'please'?" The brusqueness, the offhand dismissal, was wearing me down.

"I know all the places you mention. It won't be easy. Not easy at all. That's why you are lucky you have me. I am one of the few guides who knows these places. Oh, they will be hard to find."

"Athlit?"

"Please." His voice was firm, final.

"Look, Yigal, enough of that. Can we or can we not see Athlit?"

"I don't think so. But we try. We try."

We walked outside. He had an elegant new pale-beige station wagon. I'd noticed that almost all the new cars in Israel were that same desert tan. My theory was that if they had to be put into military service, they would already be camouflaged. That neutral brown tint would blend with the arid wastes.

Marie and I got in, and we drove away from the Dan Carmel Hotel.

"And Dor? And Apollonia? Antipatris?" I was getting apprehensive. It was the kind of touring day I love best of all—an adventure into little-visited, weed-grown places where neither refreshment stand nor tour bus is visible.

"Ah, Mr. Green, you are impatient. You are intelligent. I knew last night when I saw your list what kind of a man you are. I respect your choice of sites. Some I myself have not seen in fifteen years. Dor! My God, when has anyone asked to see Dor? And Antipatris! Never! Apollonia? My dear Mr. Green, I doubt that anything exists at some of these places no matter what the guidebooks say. But we will try. Now, any questions?"

I exchanged a glance with Marie. Another Dani. Another sabra expert. "I assume you are a sabra," I said.

"Wrong. I am from Germany, born in Weimar. I left in 1935 when I was just a kid. Lost my parents. I speak English, French, German, Spanish, Arabic, and Hebrew. I own this car. Bought it with a loan which I will pay off maybe when I'm seventy, but this is a good living and I meet interesting people. I have two sons in the army and they are better men than I ever was. No, I am not a sabra."

We rode south on the coastal road and passed the Cave of the Prophet Elijah. Marie pointed to the right of the road. "Look. There's a dig there. Is it anything worth seeing?"

"Please." Yigal swung the Peugeot around, backtracked, and found a sandy track running along the beach. "I intended to take you there."

He had not. But no tourist was going to spot an archaeological site before he pointed it out. And it looked like a fascinating place, a spur of rocky land projecting from the sandy slopes of Mount Carmel into the water.

"Please, pay no attention to these Arab houses," Yigal said as we bounced past some shacks. Actually they did not seem that shabby. "This used to be a beach for rich Arabs. Now it is a slum."

We parked the car and started up a slope toward a cluster of tents. There seemed to be two digging sites. One, in the distance, had an older and more eroded look about it, and there did not seem to be any activity in it. In the area nearer the tents some workmen were digging and pushing wheelbarrows. To one side was the familiar sorting table, laden with pottery fragments and the usual hillock of discards. This latter, while large, was nothing compared to the Mount Blanc of junk I had seen at the Western Wall.

"Tel Shikmona, Tel Shikmona," Yigal said as we approached the tent. "That is the name of this place, Shikmona. In Greek, *sykamon.* 'Sycamore tree.' The Arabs call it Tel Samak, the 'Tel of the Fish,' and it was probably once part of ancient Carmel."

It was an enchanting place, the surf breaking on the black rocks of the projecting spur, the trenches themselves softened by the morning light and appearing less to be man-made intrusions on the bare seaside slope, than natural formations.

"They have been digging here since 1963," Yigal said. "Dr. Elgavish, of the Haifa Museum, is in charge. It is financed by the municipality. There's a lot of interest in it. They say that during Byzantine times Shikmona was known as Sycamina Iudaeorum, Jewish Shikmona, because of the large community and because of its strong faith. They battled against conversion, told the Emperors Maurice and Phocas to do their worst—they would not become Christians." There were two young men in shorts sitting in the tent. One spoke no English, the other, a dark fellow in his thirties, with the calm, pipe-smoking look of the academic, spoke it reasonably well but had no desire to communicate. Yigal talked to him briefly.

"He is one of Dr. Elgavish's assistants," our guide said. "Dr. Elgavish will not be here today. He is in Haifa."

"Can he show us around?"

"No."

"Can he talk to us about the site?"

Yigal held his hands up to stop me, a gesture he would use all day. "Please. Please. Impossible. Only Elgavish is allowed to show people around. This gentleman can do nothing for us."

"He won't even identify the trenches? Or tell me what they have found?"

The guide took my elbow and started moving me away. Clearly I was being a boor. "No, he can say nothing. Only the professor is allowed to talk. I know a little about the place. Besides, this fellow says there was an article in the Jerusalem *Post* this year."

"He runs a tight ship, Elgavish."

"Well, it is in your interest. The assistant might mislead you."

"Then he has no right to be an assistant."

"A Talmudic point. Look—in the distance is the Persian city, from the sixth to the fourth century B.C. It was inhabited by Phoenicians at the time, under Persian rule, and they planned a lovely town. Shikmona is probably only twenty-five hundred years old. The trenches nearer to us is the Byzantine city, which is of less interest."

"Except that the Jews defied them when they tried to convert them."

"Yes. During the time of the Hasmoneans Shikmona was a port for the Seleucid troops. When Alexander Jannaeus was attacking Acre, which was the main port, north of here, Ptolemy brought thirty thousand soldiers here to help the Greeks at Acre. So you can imagine this was a big harbor and big city if it could hold thirty thousand troops and their equipment."

I later found the *Post* article on Shikmona. In it the elusive Elgavish paid tribute to the early Phoenician settlers as expert "town planners." The streets of seaside Shikmona, he said, were of remarkable regularity, showing much forethought. In fact the Greeks may have adopted town-planning from them. Another conclusion reached by Dr. Elgavish was that the early Persian period was a peaceful and secure one, since coastal settlements like Shikmona flourished beyond the fortified hilltop citadels. It must have been a good life, I concluded, right on the edge of the bright, sparkling Mediterranean, sipping the dark wine of the Carmel.

Did the invigorating wine and the life-giving sea endow these Jews with their stubborn courage when under the rule of the later Byzantines? A Greek traveler who visited Shikmona commented on their resistance to Christianity, observing that they were convinced the Roman Empire would fall and with it the new faith. Hence they had no desire to join a doomed enterprise. "They proved from the Torah and the Prophets," the Greek wrote, "that the Messiah had not yet come and that the time was not yet ripe for holy baptism."

As we continued down the coastal highway to Athlit—Yigal warned me several times we might not be allowed in, but if anyone could get us in, he could—we got into a discussion of the Temple in Jerusalem. I had said to him that I had trouble identifying with the Western Wall. I appreciated the devotions of Jews who prayed there, but to me the Temple was a foreign, forbidding place, the chief activity of which had been the slitting of animals' throats and the burning of offal.

"Ah, you are totally out of touch with the reason for the holiness of the Temple," he said. "I count myself a modern man, a modern Jew, but I understand it. It is the godly presence in the Wall, the *Shekina*, that Jews celebrate. That divine presence will never depart from the Wall."

"But a godly presence should be *everywhere*. One geographical location should be no more important than another in a religion based on morality, ethics, and law. Those old stones tell us of a lot of bloodshed and murder and dreadful deeds, as well as the faith. I'm just not comfortable there."

"You refer to Herod?"

"And others. But Herod is as good a place to start. That wall is his. All those buildings around it, his. I know that he was a great builder and diplomat, but he was a rat, a bloody killer and a psychopath, and it seems all that praying at the Wall gives him too much credit."

Yigal's eyebrows rose. He saw he was in a fight; he liked the idea. "Herod has nothing to do with it. The Wall has nothing to do with it. The physical artifacts, nothing. We pray only to the site, to what the Wall represents as a standing witness to the Jewish tradition, do you understand? Of course, there is a wide variety of opinion even among learned Jews as to the significance of the Wall. But all agree that it is vital to us. Look—suppose the Temple was restored today, just as it was in ancient times. Would we go back to animal sacrifice, which seems to bother you so much? Of course not. Even the Orthodox don't want that. And believe me, I'm no friend of the Orthodox. Judaism stood still for centuries because of them."

"They are the main votaries of the Wall. They are the ones who have kept alive the concept of the Temple."

"For that I give them credit. The Western Wall is a symbol, and yet it is more than a symbol. It is ... an instrument carrying the spirit of the Jewish people. Listen, once I took a Polish tourist there. He was once a Jew, but when he was hidden by a Polish family during the holocaust he converted to Catholicism and he was still a Catholic. He stood outside the Wall and saw the people praying, and he wept—he *wept*. A childhood remembrance, he said, of his parents' prayers: 'Let the Temple be built.' "

"I don't deny its emotional impact, its force as a symbol of our history. But I am unable to summon up such emotions. It is the abstract systems of Judaism, the moral codes and the rules of behavior, the grand continuities of thought that interest me, not a pile of stones hewn by slaves."

"I respect your feelings. Let me put it this way. The Temple and the Wall—they are our holiest of holies." He looked at me, smiling, and I knew he was not finished. "But ... we can also live without them."

The blacktop road to Athlit disappeared. We found ourselves on a sandy expanse of newly graded earth, winding amid bulldozers and earth-movers. A workman told Yigal that the road resumed some distance ahead. "As I thought," Yigal said mysteriously. "Something is going on there."

On our left was a grim, deserted camp, surrounded by more than the usual protective spirals of barbed wire. Inside I saw peeling, bare barracks. "And that?" I asked.

"Prisoner-of-war camp," he said. "It had seven thousand Egyptians in it after the Six-Day War."

"Empty now?"

"Yes. Ready for the next batch."

The sandy track met the blacktop again, and we saw Athlit in the distance, a sublime castle, tawny-red, looming in splendid solitude against the sea. It is one of the most superb medieval Crusader castles in the entire Middle East and one of the best preserved.

As we drove up I began to read Nagel's guide. Athlit, the "Pilgrim's Castle," was never destroyed. The giant towers and portals remain in excellent condition, and the old halls, towers, vaulted arches, and chapels are pretty much as they were when the Knights Templar ruled the coastline from their impregnable fortress.

"Trouble, trouble," Yigal said.

A chain was draped across the road. The castle was so close I wanted to run up to it, to race across the dunes and the salt marshes. To one side was a sentry booth with a warning sign in Hebrew. A young soldier carrying an Uzzi machine gun came out to talk to Yigal. Our guide nodded and dutifully turned the Peugeot around. We left on the same road.

Crushed, I asked, "What's going on there?"

"Who knows? I don't ask. But absolutely, totally, completely forbidden to anyone."

"Radar? Coastal defense?"

"I don't know. I don't ask. They tell me no, I listen to them. You know, in this country are other problems besides sight-seeing."

Sight-seeing itself seemed to be proving a problem that morning. First, nobody would talk to us at Tel Shikmona. Next, the army had barred us from Athlit. Now Yigal was expressing doubts about Dor. "Dor, Dor," he said, rolling the sound on his tongue. "My God, it must be fifteen years since anyone has asked me about Dor. And as I recall, it is not easy to find. It is hidden. Perhaps it is barred to us also, like Athlit."

"I don't see why it should be so hard. The book says it is right on the coastline, about seven miles south of Athlit. It should be near a kibbutz called Nasholim."

He frowned. "Please. Let me be the guide. Dor, Dor. It will be a miracle if we find it."

Again we wandered off the main road onto a sandy track. Some depressing shacks were thrown helter-skelter in a settlement that looked more Arab than Jewish. But it was Jewish, and Yigal apologized. "Those buildings will be cleaned up soon. That is not Nasholim." He shook his head, despairing of the dwellers, and called to a strange, dwarflike boy. They spoke in Hebrew, and the youngster shouted something after us.

"What did he say?"

"He says Nasholim is this way. And it is forbidden to steal coins or pottery pieces. Probably does it himself, the little crook, and sells them."

Nasholim, Yigal told me, means "the breakers," but it was light-years removed from Newport. It proved to be a cheerful, tree-shaded village adjacent to a wide, shimmering beach of fine sand. What looked like a group of children from a day camp had the huge beach to themselves.

"Nasholim was founded mostly by Jews from Salonika, in Greece. You know about them?"

"The Nazis killed most of them. It was one of the worst round-ups of the holocaust."

"Many of the survivors came to Nasholim. Here, this is as far as we can go."

A woman carrying groceries told us that the ruins of Dor were a short walk across the beach and up a seaside mound to our right. No, she herself had never seen them, although some of the children hiked there. I noticed as she departed down a path that the borders of the walk were marked with the bases of Roman columns!

"Come along," Yigal said. "An adventure."

We walked across the beach. The air was bracing, salt-laced. The sky was a crystalline blue, and the Mediterranean had never looked more invigorating, more tipped with silver and platinum, than it did on that old jagged coastline. Yigal led us through a gap in a barbed-wire fence and to the mound. Donkey droppings and an occasional tin can indicated that someone traversed the mound now and then. But apart from these signs of intrusion it had a private, untouched quality. It was covered with low scrub, obscure purple and blue flowers. Even in my ignorance, I knew it was a tel, a habitation mound, long buried and overgrown with vegetation. Its gentle contours were simply not of a piece with the coastal conformations of beach and rocky outcroppings.

"These look like trenches," I called to Yigal.

"Oh, yes, they dug here once. But it was never pursued, the way Caesarea was. Frankly I had forgotten this place."

We plodded behind him and suddenly we were on the summit of the tel, standing next to the stump of an old truncated tower. Vilnay's guide showed a drawing of a taller structure, a depiction of the ruins of Dor in 1888. The location looked the same, but the tower we stood next to was much shorter. I pointed this out to Yigal.

"Time, vandals, who knows? I would guess it was an old Crusader tower."

"And that's all there is to Dor?"

"No, no. Turn around."

Marie and I turned from the ruined tower and looked north. Below us was one of the most sublime sights I had seen in Israel. Like Chorazim, it was one of those rare places that strike the eye, the mind, and the heart full force, immediately, and are imprinted in one's consciousness forever. The instantaneous impression is so potent, so ineffably lovely, that it remains fixed in the mind, a true-to-life color photo, brimming with drama, remembrance, esthetic perfection.

"That is the ancient harbor," Yigal said.

It was of a magnificence that, like Chorazim's, was the result of many circumstances: location, age, isolation, coloration, proportions. It was a dazzling window on the past, utterly joyful and satisfying.

To begin with there was the sky. Unlike most of the mornings we had experienced, there was this day a bank of delicate white clouds hovering above. Normally the sky was an unrelieved blue; today it benefited from the sea-borne clouds. And the sea itself—dark blue as one looked westward, a pale turquoise or ultramarine closer to shore, where undersea rock formations and the packed sand worked their illusory magic on the sunlit waves. At the shoreline the black rocks of the coast and the shaped brown-black boulders of the old harbor—these latter rooted in the sand in robust rectangular formations—seemed like a chunk of the underworld exposed abruptly to daylight. On their slippery moss-covered surfaces the sea broke in muted explosions of creamy foam. There was a sandy beach, perhaps ten meters wide, a pale desert color, and then the littoral rose to a grass-covered height. Nesting in the midst of the green and beige hillocks were the remains of the harbor fortress: a large section of firm wall, the outlines of ancient buildings. I had seen many golden stones in Israel, but these were of a soft glowing hue that defied belief. Perhaps it was the angle at which the sun, still low over the sea, struck them, creating a symphony of shades and shadows on the honey-colored surfaces. The stones were huge, rudely shaped, stacked like a child's blocks, devoid of ornamentation. It was not a delicate or an effete place. It manifested a sturdy primitive beauty, a solidity and a rightness that was stunning.

"This is it," I said to Yigal. "The day is made. I have never seen anything like it. It ranks with Chorazim. Why doesn't anyone come here?"

He shrugged. "They come to swim,' over there. Dor is ignored. Caesarea gets all the publicity."

"But this is infinitely more beautiful. Look at the colors! Blue sky, dark-blue water, white foam, black rocks, golden stones. And it's a unit. It's compact. God, what an incredible combination of shapes and colors and sensations!"

"What period are they from?" Marie asked.

Yigal scratched his head. "I am not sure. Let's see what the book says."

I wanted to know everything about Dor, or Tantura, as the Romans called it. "The King of Dor in the coast of Dor" is mentioned in the Book of Joshua as one of the monarchs whom Joshua and the children of Israel "smote." The "half-tribe" of Manasseh was given the coastal plain of Sidon, which included Dor, but they were unable to hold the rocky promontory. The native Phoenicians—or Sidonians—lingered, to be replaced by a Pelagic people, these in turn to be conquered by Rameses III, who assigned the seaport to the Philistines. When the monarchy united and strengthened Israel, David captured Dor from the Philistines. There is a reference in First Kings to Solomon's giving Dor to his son-in-law Abinadab, who married the monarch's daughter Taphath. The Greek states that succeeded Alexander— ruled by the rival Ptolemies and Seleucids—fought over Dor sev-

eral times. Some inland digs, I read, had established that Dor
(like Professor Weinberg's Tel Anafa) was "very Greek."

Finally, Romans and Byzantines occupied the coastal town,
and a Byzantine church still stands in nearby Nasholim. A Crusader restoration was the last major event in Dor's history until
modern times, when Nasholim was founded and the neighboring
beaches were developed as recreational areas. But I still had not
an inkling as to what period the dramatic glowing boulders nestling in the sandy cliff represented. Nor did Yigal.

"Let's guess that they are Byzantine and leave it at that," he
said. "I just remembered that the beach down there was where five
hundred Egyptian commandos landed in 1948. Their Normandy,
they said. They were all killed."

It was hard to leave the place. The aureate stones, the rhythmic pumping of the surf, the blend of intense hues, were
theater, drama of a high order. Now that I knew a little about
Dor's history, that it was an old Sidonian place where wise Phoenicians baked glassware and taught their children an alphabet, I
was even more intrigued by it. It had the kind of glory that drew
one toward it, back into time, as blissful as a narcotic sleep.

"I must confess," Yigal said, as we walked slowly across the tel,
"I had forgotten how beautiful it is. All along the coast there are
these old ruins, but this I admit is the finest I have ever seen."

"Yigal, you have made my day. Dor was worth everything, the
frustration at Tel Shikmona and Athlit. It is a hidden treasure."

We took the inland road south. I was smugly content about
having found Dor. Along with Chorazim, it was my favorite site
in Israel. The beauty, the isolation, the colors, the historic
drama—all these blended to make them two rare antiques, singular in appearance, significance, location.

"On to Antipatris and Aphek," I said.

"How do you know about them?" he asked.

"Vilnay. Nagel. They are marked in red on a map I have. That
means they are of interest to tourists."

"The people who make those maps are optimists. You will be
disappointed, especially after Dor. Antipatris—you'll see. As for
Aphek, it doesn't exist."

"Apollonia?"

"That doesn't exist either, I have a feeling. These are names on a map and in a book. Nothing left. Of course, nobody's asked me to take them to them in years, years." He said this with an admiring wink.

We passed a road sign pointing east—inland—to Tulkarm, which I knew was a large West Bank city in occupied territory. (It was one point of the dread "Triangle of Terror" I had publicized many years ago as a cable editor at the International News Service.) It was only a few kilometers away. The proximity of towns in Israel always makes one ponder the vulnerability of the place.

"What are you going to do about the Arabs in your occupied territories?" I asked suddenly. "If you want an opinion from an outsider, I think your borders are secure, more secure than they've ever been, and you can handle the Al Fatah and even Nasser for a long time. But all those Arabs you've taken under your wing . . . Gaza, the West Bank, East Jerusalem . . ."

"Please." The admonishing palm stopped me. The "please" was more peremptory, more minatory than ever.

"Never mind the please," I said. "Doesn't anyone give any thought as to what to do with these people?"

He frowned at me. "You've been reading too much."

And indeed that week there had been two full-page articles in the Jerusalem *Post*. One dealt with a much-debated plan to resettle ten thousand Arabs from the Gaza area into small farm villages around the coastal town of El Arisha in the Sinai. The second article debunked the first.

"But what is the answer? How can you tolerate a million or more dissatisfied people in your midst, especially those hordes in the Gaza strip—embittered, shiftless, angry, a stew of hatred and prejudice, exploited by Nasser and the guerrillas. Now this idea of resettlement in places like El Arisha—"

This time he almost sang his litany. "You have been reading too much."

"Maybe I have. But maybe some of you don't read enough."

"The refugee problem, so-called, will be settled in due time. In all likelihood it will be resolved when those people make up their minds to live peacefully right where they are. Nasser and the Al Fatah must stop stirring them up, then we will do the right things for them. I am certain that we will solve it, on our time, our own schedule, in our own way."

This cocksureness can be disheartening. But I said no more. Like the archaeologist who was convinced that the Negev would be settled with Russian Jews and desalinated seawater, like my guide in Arad who had no fear of Nasser or 100,000,000 Arabs, Yigal had no worries about the suppurating wound of the refugee camps. Or at least they did not show these concerns to the world. And, I decided, why should they? If they did, the world would *tsk-tsk* and ask the United Nations to vote on it, and the petty republics of mud huts and principalities of thatched roofs would unite against those technologically advanced Jews, who, having built hospitals and schools and factories, had incurred the wrath of tribal functionaries and juju doctors still puzzled by the inclined plane. I said no more about Arab refugees.

Antipatris proved to exist, but it was by no means the old Herodian city I had read about. According to my sources, it was built by Herod in 35 B.C. and named for his father, the old Edomite chieftain and convert. It was a crossroads, the place where the Jewish High Priest Simon, in 333 B.C., long before Herod lived, greeted Alexander the Great on his way to Egypt. It was also, according to the New Testament, a site through which St. Paul was escorted by Roman soldiers while being transported from Jerusalem to Caesarea and thence to Rome. "Then the soldiers, as it was commanded them, took Paul, and brought him by night to Antipatris," we are told in Acts.

Smith's *Historical Geography of the Holy Land* says rather enigmatically that what Herod built was not a fortress but a "peasant residence," which would seem to mean a communal farm building of some kind. In the Middle Ages the site housed a four-turreted fort and caravanserai. Today, atop a green hill near the waterworks of Rosh Ha'ayin, the oldest ruin on the mound of Antipatris, is a stark Mameluke fortress.

We climbed the hill along a weed-grown path, moving toward the great walls on the summit. Ascending, we passed an Israeli father and son on a day's tour. Yigal, proud of his localized knowledge, asked the man: "You know what this place is?"

The man answered haughtily: "Of course. It is Antipatris."

We paused to catch our breath. Away from the sea, it was much hotter, windless. "Look in the corner," Yigal said. "A modern pillbox. From the war of 1948. You can see the bullet holes."

"And where is Aphek?" I asked.

"I'm not sure. I don't even think the archaeologists know. We may be standing on it."

"You mean Antipatris and Aphek are in the same place?"

"Possibly. I've also heard it is under the Rosh Ha'ayin pumping station, over there."

On a hill across the road we could see a large covered shed. Yigal explained that the pumping station tapped the main sources of the River Yarkon and sent the water southward into the Negev.

"Aphek was an important place," he said, as we walked slowly down the narrow path. The Mameluke fortress was absolutely silent, deserted. Only true *aficionados* came to commune with its bleak stones. "Like a lot of these cities, it was on the Via Maris. By now you know all about the road; it was the one the Egyptians and the Assyrians used whenever they came in to conquer. It's also the place of a terrible defeat for Israel."

"In 1948?"

"In 1066 B.C. Read it in Samuel. 'Now Israel went out against the Philistines to battle and pitched beside the Ebenezer: and the Philistines pitched in Aphek.' Right here, where we are standing. Three thousand years ago. Well, you know what happened. The Philistines killed a lot of our people. So they brought the Ark into the Israelite camp at Shiloh to strengthen them. It didn't stop the Philistines. They attacked again and killed thirty thousand Hebrews and stole the Ark."

"There is a lesson in that, I imagine."

"Oh, yes. The Ark is fine. So are prayers. But also you should have a better army."

Yigal drove east to the coast for our last stop before Tel Aviv, Apollonia. I felt that everything was coming full circle. We had started our tour with a biblical lesson from Dani on the capture of the Ark by the Philistines and how possession of the holy crate wreaked havoc among them. I remembered their god Dagon, fallen on his side, beheaded, hands amputated, after spending a night with the Ark. Not to mention the "emerods in their secret parts"—condign punishment for those blasphemers! Centuries pass, and David brings the Ark back and dances around it.

Once more we had to do some twisting and turning on roads running along the beaches. We were only a few miles north of Tel Aviv, but no one knew anything about Apollonia. "I don't think it exists anymore," Yigal said. "But we'll keep trying. I have a feeling there's nothing left."

There were no signs, no directions to Apollonia. It was like Aphek, a name in a guidebook, unvisited, unknown, vanished. Finally he parked at the edge of another beach. To our left was the elegant minaret of a Moslem building of some kind. Yigal was not sure whether it was an actual mosque, but it was a Mohammedan shrine, the Sidna Ali, "Our Master." It endowed the beach area with a dignified quality.

"I think it is off to the right through the dunes," he said. We climbed the sandy cliffs and began walking north. Below us I could see deserted beaches of tan, hard-packed sand, spotlessly clean, occasional rocky formations, and a pure cobalt-blue sea breaking. I was amazed that no one swam there; I had seen the mobbed beaches of Ashkelon and Caesarea (Tel Aviv's are a nightmare), and I wondered why these superb stretches of sand were deserted. Then I recalled Dani's explanation to me on the shores of the Kinneret: bathing was forbidden where there were no lifeguards, and violators were punished.

"Yes. Apollonia, Apollonia," Yigal mused. It was an enjoyable stroll, up and down the hard-packed dunes, the tough desert grass nipping at our ankles. the surf pounding softly below. "I read up on it, and it all comes back to me. Arsuf is its Arab name. That is a whole story in itself. Arsuf may be the same word as Reshef, and Reshef was a sun-god of the Canaanite people, the Semitic equivalent of Apollo. Hence, Apollonia. Perhaps the earliest name for the city was Rishpon, which is found in Assyrian texts. Rishpon, Reshef, Arsuf—all related names. The Crusaders called it Arsur, and they won a big battle against Saladin here in 1191, four years after the battle at the Horns of Hittim."

We had walked almost a half mile over the undulant dunes, and there was still no sight of ruins. One guidebook had told us to expect the remains of a fort, walls, moat, and harbor. I was expecting another Dor. But there was nothing in sight.

"There it is," Yigal said.

"I don't see anything."

"Rocks, rocks, big rocks. I remember it. I was here maybe sixteen years ago."

Embedded in the facade and the summit of the cliff were huge gray ashlars. But they were so deformed, worn, and set at such haphazard angles as to have become, after millennia of patient residence on the salty littoral, part of the landscape again. It was as if they had sought surcease from their bloody history by rudely discarding any hint of man's artifice—shaping, placement, adornment—and merging once again with nature.

"I don't see a moat, or a harbor, or a fort," I protested.

"They're there, they're there," Yigal said. "You must use your imagination. Look below you. What you see is a deep ditch, full of bushes, rocks. Watch it, don't fall in. What is it?"

"The moat?"

"Of course. On the beach you can see the ruins of the harbor, under the waves, like at Dor or Ashkelon. Oh, it is there, but you must look for it. And these remains up here—the fort."

"It isn't much."

"You wanted to see Apollonia."

"I'm not disappointed. It's here. In fact, I like it this way. 'Imperial Caesar turned to clay, might stop a hole to keep the wind away.'"

"Very good, very apt." Yigal frowned and folded his thick arms. "But here, the imperial ruins don't even do that. Canaanites, Assyrians, Israelites, Egyptians, Arabs, Turks—nothing left. But, you insisted on seeing it."

"And I have no regrets. There should be places like this— absolute, total, unimaginable ruins, places that have gone back to earth, leaving almost nothing that suggests a mighty city. It keeps us on our toes."

CHAPTER XIII

The Starkey
Heritage

A stout, large-featured Englishman in a light-colored vested suit, pointing to a pottery fragment; this is the way J. L. Starkey, the discoverer of Lachish, appears in a small photograph in the dedicatory preface to one of the huge volumes that grew out of his pioneer work.

I had been intrigued with Starkey ever since Dr. Nelson Glueck had told me about his murder in 1938. Somewhere I had read that he was largely a self-taught archaeologist, that he had come to his calling late in life. Recently I went through the published record on Lachish in the New York Public Library, but I could find nothing much on Starkey's life. Beneath the small photograph of him—I assume he is studying one of the famous Lachish letters—is the notation that he was born on January 3, 1895, and died on January 10, 1938. At the bottom of the page there is a paragraph:

This volume records only a small part of five years' work begun by Mr. Starkey as Director of the Wellcome-Marston Expedition. Tell ed-Duweir had already revealed much to his observant mind when his tragic death on a lonely road near Hebron deprived the world of a brilliant archaeologist and the expedition of a beloved and trusted leader. Though the preparation of this account has been in other hands, the inspiration and the results remain his.

Elsewhere in the book—it was titled *Lachish II*, one in a series published by the Oxford University Press—I learned that Starkey first broached the idea of the Lachish dig in 1932 to Sir Henry Wellcome and two other influential persons. Work began in October of that year, with English supervisors, two trained Egyptian workers, and a labor party of Bedouin and local Arabs. In January, 1938, the passage continues, "the tragedy of Mr. Starkey's murder by bandits on the Hebron–Jerusalem road brought work to a temporary halt, but it was then resumed and continued through May, 1938, when it was terminated."

I have been unable to find any additional information on Starkey. Indeed, it was maddening to discover that in the card catalog of the library he is *John* Leslie Starkey, but the dedication in *Lachish II* lists him as *James* Leslie Starkey, while the secondary accounts of his work call him John L. or sometimes merely J. L. Starkey.

I recalled Dr. Glueck's theory that Starkey had perhaps revealed information about Arab terrorists to the British and had earned their hatred. There is a hint of this in an article by G. Ernest Wright on Lachish in *The Biblical Archaeologist Reader* (Vol. 2, New York, 1964) which states that Sharkey was "murdered by Arab enemies." Now, an enemy is rather different from a bandit; and I had the feeling that Dr. Glueck was closer to the facts of the case.

Lachish is on no organized, or even specialized tours that I know of. It is—like Dor, and Chorazim, and Maresha—one of those mysterious, weed-grown, dusty sites that the archaeology buff must seek out on his own. Toward the end of my stay in Jerusalem, after Marie had left, I consulted a map and discovered

that Lachish was not more than forty miles from Jerusalem—
south and east by way of Beit Shemesh—and that it was near
another old site I had read about, Tel Maresha. Having felt the
firm fatherly hands of several guides already, those knowledge-
able and authoritative fuglemen, I decided to make the trip on
my own. Bus service proved to be chancy. I could get to Beit
Guvrim or Kiryat Gat, the two large modern towns in this fertile
area between the Judean hills and the coastal plain of the
Sephaleh, but I was warned that local cab drivers, even if available, might be calculated risks.

A private car and a good road map seemed in order, so I called
the Nesher cab company (which I highly recommend) and asked
for "Sheshin the Chazan." This sounds like a line from an S. J.
Perelman parody of Raymond Chandler, so I had best explain
that a few days before, touring the Mea Shearim, I had ridden
with a cab driver who without warning had burst into song, high-
pitched falsetto warbling that could only mean he was a cantor.
He was a handsome, husky fellow in a red beret, a certain Avram
Sheshin, and he was indeed a cantor, who plied his melodious
trade between Israel and America, depending on the season, the
bookings, and his mood. "Oh, yes, I have sung in Brooklyn—
Ocean Parkway, Eastern Parkway—in Manhattan, on West End
Avenue. Baltimore, Washington, St. Louis. Even Mexico City.
When I am not working as a cantor I drive for Nesher. Here is my
card. If you need a driver ask for Sheshin the Chazan."

Unfortunately the cantor was off that day, but the dispatcher
promised to send over one of his brightest young men, who spoke
some English. In a little while one of the inevitable sand-colored
Peugeot station wagons pulled under the porte cochere of the
American Colony Hotel. We studied the map briefly and took off.

"My name is Reuven," the young man said. "I have an uncle in
Los Angeles. I visited him last year. He is rich. He owns a big gas
station and has a big house. But at night he goes home and locks
the door and watches television. His daughter is afraid to go out
at night. When she does, my uncle stays up worrying about her.
He has no one to talk to, no neighbors, nothing. Just television. I
liked it there, but I could never live in America."

"People are friendlier here?"

"Of course! We are one people. We all know each other. There is always someone to talk to, and we enjoy talking, and we want to know each other."

"Does that include your Arab citizens?"

"Yes. I am a sabra. I was born in the Old City of Jerusalem. I had many Arab friends as a boy, good friends, wonderful people. I am sorry we cannot be close friends anymore, but that is the work of the Arab politicians—people like Nasser. I like the Egyptians, they are all right, good people. But Nasser . . ."

Reuven had the lustrous tan coloring and sharply angled features one finds in many young Israelis. He was short but wiry, narrow-waisted—a common physical type. His parents, he told me, were from Zagreb, Yugoslavia. They had gone to Salonika and then settled in Jerusalem. During the Six-Day War he had driven a Centurion tank in the Sinai; he knew Egyptians from firsthand experience.

"Perhaps you would like to stop at Beit Shemesh," he said. "Shemesh is the same as Shimshon—you know, who pulled the temple down."

"Samson."

"Yes. I am sorry, I am not a trained archaeologist or guide."

"That's perfectly all right." It was, in a way, a relief to be less pressured, less under the paternal thumb of a professional. We climbed the mound of Beit Shemesh. The old foundation stones were peculiarly cemented, and the round platform seemed to have been stuccoed over. It was not the way I like my ruins. But the history was interesting. Beit Shemesh was the place where the Philistines brought the Ark with such embarrassing results.

Samson's country: We had crossed the Brook of Sorek, the place where the strong man courted Delilah, and Zorah, his hometown. Inevitably there was a Samson Cement Factory, something that sounded as if it had been invented by Milt Gross.

There was a roadblock beyond Beit Shemesh and we sped around it, Reuven waving to the policemen. "The police in Israel are very good. We have the best police in the world. They want to help people. But it is a hard job. Long hours, especially now."

The roadblocks were understandable. As we headed south, a good chunk of occupied Jordan, the Bethlehem–Hebron area, was on our left. I pointed this out to Reuven, and this reminded him of another historic place nearby. "In there is the village Kfar

Zechariah. The Arabs call it Kis Faluja. *Kis* means 'a pocket.' In the War of Independence, our soldiers captured a young major in the Egyptian Army there. He was Nasser, the same one giving us the trouble today. They had him in handcuffs. I am sorry they took them off."

We proceeded along an excellent blacktop road, passing farms, fields, barren hillsides covered with brooding rocks, small villages nestling at crossroads. I began to read about Lachish.

Its modern prominence derived from the Lachish letters, a collection of twenty-one inscribed pottery fragments found by Starkey in 1935, most of them buried deep in the guardroom of the fortress gate. The most dramatic was written by one Hoshaiah, an Israelite commander stationed north of Lachish and its sister fort, Azekah, at the time of the Babylonian invasion in the sixth century B.C. Nebuchadnezzar's savage troops were overrunning Judean towns. Only Lachish and Azekah still stood.

"And let my lord know that we are watching for the signals of Lachish according to all the indications which my lord had given, for we cannot see Azekah," Hoshaiah had written. A certain Lord Ya'ush, about whom nothing is known, was the Lachish commander. Neither he nor his comrades were able to send up the hopeful fire signals. Flames did arise from Lachish soon enough—but they signalized the destruction of the city by the Babylonians, probably in 598 B.C., according to Starkey's reckoning.

The mound was an ancient one. Remains of a small Canaanite temple were found on the fortress slopes, a building dating back to the fifteenth and thirteenth centuries B.C. It was presumably destroyed by the Israelites when they subdued Lachish shortly before 1200 B.C. There then followed a period in which the mound was deserted. Early in the tenth century, it is believed, King David revived the settlement. A provincial official's building was erected over the Canaanite ruins. Under Solomon's son Rehoboam, sometime after 922 B.C., the main fortifications of Lachish were built, and it was to become one of the largest cities of Judah, with a summit of about eighteen acres, larger than Megiddo and Maresha and about the same size as Gezer. Rehoboam's fortifications were obviously designed to protect a city of some magnitude. The summit was protected by a brick wall, nineteen feet thick, and studded with recesses and salients. Fifty feet below, on the slope of the hill, a second wall of stone and brick, about thirteen feet thick, was built. This barrier was formed of alternating projecting and recessed panels, a formidable impediment to a besieger.

But besieged it was, first by the Assyrians under Sennacherib in 701 B.C. Vilnay's guide reproduces the famous relief from Sennacherib's palace, now in the British Museum, that shows the siege of Lachish and depicts clearly the complex fortifications. The city was captured and became an Assyrian military base. The Nineveh stone reliefs are full of drama. The mighty Assyrian battering rams pierce the walls of Rehoboam. Jewish captives leave the city with packs on their backs. Jewish soldiers, naked, are hanged. A naked defender falls from the walls. And Sennacherib himself is seen seated on a throne as he receives the loot of Lachish. Two subjugated Israelites, barefoot men with tightly curled hair and beards, wearing loose ankle-length robes, kneel in supplication.

Lachish revived in the latter days of the Judean Kingdom, only to be assaulted again by the Babylonians. It is from this period that the letters date, the time when the querulous Hoshaiah watched the horizon for signal fires from Lachish, saw none, and knew that the city had been subdued again.

In addition to their historic import, the letter-potsherds revealed, according to Harry Torczyner, writing in the official report *Lachish I*, that "the ancient Jews could write quickly and boldly, in an artistic flowing hand, with the loving penmanship of those who enjoy writing." This observation I found particularly engaging—an archaeologist, studying the evidence of a dreadful blow to his antecedents, who could nonetheless take heart from the fact that they had good handwriting! It reminded me of the craftsmanship of the Jewish artists in the Terezin concentration camp: excellence in the shadow of the gallows.

Apart from the letters, the Canaanite temple, the double walls, and the other structures, one of the most intriguing finds at Lachish—and the grimmest—was a large pit on the northwest slope of Tel el-Duweir and five smaller pits nearby. They had been used as tombs. But what grisly tombs! The main hole contained the remains of about fifteen hundred bodies in a hopeless jumble.

Moreover, the skulls had all rolled to one side of the cavity. There were signs of burning on many of the bones, and at least three of the skulls showed evidence of trepanning, the first such sign of this kind of surgical procedure ever found in Asia. On two skulls the rough marks of the surgeon's saw were still visible around the hole where bone had been removed to relieve pressure on the brain. On a third the bone had begun to grow together and obliterate the saw-marks—a sign that the patient had lived for some time.

This manifestation of medical excellence did not relieve the grisliness of the charnel house of Lachish. Over the solid mass of vertebrae, limbs, and skulls had been thrown a blanket of animal bones, most of them from pigs, an unclean creature forbidden to the Jews. There was also a conglomeration of pottery fragments of household vessels not normally placed in tombs. Hence it was concluded that the skeletons were swept up in one great heap and tossed into the pit along with pottery and other detritus from the mound.

It was a terrifying and puzzling find, and after examining all the evidence Starkey concluded that the great stew of human and pig bones and broken pots was the result of a clean-up of Lachish after the siege of Sennacherib, not the later invasion by the Babylonians. To support this conclusion Starkey pointed to the lack of older people in the mass grave, whose bodies would have been present had an existing cemetery been cleared and transferred to the pits.

But what about the pigs? Israelite dietary laws are ancient, and the pig has long been a proscribed animal for practical reasons. In hot weather its meat can be treacherous and disease-laden. However, the neighboring Semitic peoples did not have any such bias. Starkey reasoned that the pigs of Lachish were part of the stores brought there to feed the Assyrian garrison. And it would be in keeping with the tender mercies of conquering armies of that era if, not content to toss fifteen hundred bodies into a mass grave, they then dishonored and humiliated the dead by throwing the gnawed shanks and ribs of the abhorrent hog on top of them.

I told the story to Reuven as we sped south. He nodded thoughtfully. "No one will ever throw pig bones on us again."

The map indicated that we would come to Tel Maresha first,
and since the guidebooks recommended a visit to this other
Judean town, I asked Reuven to look for the track to the tel
before we stopped at Lachish.

He wasn't sure where it was, but he would ask. Beneath a
grove of trees we saw a group of Israeli soldiers in green fatigue
suits. He pulled the Peugeot off the road to ask directions of
them. As I looked out of the window of the taxi, I did a take:
There seemed to be several disfigured corpses sprawled on the
ground. Then I realized that these were dummies—old fatigue
suits stuffed with straw, such as are used in bayonet practice. The
soldiers were busy ramming dry grass into collars and sleeves.

"The road is on the left, a small dirt road," Reuven said. "He
says we should be able to see the tel from the road, and then we
follow the main track."

Back on the road again he told me that the soldiers to whom he
had spoken were—through mere coincidence—with his old motorized unit, and that some of the noncommissioned officers and
drivers were just ahead. Would I mind if he stopped off to talk to
them? I had no objection.

About a mile beyond, under another grove of shade trees, were
parked a dozen half-track armored vehicles. The sight of them—
olive-green, ungainly, deadly looking—made me think of Paul
Schutzer, the *Life* photographer who had lost his life atop a
half-track during the Six-Day War. We had known Schutzer and
his family in Paris; his death had been a tremendous shock to
everyone who knew him. He was a quiet, handsome, artistic boy
from Brooklyn, with the natural grace of a small man.

"Very good vehicles," Reuven said to me. "Better in desert than
tanks."

At once he found a noncom who had been an old army buddy
and they began to talk, quietly, gently, in an offhand way. The
soldier was another one of those string-bean sabras—painfully
thin, but a controlled power in his limbs, an expressionless tanned
face, curly blond hair. He was demonstrating the proper use of a
lubricating gun to a dark, almost black, Oriental boy, showing
him how to shoot grease into the wheel bearings of the half-track,
and he did so daintily, holding the gun away from his fatigues.

When Reuven came up he wiped his hands on a rag, and they chatted.

It was a brief visit, but impressive nonetheless. I noted the sobriety, the taciturnity of the men, GI's and noncoms. An American army unit (or at least the army I remember from World War II) out on field maneuvers would have resounded with profanity, coarse humor, insults, taunts, songs. These young men were subdued, deadly serious about their work. Even when lunch was served, they stood around the chow truck, quiet, orderly, waiting their turn. It was, I should add, a meager lunch, but they did not complain. Each man got a half loaf of brown bread, a bunch of fresh green scallions, and some tomatoes. No meat was served, as far as I could see. It was surely one of the gentlest—but also most confident and determined—of army groups.

"I sometimes miss the army," Reuven said, as we made a sharp left turn off the road toward what we thought was Tel Maresha. We had left the village of Beit Guvrim behind us. Both Maresha and Lachish should have been just a mile or two to the south. "But . . . I will probably be driving for them again."

We bounced along a dirt track. One of the sights we were supposed to look for was the ruins of the Crusader church of Santa Anna. Nothing like it materialized. The day was hot, preternaturally bright, the sky dotted with clouds. A warm wind was rising. The hills around Maresha were desolate, silent. The road became rougher, more potholed and ridged, narrower. Finally, the Peugeot protested. Reuven parked it in a circular cul-de-sac that seemed to mark the end of the road. Around us were fantastic natural formations in the sandstone rock—enormous irregular gouges in the mountains, baroque holes and caverns, amorphous pillars and columns. Obviously the work of wind and erosion and shifts in the earth, they had a haunting man-made quality, as if some flamboyant abstractionist had blasted at them with explosives after studying Henry Moore's apertures.

"Do you think this is Maresha?" I asked.

"I don't know. Why don't we walk on top?"

The ground rose sharply in front of us, the sandstone hill ascending to what seemed to be a tableland, the kind of upper slopes I had come to associate with a tel. But it seemed exces-

sively overgrown with scrub, nettles, thickets. We climbed it.
Around us were more grotesque caves—looming arches, bottomless dark pits, curlicues and cornucopiae of rock, sweeping formations suggesting a giant's earlobes. Maresha was excavated in
1900, I had read. It could explain the manner in which natural
contours and desert vegetation had obliterated the site.

"Here is something," Reuven said. He pointed to a row of
stones, a long trench. I had not the faintest idea if I had found the
old city or not. I could no more read the signs of the old stones
than I could the Lachish letters.

"I don't know," I said. "The book shows this shape, with towers
on the four corners, a citadel. I see nothing like that here."

We trudged about the hilltop, burrs sticking to our socks and
trousers, and finally I decided we were on the wrong summit.
Back at the car, on the sandy cul-de-sac, we saw a small truck
pull up.

It was a remote place, with neither farm, nor village, the sandy
road coming to a dead end amid the grotesque caverns. I wondered what the small panel truck was doing there. A middle-aged
man and a girl in her twenties were in the cab. Seeing us, the
man came out and spoke to Reuven.

"Tel Maresha?" the man asked. And he pointed south.

We turned, and there, almost bleached out of the skyline, was a
gray-white mound, perhaps half a mile away. It had the typical
flattened crown, the gently sloping sides, but it was cunningly
camouflaged amid the surrounding hills. We had missed it completely, wandering around a hillside to the north.

This time we were certain we had found the right road. A short
distance in we saw the ruins of the Crusader church with its
unmistakable round apse, like a pale, dried, antediluvian shell
left on an old sea bed.

Maresha was the home of the prophet Eliezer, who, according
to Second Chronicles, prophesied against King Jehoshaphat, of
Judah, because the latter had made an alliance with the Israelite
King Ahaziah. This was about 852 B.C. Later, in the reigns of
Kings Jotham, Ahaz, and Hezekiah, of Judah (758–698 B.C.),
Maresha produced another prophet, Micah, described as a "Mor-
asthite." It was Micah who uttered the words: "What doth the

Lord require of thee, but to do justly, and to love mercy, and to walk humbly with thy God?" He was exalting this mode of conduct above the sacrifice of animals, and asked, "Will the Lord be pleased with thousands of ram, or with ten thousands of rivers of oil?" Micah, a man after my own heart, evidently was in step with the mood of his time. The Judean King Hezekiah became an antisacrifice man and reformed the rituals.

Maresha had produced some distinguished Jews. But before the time of the prophets, Maresha was one of King Rehoboam's "cities of defense." Around 920 B.C. he fortified it—along with many other places, like Gath and Lachish and Azekah—and "put captains in them and store of victual, and of oil and wine."

The great achromatized table grew larger, dominating the landscape, and the road became a rutted trail. Reuven had reduced the Peugeot to a crawl, maneuvering it between white boulders and potholes almost as bad as those in Queens or the Bronx in February, after the first thaw.

Maresha loomed above us, barren, flat, fearfully old and parched, its summit devoid of any structures. On its steep slopes were a series of eroded gullies cluttered with chalky white rocks. The base of the tel was surrounded by a necklace of bonelike stones, and finally the Peugeot could go no farther. We got out and began the ascent.

The wind had risen again, a warm, harassing breeze coming from the sea. To the north we could see the houses and farms of Beit Guvrim, but apart from this sign of habitation the area around us was desolated, a serene and silent place, a landscape burned out and burdened with too much history. On the summit I was astonished by the absolute flatness of the ground, the absence of any formations to denote old walls or structures. Evidently the last diggings, seventy years ago, had long been covered and any stones of consequence removed. As we walked about the heights, the wind blowing briskly and kicking up small dust devils, I felt it a major triumph when I located the ruins of defense towers at the corners of the mound. A deep hole near the edge puzzled me. Was it merely the remains of an archaeologist's trench? A well? An underground room? I would never know. The scary bleakness of the citadel was accentuated by what now appeared to be the skeletal remains of old walls on the lower ground. What were they? Part of the old city below the fortress? Had the rocks been stacked and lined up by the archaeologists in 1900? Whatever they were, they were dreary, truly the detritus of a destruction too calamitous to contemplate.

Although I am usually adept at following maps and diagrams, I was unable to get a fix on two of the more interesting sites near Maresha: the painted burial caves and the underground columbarium. Time and again I squinted at the maps in the guidebooks, tried to get oriented, looked for signs—and failed. The heat beat down on us like the exhaust from a blast furnace. My eyes had trouble focusing. Reluctantly I decided we should leave Maresha and press on to Lachish.

In the car I made a note to come back with a guide and find the caves. In a way my frustrations at not seeing every stone, every cave, every ruined building have fringe benefits. The unseen tomb, the missed bridge, the hidden temple, are bonuses I can look forward to on a second trip. (Florence, incidentally, is the bottomless barrel for this type of thing. I have been to Florence six or seven times, and I have yet to see the city entire, and am always astonished and delighted by the fresh works I find on each visit.)

One of the burial caves of Maresha, located east of the tel— which might have placed it near the weird natural formations we had seen on our first turning—was once a rendezvous for lovers. I learned this from Vilnay's book, which reproduces a Greek inscription on the tomb wall. It reads: "There is nought that I may do for thee or wherein I may please thee. I lie with another, although loving thee dearly. But, by Aphrodite, of one thing I am very glad: that thy cloak lieth in pawn . . . do what thou willst. . . ."

I thought of the couple in the panel truck. Apparently they were following an ancient tradition.

The tel of Lachish was easier to find. Its flattened summit rises from a rich agricultural area, Hevel Lachish. Where the slopes of the old mound end, a lush fruit orchard begins. Beyond are green cultivated fields, farm buildings, pasture lands. The great tel cannot hide in the desolation of the surroundings the way Maresha does. It rises, exposed and parched, a relic of a poorer, harder age.

We walked up the slopes where once the legions of the Assyrians of Sennacherib and the Babylonians of Nebuchadnezzar, and long before them the armies of Joshua, had marched.

It was a gratifying and provocative place. In terms of beauty it was not in the same category as Chorazim or Dor, but it was satisfying in its venerability, its consistency.

"You know," Reuven said. "I just remember. I came here as a boy, eleven years old. They took us from school in Jerusalem to see where Joshua fought."

This seemed logical. It was like taking school kids in America to see Bunker Hill and Valley Forge. Though there is something to be said for excursions for school children to historical sites three thousand years old!

Reuven's memory was good and so was Vilnay's map of Lachish. With no effort we discerned the outer wall—not much more than a weed-strangled ditch, but clearly part of Rehoboam's outer fortifications. Then we approached the inner wall. Stupendous gray boulders stood in rows, irregular ashlars suggesting the section of ancient Cyclopean wall near the main railroad station in Rome. A definite gap in the wall was evident. I felt as triumphant as Joshua as I walked through it with my sabra companion. The stones on either side were of greater dimension, mammoth boulders piled to a height of about five feet, and between them were unmistakable steps. We had entered Lachish with a lot less difficulty than Sennacherib's Assyrians, with neither battering ram nor siege engine. It seemed to me, as I strolled about the grassy heights, that they could not have felt more thrilled than I. They had come for blood and booty, and had drunk delight of battle with their peers. I had come unarmed, with a young Centurion tank-driver, now employed by the Nesher cab company. Latter-day Assyrians and Babylonians now had *him* to contend with, and he would prove (along with those silent soldiers I had seen at the half-tracks) somewhat tougher than Ya'ush, the doomed commander of Lachish, or his lieutenant, letter-writing Hoshaiah.

"And here is the palace," Reuven said. "Ah, I remember it well when we came here as children."

A stunted stone foundation rested high on the tel. It was apparently the composite remains of what the diggers referred to as Palaces A, B, and C. The earliest parts of the building were believed to date from the late tenth or ninth centuries B.C. The later additions lengthened and widened the official residence, but the dates are a matter of conjecture, and the C and B versions of the building are believed to date anywhere between 900 and 750 B.C. It was a ruinous site, but it had a palatial air about it. Its dreariness was regal. Its barrenness had a magisterial quality. Perhaps it was the fact that it stood higher than the rest of the mound—or the utter loneliness of the place, the way the tel was detached from the farms and orchards surrounding it; a pariah.

There were a few other structures on the summit. One flat stone I assumed—perhaps mistakenly—to be the remains of the sun temple. There were some odd trenches and pits, but whether these were the work of Starkey and his successors or part of the early conformation of the tel (a well? the burial pits with their ghastly hoard?) I could not be certain.

I rested on the hot surface of the sun temple and thought about the repeated bloody assaults on Lachish and its eventual obliteration. Months later I read in Olga Tufnell's account in *Lachish I* (she was one of Starkey's successors) of how archaeologists concluded that the city had been razed in the Babylonian conquest of the sixth century B.C.:

> Masonry, consolidated into a chalky white mass streaked with red, had flowed into a liquid stream over the burnt road surface and lower wall, below which were piled charred heaps of burned timber. In the angle below the north wall of the bastion, and the west revetment, breaches which had been hurriedly repaired with any material available were forced again; indeed evidence of the destruction by fire was not difficult to find anywhere within the circuit walls.

At Masada I had been engloomed by the repeated emphasis on the Zealots and the way in which they put their throats to their

own knives to frustrate the Romans. I could understand the
Israeli obsession with the story, and the cry, *Masada shall not fall
again*. The trouble for me, I suspect, was the absolute bleakness
and inhospitability of the land around Masada. It spoke to me of
a hard, hard life, of a nature so perverse and malignant as to
make daily existence a trial—let alone the challenge of building
a new society or confronting a savage enemy.

But at Lachish I was not depressed. In spite of the direful history of bloodshed and holocaust, of unseen fire-signals and roar-
ing cones of flame in the ultimate disasters, the place is reassuring
because of the pastoral, prosperous farms around it. If the tel
speaks of a terrifying past, the peach orchards and wheat fields of
Hevel Lachish confirm something valuable and positive and
uplifting.

Our throats parched, we went into a small general store serving
the community of New Lachish. It was crammed with goods—
groceries, dairy products, household needs, pharmaceuticals—a
cheerful, cluttered little place. A few farmers, sun-blackened,
thick-limbed men, came in to shop. Two women in print dresses,
one pregnant, one pushing a baby in a stroller, entered and began
to buy food.

Reuven and I sipped Jaffa grapefruit juice. It was liquid gold,
better than all the champagnes of France.

"*L'hayim*," Reuven said.

"*L'hayim*," I responded. "And to the memory of a good Englishman—Starkey of Lachish."

CHAPTER XIV

Zev Vilnay's
Jerusalem

Zev Vilnay, Ph.D. in Oriental studies (Dropsie College, Phila-delphia), archaeologist, writer, king of guides, biblical scholar, army intelligence agent, gunrunner, and Zionist historian, is, by a generous margin, the most memorable figure I met in a nation noted for individualists.

I first heard of him from my sister, who had used his guidebook on a trip to Israel some years ago. Someone had borrowed it, failed to return it, and she was brokenhearted. "Get one," she told me. "It's the best guide to Israel. But they're hard to find in New York."

They are hard to find because they sell out almost as soon as they reach the States. Luckily, I found one through a fine book-store (and publisher), Bloch's, on West 31st Street in Manhattan. Thus I knew Zev Vilnay from his writings before I met him.

One night in Beersheba, when I retired early with a heat-induced migraine, Marie met Vilnay. He had spoken to a touring group under the auspices of the Hebrew Union College. The wife of the tour director was related to one of our neighbors; she and Marie struck up a conversation and Marie met Dr. Vilnay. To say that she was impressed was an understatement.

"He's like . . . well . . . a Tatar prince. Or a professional football coach," she said. "Rugged, charming, funny, intelligent. Like a combination of Gregory Ratoff, Ezio Pinza, and Samson."

Apparently he was impressed with Marie. I called him some weeks later in Jerusalem. "Dr. Vilnay," I said, "I am a great admirer of your book."

The accent was as thick as meat borscht, as rich as potato pirogen. "What? What do you say? Who is this?"

"This is Gerald Green, an American writer. I said I am a great admirer of your book."

"Hah! Yes! Green! I am a great admirer of your wife!"

"I'd like to bring you a copy of one of my own books in apprec—"

"Don't bring a book! Bring your wife!"

We met Zev Vilnay in his Jerusalem apartment a few days later. He grabbed me in a rib-straining embrace, then hugged Marie.

Mrs. Vilnay—Esther—a tall, beautiful woman with handsome gray hair, was introduced to us. A woman of great warmth and elegance, she speaks fluent English, Hebrew, French, German, and Arabic. She lived for many years in Egypt and counts many Egyptians among her close friends.

I studied Vilnay. He has close-cropped gray hair, a wide, frank face, large features, and shoulders as wide as a middle linebacker's. His torso is huge; he is a great hard barrel of a man, full of strength and vitality and humor and strong opinions. As a talker, he is superb. Whatever his shortcomings (and they are few) in English, he makes his points with a rough elegance, a vigor and an enthusiasm for his craft, his people, his homeland, that exhilarates anyone listening to him. He is a kind of Israeli Samuel Johnson, a man with a great zest for life. The guides he trains for Israel—I was to see dramatic evidence of this a few days later—love him.

"Well, Gerald, my boy, I will tell you where I get my strength," he said as Esther served coffee and home-baked apple pie. "I am a Bessarabian."

"My father is a Bessarabian."

His eyes, somewhat secretive behind thick glasses, widened. "You . . . you . . . are Bessarabian, too?"

"Half. My father was born in Kishinev. My mother is a Litvak. My father was born in 1886 and died in 1952. I brought you the novel I wrote about him, *The Last Angry Man*."

"Ah, Gerald, Gerald, I knew all along there was something, something . . ."

He had leaped from the couch and was hugging me again. Released, I was silently grateful that I was not a full-blooded Bessarabian.

"Bessarabian men," Vilnay boomed at Marie, "know how to eat, drink, and make love. They grab for women, no preliminaries."

"Well, he does like to eat."

"Ah, I think he is a real Bessarabian. I also was born in Kishinev. My father came to Haifa in 1907 when I was a kid. They were crazy, all those Bessarabians. Ten Jewish farmers, they were going to start vineyards and make wine on Mount Carmel. But it didn't work out. They turned to olive oil instead, bottling oil with the Holy Land name on it. Oh, we were poor. I remember, we lived in shacks. No running water, no toilets. But those Russian Jews, they were crazy, they were all a little crazy. Listen, Russian Jews built the kibbutzim and made them great! They had visions, ideas. But crazy people make history. Normal people only make hysteria."

I asked him about the military situation, the raids on the borders, the threats of the Al Fatah, the bombings of Israeli offices, the assaults on airliners.

"It will end. It will be controlled. My older son is a major in the paratroopers. He is in charge of a large area where they go out every day and shoot a few Al Fatah *kockers*." He suddenly noticed my Abercrombie and Fitch shoes. "Ah, Al Fatah shoes. If my son saw you in those, he would shoot you first and interview you later."

The army was dear to Vilnay. He showed me a plaque with his name, an inscription in Hebrew, and the symbol of the Israeli

Army, the Zahal—the sword and olive branch inside the Star of David and the winged parachute of the Israeli paratroopers. "This was given to me for service in the Six-Day War. They came to me for information on the streets of the Old City, the alleys, the strong points. Also for the Sinai. I knew all the old roads, the mountain passes. It would take a biblical scholar to know them. Our army is the yardstick, the measure we use to judge everyone in the country."

I asked him how this squared with the views of the extreme Orthodox, the majority of whom refuse to serve. Many Israelis denounce them as parasites, troublemakers.

"Quite right," Vilnay said. "If you will not serve in Israel, you are not truly part of us. Still . . . the Orthodox have their role to play."

"What do the Arabs think of the Orthodox?" I told Vilnay of having asked an Arab driver at the Dung Gate to take along a soft-eyed, lost-looking bearded chap in a kaftan and a *shtreimel.* He looked stranded; I would have been glad to have paid his way to West Jerusalem. Nostalgically I recalled my late father often giving rides (he was a pork-eating Jew, a muscular physician who never went to shul) to old bearded fellows tottering along the dirty streets of Brownsville. The Arab driver, with a querulous look on his face, had said, "Oh, no, sir. He is from Mea Shearim." I told Vilnay that this sounded to me as if he were *afraid* of the Orthodox fellow.

"Not really, not afraid," he said. "Many Arabs are superstitious. They regard our Hasidim and the others as holy men, insiders, people with special knowledge. And of course the Arabs have a more practical reason for liking the Orthodox."

"I can guess. They like them because they don't bear arms."

"Precisely. Any Jew without a gun, without the will to fight, is fine with the Arabs."

"The Arabs are a difficult people to understand," Esther Vilnay said. "And they are widely different. You know, I lived in Egypt many years, and I know them well. I like them. They are a dear, sweet, kind people, with no anger or malice."

My eyes goggled. "But those street demonstrations? Those mobs screaming for Jewish blood and revenge?"

"Oh, anyone can raise a mob in Egypt," she said. "What they

say in public, no matter how loud, and what they want are two different things. When the Six-Day War started, of course I was not glad about it, or absolutely sure we would win as quickly as we did, but I knew that those sweet Egyptians, those soft people—they speak the softest, gentlest Arabic in the world— would never be able to fight us."

"Yes, that is the crazy thing," Vilnay said. "I am fond of Arabs too. Some years ago the government sent me around to American colleges to debate Arab students and diplomats. I spoke at USC, Columbia, Penn, many places. But it was not a contest. I like to feel I have an adversary. This was too easy, so I gave it up."

The Vilnays' younger son, Oran, entered the room; he crushed my hand in an iron fist. He was bigger than his father, broader, a dark-haired, fair-skinned young man. But his voice was low-keyed, unemotional. He was, Zev had told me, a reserve officer in the army engineers and was presently teaching engineering at the Technion in Haifa.

"What is wrong with you Americans?" he asked me bluntly.

"In reference to what?" I asked.

"Vietnam, for one thing."

"Well, I agree it's a mess. We should get out."

Young Vilnay lifted his eyebrows. "Out? You should clean out those communists in the north, and with no mercy. When you are in a war—win it. You should invade North Vietnam. Hit them with everything."

Again, I had to swallow. "Atomic weapons?"

"No. You would not need them. Your generals are right. Half-measures do not win wars. We have learned that."

"I think your situation is different. You are fighting for your homeland, for earth in which you are a majority, a united people. The North Vietnamese and a lot of South Vietnamese feel the same way, whether we like communism or not. They think we're the invaders. We're—to many of *them*—the Egyptians and the Syrians and the Al Fatah of the Middle East."

He shook his head. "No, no. It is part of your whole policy. You do not stand up. Look at the business with the TWA plane." A few days earlier, Arab guerrillas had hijacked a TWA jet bound for Tel Aviv and forced it to land in Damascus. The Syrians were still holding two Israeli men hostage.

"What did we do wrong?"

"The TWA crew should have refused to leave. Insisted on their rights to stay in Damascus with the passengers. The United States should have told the Syrians to hand those Israelis over, or get everything thrown at them. Even the language should have been stronger." The huge man sighed. "Ah. America, America."

Apparently the Vilnays, in varying degrees, felt the same way. They were the hard-liners, vis-à-vis communism and countries helped by the Russians. And who could blame them? Too long, I think, Jews have been automatically associated with the Left. Let all who think that this politico-racial relationship is immutable talk to some Israelis. As an American journalist—a Christian—said to me one night, "The only people in the world who hate the United Nations more than the John Birch Society are the Israelis."

"And you are from Stamford?" Zev Vilnay asked. "In Connecticut?"

"Yes."

"I knew it well in 1946 and 1947. I bought guns from the Colt Company, good American guns, for the War of Independence. Also in Connecticut was Winchester, who also sold me guns. I was an efficient buyer. We took whatever we could get in those days."

Archaeology and ancient history were my main interests, and I asked Vilnay about one place that had intrigued me. Gordon's Calvary, or the Garden Tomb.

He held his hands to his cheeks. "*Oi*, Gordon! Gordon was crazy, just crazy. That was no more the site of Calvary than the Holy Sepulchre. Neither have any claim. It is a complicated matter, but the fact is that the walls of Jerusalem, Agrippa's Third Wall, was *outside* both places, so neither can be regarded as correct. Where it took place, who knows? You should read Gordon's book on the whole thing. The work of a *meshugeneh*."

I asked Vilnay to name for me his all-time list of the ten sites he most liked to visit in Israel.

"That is hard to do, and whatever list I give you is subject to change. But for a quick reaction: Masada, Bar'am synagogue, all of Jerusalem, Mount Tabor, the pools of Solomon, the Herodian fortress near Bethlehem, the Wadi Kelt, which is the biblical valley of Achor, Shiloh, the Monastery of Mar Saba, also near

Bethlehem. That is a rough list. Except for Masada and Jerusalem
I could give you another list tomorrow. I love it all."

It saddened me that I had not seen half these places, and my
time in Israel was drawing to a close.

"Listen, Gerald, let me tell you about those guns I used to buy
from Colt and Winchester," Vilnay boomed at me. "Oh, did I
have a time hiding them. You know where? On chicken farms in
New Jersey. There were a lot of Jewish farmers there. We con-
tacted them and hid our weapons for the Haganah. A hen would
sit for us on a grenade. Inside the bags of chicken feed were rifles
and pistols."

"I've seen the display at Yad Mordekhai," I said. "Those few
rifles and machine guns. And those poor farmers, with the shells
blowing up their water tower and killing the chickens."

"Yes, yes, we learned from that. Never again, my boy, never
again. The Orthodox keep telling us that God will help us if we
study the Torah, that one overcomes an enemy not only with
swords and strength, but with the spirit. If you are absorbed with
the spirit of learning, if you are soaked in the law, you will overcome."

Oran Vilnay snorted. I could scarcely imagine him or his brother—the paratroop major cleaning up Al Fatah infiltrators—suc-
cumbing to abstract pacifist sentiments.

"I take it you hardly believe that," I said to Zev.

"Ah, I am glad they have the Wall, and the Torah. I am glad
they can pray there and experience the spirit of the Ark, the Holy
of Holies. But someone has to buy the guns and use them." He
looked up, his broad face beaming. "Gerald, I have a marvelous
idea. The first chance you get, I will take you on Zev Vilnay's private tour of Jerusalem—how the war was won here. We will ride
around, and you will have a lecture in history, military strategy,
and archaeology."

Of course, I was honored. Vilnay is one of those rare men in
whom talent and enthusiasm are present in generous and equal
amounts. I have always felt indebted to gifted people who are
eager to impart their special knowledge to those who want to
learn. It is surprising how many brilliant people are niggardly,
secretive, and snobbish about their hoards of skill and informa-

tion. Writers, especially novelists, are among the worst. It is difficult for me to recall a witty, original, or profound comment made by a novelist—in conversation, not in his works—in the last ten years. They are the true misers of the art world.

On the other hand, I have known men who possess impressive minds and are guardians of much specialized and intriguing information and who dispense it freely, happily, and with much clarity. The man I admired most in the world, the late Joseph Wood Krutch, was the paradigm of this kind of generous scholarliness. Mr. Krutch had a formidable mind, and was an erudite critic, teacher, philosopher, biographer, essayist, and naturalist. And he enjoyed talking to people about any of these subjects.

Zev Vilnay was of this breed of man. Scholarly, wise, his mind imbued with the drama and color of the Holy Land, he approached his calling with a vitality and a joy that immediately involved the listener. He must have been a marvelous teacher. I had the feeling that the Arab guides he was now training at Israel's behest would be the best in the Middle East.

A few days before leaving Israel, I was back at the Abu Tor observation point, near Aunt Susie Schwartz's forlorn snack bar. ("A tragedy for the poor woman," Zev said as we drove up in his car. "She just put in six new toilets. Then we win the city, and people don't have to come here to look.")

It was a Saturday in late August. The combination of torpor, of silence, and the saunalike heat gave me a sense of disorientation. There was almost no traffic on the streets. On Abu Tor, the bombed-out houses of the former Jordanian quarter never looked more dilapidated. This time there were no Arab urchins in sight. The sun and the sabbath appeared to have driven the world to cover.

"Now, Gerald," Vilnay said, "you have been here before, and you have done much walking in Jerusalem, so you know where we are. We are looking out to Mount Zion, just outside the walls of the Old City. You know what the tower is?"

"Yes, the Dormition Abbey."

"Very good. Now, you will see that the city is well protected. There is the Kidron Valley on one side, and the Hinnom Valley,

Gehenna, on the other. It is a good place to defend, as many have found out. The Jordanians had good positions around it. We had to keep an eye on them, so for many years we had an observation point in the bell tower of the Dormition Abbey, which you can see is a high point. But the Pope didn't like this. He didn't want us for tenants. He kept complaining we should get out. We were sorry for him, but we stayed. You see, he didn't have key money."

Someone had told me that James Michener had based the character Schwartz in his novel *The Source* on Vilnay—a salty, irreverent, robust fellow, who, on learning that the Pope is to visit Israel, wants to put up a sign reading "We Did So Kill Him." With all due respect to Mr. Michener, who has a talent for creating memorable characters, he did nobly with Schwartz, but Vilnay is Vilnay, and the fictional creation was more subdued, not quite as forceful as the model.

"When the Six-Day War began," Vilnay went on, "we had only one brigade in Jerusalem, about two thousand men. The Jordanians had artillery positions back there, right on Abu Tor, and also in the Augusta Victoria Hospital on the Mount of Olives. We didn't have enough men to storm them. The High Command needed troops for the offensive in the Sinai. I was attached to the Jerusalem command as an adviser. In 1948 I was an operations officer, but this time they told me I was too old, so I settled for being an adviser."

Below us the city shimmered in the burning light. The Dome of the Rock was a fiery golden ball. It was hard to imagine this somnolent, motionless harbor of sanctity ablaze with bombs and shells.

"We were content to wait in Jerusalem until the Jordanians did something that provoked us," Vilnay said. "That house up there, that was the U.N. Truce Organization headquarters. It used to be the British High Commissioner's place. Abu Tor is also called the Hill of Evil Counsel because Caiaphas had a house here where he conspired to get rid of Jesus. Hence, Evil Counsel. Also, a legend says Judas committed suicide there. Anyway, with the United Nations here, we felt the name Evil Counsel was appropriate."

"What did they do when the Jordanians occupied their house?"

"Not a bloody thing." Vilnay was wearing a yellow Panama

hat low over his eyes. His square jaw set, and the muscles at the
side of his wrestler's neck tightened. The U.N. has this effect on
Israeli patriots. "Those Jordanians marched up the Bethlehem
Road and right into the United Nations. And those bloody U.N.
people did not raise a word of objection, nothing, just the way
U Thant pulled his men out of the Gaza strip at one word from
Nasser. Dirty, bloody, no-good . . ."

"Zev, it is too hot to get excited," I said.

"Hah! I am still angry just thinking about it. They were scared
to death, those U.N. officials, making in their pants. They ran out
of toilet paper, that was their main problem. Do you realize what
the Arab artillery could do to us from up there? They could cover
the entire southern part of Jerusalem with their fire. And if they
brought up tanks, they could penetrate. It was a bloody bad
show! As I have told you, we had one brigade in Jerusalem, and
they were reserves—doctors, lawyers, professors. Not even regu-
lars. But we were furious. My job was to prepare a reconnaissance unit. Not to attack, just to have a look. I met with this
young officer. I can't tell you his name. We discussed the 'recky.'
What a kid he was! He looked me in the eye, and he said, 'I'm
ready to let them have it.' Like all of us Jews, he was a philosopher also. 'Let's try them out,' the boy said. 'Let's see if the bas-
tards will fight. All life is a trial.'

"So the reconnaissance unit marched up to the U.N. house.
They shot a bazooka shell at the house. Some of the Arabs ran.
The others fired back. That is how the war in Jerusalem began. It
was tough fighting—for a while. Suddenly in the middle of everything the Swedish General Bull came out. He was the U.N.
boss. His chest was full of medals but he never fought a battle in
his life. You know what he asked us? Please get out. We might
hurt some U.N. people. Please let us give the house to the Arabs.
Ah, but not a word to them when they seized it illegally! We said
that after we cleared the Jordanians out, we would escort all the
United Nations people out safely."

"It seems you are angrier at the U.N. than at the Arabs."

"Yes. One is an enemy who makes no pretense. He says, I want
to kill you. The other smiles and bows and talks sweet, but he
will help kill you also. By four in the afternoon the building was

in our hands. The hills around Jerusalem were all battlegrounds by then. We were going to get rid of them—and we realized we could."

"Why were you so certain?"

"Because in the battle at the U.N. headquarters, they ran. They were the same *kockers* we fought in 1948 and 1956. They were good to make parades and wear fancy uniforms, but that was all. So we were secure. We had kicked them out of the Hill of Evil Counsel, and we were fighting them north and south, up to Latrun, and south to Bethlehem."

"What about the U.N. personnel?"

"We escorted them out safely as we promised. We took down the U.N. flag and put up our own. And we were hospitable to the U.N. generals with their medals. We put them up in a kosher hotel."

We drove to Mount Zion, through the Yemin Moshe and past the Jaffa Gate.

"So while the war was starting here, the army was chasing the Egyptians in the Sinai," Vilnay went on. "The High Command realized they would not need so many men in the Sinai. There was a paratroop brigade under Captain Moti Gur, waiting for an assault jump on El Arisha in the Sinai. Instead they were ordered to Jerusalem. We were going to take the Old City. This was the strategy. One battalion of this brigade was sent out on a diversionary action, as if they were going to take the Dung Gate, to get the Jordanians to move their forces. The Jerusalem brigade, the reservists, stayed on Abu Tor and secured the roads to Bethlehem, Hebron, and Jericho."

We were riding slowly down the Jaffa Road, passing the Citadel, the Tower of David. "This was a no-man's-land here," he said. "Terrible shelling. In those houses opposite the Tower of David—the wrecked ones—a lot of poor old Jews took a terrific pounding. Many of the poorest Orthodox people in the city, the Persians, the Bukharians, were nearest the Jordanian lines, and they took a lot. Believe me, they were brave."

Vilnay stopped the car near the New Gate, across the street from the Notre Dame monastery. "They brought the paratroopers up in plain buses. A staff conference was held. They would attack to the north at one A.M. The paratroopers, Captain Moti Gur's unit, would attack across Mount Scopus and the Mount of Olives and then through the Shechem Gate. You know the Shechem Gate?"

"St. Stephen's. The Lion Gate."

Vilnay was squinting, his eyes seemed misty, at the high walls of Notre Dame. "Ah, Gerald, my boy, I must digress to tell you what happened here in 1948, in the War of Independence. This was the high point of the battle for Jerusalem in those years. I will tell it so you can compare how we were equipped then, and what we had in 1967.

"Look how Notre Dame dominates the area. Right on the boundary, high on a hill, it overlooks the steep road up from the Damascus Gate. We were holding the top of the hill—right where we are now, on Jaffa Road. The Arab Legion was going to send a column of British tanks up the street, up Suleiman Road, parallel to the Northern Wall. We could see the *momserim* getting ready. What were we to do? We had not a single tank, not a single anti-tank weapon, not one piece of artillery. All we had were rifles, dynamite, and Molotov cocktails. What does one do as he sees death approaching?

"Gerald, I was standing right at the summit of the hill, at the northwest corner of the city wall, and I felt we had had it. If the tanks got through, that could be the end for our Jerusalem. It was the worst night I ever spent. We stood there, and like all Jews we talked, we reasoned, we wondered what would happen when those tanks broke through. It wasn't really an army unit. Just a bunch of diverse people. Some young kids. We were *chaverim*, as you say, buddies.

"One of the kids said, 'Zeve, let us go into the monastery of Notre Dame and defend ourselves there.' An older fellow pointed out that we were under orders to stay out of the monastery. So another kid spoke up. 'Let's go in. I don't care what the Pope or the President says. They didn't say anything when the Germans murdered six million Jews, so why should they say anything now? What we are going to do isn't as bad as killing six million Jews.'"

Vilnay mopped his forehead. He was staring at the bleak high wall of Notre Dame; the day was fresh in his mind. "I tell you,

Gerald, at that moment, I realized I was getting old, that I was a member of the older generation, and that these kids were taking over."

"You decided to go in?"

"Yes. We knocked on the door, and walked in. The monks were reasonably friendly. Assumptionists, very intellectual. I sat down with them in the basement, and explained the theory and practice of Zionism. Meanwhile the boys prepared a defense against the tanks. It was late at night, and we had a feeling they would come up the Suleiman Road soon. It was decided to blow out a section of the wall of the monastery on top of the first tank and block the street. So they set dynamite charges in the wall. Look, you can still see where they went off."

In the wall of the monastery I could see a huge vertical gouge. "It worked?"

"Better than we dreamed. A tank came up and the boys blew out the wall. It fell on top of the lead tank. The others were bunched up in back. As soon as the tanks were stalled, the kids threw Molotov cocktails on them and burned the Arabs alive. We didn't call them Molotov, but *mazal tov*, 'good fortune.' Ah, I can remember it so clearly. It was at two in the morning the battle started. It was over in less than two hours. I can still remember Lash, he was the British brigadier commanding the Arab Legion, yelling at his drivers. '*Roho, roho!*' That means, 'Move, move!' But they refused to move. When the first tanks ran into the rubble of the monastery, they stopped. The others found the best gear was reverse. They ran. It was a victory for Jewish *kop*. You know what is *kop*?"

"Since I was five years old."

"The kids came out of the monastery and got one of the Jordanian tanks out of the pile of bricks, and put an Israeli flag on it and drove it around. If I hadn't been so tired, I would have cried."

"What did the Assumptionist fathers say?"

"I don't recall. They were praying a lot that night."

We drove by the broken stump marking the Mandelbaum Gate in north Jerusalem.

"We had to seize the northern part of the city to be absolutely secure. There was terrific fighting around the Mandelbaum Gate, right where we are passing now. It was taken by a column of paratroopers. Look—there is a monument to the Jordanians killed here in 1967. Never finished, but we let it stand. Listen, they died also, and they could be brave. It is only their rotten leaders.

"The emphasis was on the northern approaches. Mount Scopus, the police school, and Ammunition Hill had to be taken. This would be the northern attack on Jerusalem. There would be a second, from the south, from Mount Zion and the Hinnom Valley and Gethsemane, also to the Shechem Gate. If it were needed, a third would be ready, a direct attack on Jaffa Gate. But in the north—right through here—was the main fighting.

"This is the Sheikh Jarrah quarter, Jordanian, next to our Bukharian quarter. In between was a no-man's-land. That building up there is the Jordanian Police Training School, a fortified place that we could not take in 1948. This time we took it. You see, on the Israeli side, those modern apartment buildings? We built them in 1963 next to Sheikh Jarrah, and we moved in ex-soldiers and their families. There are bomb shelters is the basement. The night before the battle for the police school, the brigade of paratroopers, two thousand of them, were moved into the apartments. The ladies baked cakes, fed them, gave them the best rooms. The rule was, every woman had to bake at least one cake. The boys made phone calls home, took hot baths. It was embarrassing. We had more cakes than we had soldiers.

"At one A.M. the order came to move out of the apartment houses. They attacked the police school, and it was no easy job. There were deep trenches and barbed wire. And the Arab Legion put up a hell of a fight. And beyond the police school was the real objective, a place one had to seize to secure the northern road to the city—Ammunition Hill."

We were driving up the Mount Scopus Road, which leads north to Nablus and Ramallah. It was a Saturday, early in the afternoon, and most sensible people were asleep behind shuttered blinds.

"This was the second day of the war," Vilnay said. "And now we had taken the police school and were moving up to Ammunition Hill. But the fighting at the police school was a bloody mess. We lost a lot of men there. One platoon was almost wiped out."

"Why all this emphasis on taking the Jordanian forts to the north of the city?" I asked.

"To break their back. This was the Jordanian defense system. If we knocked them out, they could not escape from the Old City, nor could they send reinforcements in."

The Ambassador Hotel was on our right as we drove ahead. Two Israeli soldiers with Uzzi machine guns sat motionless on the veranda.

"Headquarters for the West Bank," Vilnay said. "It was a ruin during the fighting here. We took it on the way down."

On our left there appeared a huge soccer field and parade ground. In the blazing heat, it looked dry, dead. "We will drive in here and I will show you Ammunition Hill. That was the crucial battle. After the school fell, this was next. It was a shell depot for the British Army during the Mandate. A mound, not very big, maybe fifty meters across. But a lot of blood, a lot of blood was lost here."

We turned left and drove past the drill field, the car bouncing on a dirt road. I was surprised to see that the parking area ahead was full of tour buses. Normally no tours run on Saturday, certainly not in Jerusalem.

"In Hebrew this is Givat Ha Tachmoeshat—the 'Hill of Ammunition.' What they had at the police school was nothing compared to this. Trenches, bunkers, machine guns, a small fort with everything—to protect the road to the north. In the old days this was the road to Mount Scopus, which was our Via Dolorosa. We had an enclave there and were supposed to have access. It was always under fire. Once every two weeks we were allowed to change the guard on Mount Scopus, and every now and then the Jordanians would say no more convoys and we would say we will get up by force. That is one of the reasons the Arabs fortified Ammunition Hill: to shoot at our convoys and knock them out if we tried to fight our way to Mount Scopus. They are very good at shooting at unarmed trucks. They are still geniuses at that. On the road to the old Hebrew University you will see a monument to seventy-eight Jewish doctors killed on the road, aboard a bus. The British stood on the rooftops and did nothing when Arabs murdered them. So you see, our soldiers had strong motivation to take this place."

We walked up the fortified hill, which was packed with groups of sight-seers, apparently all of them Israelis. Tours on Saturday?

"Hussein used to watch his soldiers parade on that field," Zev said. "Beautiful uniforms, shined shoes, lots of starch. He used to say to them, 'If I lose this hill, I lose the war.' He was right. He lost both."

At the entrance to the battlefield there was a large sign in Hebrew. Vilnay translated it.

"'Honorable visitor, you are at Ammunition Hill, which was sanctified by the blood and heroism of our paratroopers, the redeemers of Jerusalem, who gave their lives and their souls for it.'"

In a valley below the hill I could see a complex of modern apartments going up. It was the usual Israeli pattern: build at once, settle, cultivate, right in the hottest zones. The five-story dwellings, of typical tan-pink Jerusalem stone, could not have been more than a hundred yards from the old trenches and the twisted, rusting iron of Ammunition Hill. Someone had called it "political construction." I was told later that thirteen acres in the area—the new suburb is called Eshkol, after the late Prime Minister—were in the process of being cleared for high-priority construction.

"It was a bloody fight up here," Vilnay said, as we hopped over a trench. "It lasted from about one A.M. to ten A.M. All of the Arab Legion soldiers in the trenches were killed. At first our boys could not even see them. They were deep in the trenches. The pillboxes were tough—concrete vaults, double walls. Our Yemeni soldiers were especially brave, dropping grenades into the slits, placing dynamite charges against them. No one can say anything against an Oriental in front of me! We lost thirty-six men on the assault. They started with three platoons and ended up with less than one. But we had the bloody hill."

A young man in a yellow shirt walked up to Vilnay and introduced himself. He was a tour guide, taking a party of Israelis around. Zev introduced me. "He is an old pupil of mine," he said. "I trained him to be a guide."

"And also me," a short, burly man said. He was guide to another group. "Dr. Vilnay trained all of us."

Zev embraced his former students. They spoke in Hebrew; I

gathered they wanted him to address their charges. The tourists
were no ordinary visitors. They were workers from an ammunition factory near Tel Aviv; Saturday was the only day they could
travel.

Before I knew what was happening, Vilnay was being introduced to a crowd of about three hundred Israelis by the man in
the yellow shirt. Of course, I did not understand him, but he
made repeated references to Vilnay and the crowd laughed and
applauded enthusiastically. Then Zeve himself climbed on top of
a fallen chunk of masonry from Hussein's ruined fort and took off
his hat. If he had decided to run for the Knesset at that moment,
I am certain he could have been elected overwhelmingly. How he
spoke! Forceful, witty, histrionic, gesturing expansively with his
mighty arms, his great voice booming out over the battleground.
He roused them (I imagined) with the saga of the fight on the
hill and the importance of the victory. When he had finished they
applauded and cheered. They laughed; they pressed forward to
shake the big man's hand; they wanted more.

I think what delighted me as much as his patriotic speech was
that noticeable element in their reaction which clearly connoted
respect for a scholar. When the young man had given Vilnay's
background, and several times stressed the word *Doktor* (did I
also hear Dropsie College?) there was an audible murmur of
reverence.

"What did you tell them?"

"About the battle. How the Zahal drove the Arab Legion out. I
also told them a little history. Jerusalem is almost always attacked
from the north. When the Romans under Titus got ready to
march in, they came from the north, from Mount Scopus. The
best soldiers in the Roman army were in the Tenth Legion, the
Fratensis. The Tenth destroyed Jerusalem, burned the Temple,
stole the Menorah, and brought it to Rome."

"I have seen the relief inside the Arch of Titus."

"You know the story. In 1967, while our men were fighting on
Ammunition Hill, the Tenth Brigade of the Zahal was brought up
to take Jerusalem. I was just outside the Old City and these soldiers came by. I had no idea what unit they were, and I told
them casually, the story of Titus' Tenth Legion. One of the boys

yelled at me. 'Well, we are the Tenth *Brigade*, and we will retake Jerusalem!' "

"But you said something else . . . at the end . . . When you pointed south."

"I told them we had Jerusalem now, and we would have it forever, and nobody in the world could get us out."

We returned to the car and drove a mile or so farther north. The road widened, the hills became more barren. "So the strategy was to secure the flanks. Without secure flanks you can turn a brigade into a cemetery. We had Ammunition Hill, and the next step was right here—Hamiftar, the cut, the gap on top of Mount Scopus. We brought up tanks and men, and that was that. The Jordanians could not come down the road any longer. Over there—that is called French Hill. More Arab Legion artillery. The air force made it into a junkheap. Of course, the Tenth Brigade did not march on the road the way Arabs often do. They advanced along the ridge outside and flanked the enemy, most of whom were running now anyway. But we made one very bad mistake."

"What was that?"

Vilnay pointed to the distance. Where the road bent, a sprawling, low building was visible. "That is Hussein's palace. He never was able to finish it. He wanted another palace besides the one in Amman so he could be near his people on the border. All we have now is a half-finished building. If we had waited six months we could have had the whole thing, brand-new."

We made a U-turn on the Nablus Road near Hamiftar and turned south again. "Now we were able to move south with security. The paratroops fought their way down to the Old City. You saw already the Ambassador Hotel. Next, they fought down the Wadi Joss, the Walnut Valley, and knocked out the Mandelbaum Gate. Nearby is the tomb of Shimon Ha Tzadik. The Wadi Joss runs parallel to the Kidron Valley, as you can see on the map. They battled through the American Colony, and it was tough fighting, but by then many of the Arabs knew they were in trouble. Then the brigade stopped at the Rockefeller Museum and made it their headquarters. Where we are right now."

We parked in a patch of shade in the corner of the Turkish

Wall—the northeast corner, below the Stork's Tower. On our left
was the museum.

"I tell you, Gerald, in addition to the strategy meeting to take
the Old City," Vilnay said sourly, "they should have done something about the collection in there. A beautiful collection, treasures, some of the great finds. But a mishmash, a *tsimmes* you
can't believe. Who can find anything in there? Why are the labels
all cockeyed? And no guidebooks, nothing. You have to know
Nelson Rockefeller personally before they will lend you an old
mimeographed guidebook full of wrong information."

Vilnay was so outraged over the slovenliness of the museum—a
natural reaction for an antiquarian—that I thought he was going
to forget to finish the story of the capture of the Old City.

"When Captain Gur and his men came in the front door of the
museum, the Arab legionnaires were running out the back door,"
he went on, his tirade against sloppy museums ended. "So the
paratroopers had to decide how to enter the Old City, and they
had to do it in a hurry. Already there was pressure for a cease-
fire, and the people at the U.N. were terribly worried that maybe
Jews would get their own city back. What a scandal."

"I've seen a memorial down near the Virgin's Tomb," I said.
"A jagged sort of thing. Is it connected with the attack on the Old
City?"

"A tragic incident. The kind of error our army doesn't like to
make. They sent a reconnaissance unit out along the Jericho Road
that night. Instead of making a turn by the gas station, so they
could hug the walls and be protected, they went down the main
road. Near the Virgin's Tomb they were ambushed and eight men
were killed. They were caught in a crossfire from the Mount of
Olives and from the walls of the Old City. The statue you saw—it
is an eagle's wing, broken. It was the Arab Legion's biggest victory."

He backed his car out of the angle of the wall, and we turned
right, around the Stork's Tower, and parallel to the Eastern Wall.
It was appallingly still on the scorched slopes of the Old City.
The summit of the Mount of Olives distantly glinted in the afternoon sun as the windows of the Intercontinental Hotel sent out
blinding shafts of light.

"On Wednesday morning our planes and guns started hitting

the Jordanian positions on the Mount of Olives—the Augusta Victoria Hospital—and also up Mount Scopus. The Augusta Victoria didn't fight much. We lost one man there, and that was that. Down here, on this street, the Third Battalion of the paratroopers were ready to go into the city. Our tradition says that the Messiah will come through the Golden Gate, which is farther along in the wall and leads into the Temple Mount. It is said he will be preceded by the prophet Elijah, blowing a shofar. But Elijah is a Cohen and therefore cannot enter a cemetery. So the Arabs made a double barrier at the Golden Gate. They put bricks in the wall and built a cemetery in front of it. To keep us out forever. They should have saved themselves the trouble. The Golden Gate was closed, but Gur and his paratroopers went in by the nearest gate to it, St. Stephen's, Shechem's. So that was one tradition we ended. And another one, the one that said Jerusalem could be conquered only from the north. Wrong again. We came in from the east.

"We had come back. By ten in the morning, the fight was over in the Old City. A little sniping, that was all. And soon our soldiers were praying at the Wall. With machine-gun belts around their necks, instead of the *tallis*. Do you know the legends? The Wall was built by the poorest of the Jews, and that is why the *Shekina*, the divine presence, is in it. Forget all that nonsense about killing pigeons and lambs. It is the *Spirit* in the Wall that we honor. When the Roman soldiers tried to tear it down, they saw angels who warned them, 'This wall built by the poor shall remain.' A Roman general picked up a sledgehammer. He fell dead. Titus himself tried, and his right arm dried up. And at that moment, the people saw six angels on top of the Wall, weeping. Their tears hardened the cement between the stones to make it last forever. *Forever*, my boy."

We walked up the steep path leading to St. Stephen's Gate. I could see the lions in bas-relief, the merlons, crenels, and machicolations on the high Turkish facade. A handsome gate. Vilnay and I seemed to be the only ones in Jerusalem.

"Legendary prophecies are not my cups of tea, Zeve," I said. "But here I will make an exception."

His brawny arm clamped itself around my shoulder and I gasped. "Hah! We have made a believer out of you!"

Golden stones—burning sky—desert air. I was vaguely, pleasantly, dizzy. Nelson Glueck was right: This is a land of extremes. Yet how could they go about their day-to-day existence, burdened with all that history, all those responsibilities? How does a small nation stage concerts and educate children and cure diseases and build apartments and grow wheat—and still fight an endless war?

"Zeve, you are a people who don't give a visitor any choice. You make us believe. You forced me to believe in you."

He squinted at me from beneath the brim of his Panama hat. "What is this 'believe in *you*,' Gerald? If you believe in us, my boy, it means only one thing. You believe in yourself."

And, of course, he was right.

Index